BE TRUE
TO YOUR
SCHOOL

A DIARY OF 1964

Bob Greene

BALLANTINE BOOKS · NEW YORK

FOR MICHAEL S. MELTON   1947–1967

Library of Congress Catalog Card Number: 86-26594

ISBN 0-345-35394-3

This edition published by arrangement with Atheneum Publishers, a division of the Scribner Book Companies, Inc.

Manufactured in the United States of America

First Ballantine Books Edition: June 1988

PREFACE

IN 1964, the year I turned seventeen years old, I kept a diary. What had happened was this: At a convention of high school journalism students from around the state of Ohio, a teacher had recommended that the best way to make oneself a good reporter was to keep a daily journal. The teacher said that the discipline of making yourself write down exactly what happened to you every day, even when you didn't feel like writing, was good training.

So for that one year I did it. I would write the diary late at night, just before going to bed. I didn't tell any of my friends about it; there were probably millions of teenage girls who were keeping diaries that same year, but for a boy to admit to his buddies that he was keeping a diary would be—to use the only appropriate term of the era—queer.

I wrote every night. The notations in the diary were pretty much in the style of the late Walter Winchell—quick observations, bits of dialogue, pithy descriptions of the people I met and the places I went. When 1964 was over I finished the last day of the diary, and that was that.

Years later, I found the diary in a drawer, and I read it again. It startled me. At the time I wrote it, I didn't think of it as much more than a sort of journalistic exercise—a high school student's way to train himself to observe things and record his thoughts. But when I looked at the diary after years had passed, I realized that what I had here was something money could not buy: time preserved. Most of us tend to look back on our teenage years as if they were some pleasant, seamless movie made up of endless pleasure, bathed in a warm, unfocused glow of nostalgia. My 1964 diary gave me no such luxury. Yes, the great times were there, in generous quantity, but they were mixed with heartache and hurt, one set of emotions sometimes replacing the other within a twenty-four-hour period.

In short, I had—in the most stark, specific terms—that year available to me, as current as the days when I had first written about it. And that diary is what led to this book.

The closest I can come to explaining how I wrote the book you now hold in your hands is to say that it felt very much like restoring a cracked and faded old photograph. All of the characters and events and quotations were in the original 1964 diary, but they were not in narrative form. It was startling to me how the cryptic sentence fragments and disjointed conversations and hurriedly written descriptions of emotions in the diary brought back so vividly the days and nights when they had first happened. My job was to use the details in the diary as notes, and to build this book using those notes. I have done my best not to stray from the spirit and the sequence of events in the original diary. And most of all I have tried to retain the voice of the boy who kept that diary.

All of us, no matter when we were born, have years that touch us in a similar way to how 1964 touched me. But 1964 was a unique time. America still had one foot in the Fifties, while tentatively stepping into the Sixties. When most people hear about the Sixties today, they think about the decade in terms of stereotypes: the radical change in musical styles, the revolution in sexual attitudes, the urban race riots, the student activism on campuses, the pain of Vietnam.

It is easy to forget that at the beginning of 1964, all of that had yet to happen. The year was part of the Sixties, yes, but it was very much the ending of one era and the beginning of the next. Like most other things that happen in our society, it took place so gradually that we hardly noticed it at the time.

But this book is not about politics and it is not about cultural change. It is about one year in the life of one boy and his friends who were growing up in the middle of the country. There were important events happening in the outside world that year—events that journalists of the era were chronicling every day. As you will see, my friends and I paid little attention to those things. Probably most of us, teen-agers or not, are like that. The real truths of our lives don't make the six o'clock news or the morning paper.

A note about the setting of the book: Everything happens in Bexley, Ohio, a suburb of the city of Columbus. Once you drove over the Bexley line, you were in Columbus itself, so when Bexley people went "downtown," they were going to downtown Columbus. It was as if you lived in Bexley and Columbus at the same time; your home was in Bexley, but your frame of reference was Columbus. Bexley was—and is— a town of approximately fifteen thousand people, virtually all of them white. It was the kind of suburb where teen-agers generally didn't have to worry about where their allowance money was coming from; by and large, Bexley, like so many suburbs of the Sixties, was composed of stable families where the fathers brought home "comfortable" paychecks every week. Bexley High School had a student population of eight hundred or so; everyone tended to know everyone else.

A word about technique: All of the people and places in this book are real, precisely as they appeared in the original diary. In several cases—where I felt that, even all these years later, the events depicted might prove embarrassing to a person—I have changed names. Some of the things that happen in the course of this book I am, in retrospect, not especially proud of. But my decision was not to censor myself, either in terms of events or emotions.

Working on this book has been as much fun for me as any writing project with which I have ever been involved. No matter what problems were going on in my 1980s daily life as I wrote the book, there was a time each day when I could pull the original diary out, go over the events of 1964, and then try to get them down on paper. It has been like stepping into a daily time machine; I have been able to walk away from the world I live in now, and walk into 1964.

That year was a very special time in my life. My greatest hope is that, in reading this book, you may be reminded of special times in your life, too.

BOB GREENE

January 1

RIGHT at midnight last night, just as I was kissing Candy Grossman, something popped into my mind.

It was this: I wonder if a new year is really supposed to feel brand-new?

We were all at Allen Schulman's parents' apartment; his folks were out for New Year's Eve, and they let us have the place. Allen is the only one of us who doesn't live in a house; his parents have the penthouse in the only "luxury high-rise apartment building" in Columbus, and we were all dancing to "Be True to Your School" and looking out the windows toward downtown. Columbus really looks different from seventeen stories in the air.

The dancing had me feeling good. We had been doing the Skip all night, and that makes you get all out of breath; Pongi had a date with Lindsey Alexander, and he was showing off, doing the Pony, but the rest of us were just skipping back and forth like we learned from "Dance-O-Rama" on Channel 4.

We turned off the record player and turned the radio on to WCOL, and Bob Harrington, the disc jockey, counted down the seconds until midnight. Then we all kissed our dates; I guess that's what you're supposed to do at midnight on New Year's Eve, but I felt sort of silly, like I was trying to be a grownup at one of my parents' parties, instead of being sixteen years old, which is what I am. I had never kissed Candy before—we don't even know each other all that well, she's just a friend of my younger sister Debby—but because it was midnight we had to pretend that this was old stuff to us.

So I kissed Candy and I was thinking about what the new

1

year is going to be like. I half expected, in those seconds just after midnight, to feel like everything had changed and that I was starting all over again. But I didn't feel that way, of course; I opened my eyes and I was still in Allen's parents' apartment, and everybody was still kissing their dates.

I thought about going off to find a telephone to call Lindy's number and see if she was home, but that would have been rude to Candy, and I don't know what I would have said, anyway.

I just hope that 1964 is better than 1963.

JANUARY 2

IT was snowing this morning when I woke up. The clock radio next to my bed went off, and I was hoping that the voices would say that the schools were all closed because of the weather. But they didn't; the news came on at five till seven and there was nothing at all about school closings, and then the music came back. "Louie, Louie" is number one in Columbus this week.

The reason that I was hoping for no school is that we were supposed to have a test in Schacht's Algebra class this morning, and I didn't study at all over Christmas vacation. Mr. Schacht is the hardest teacher in the school, and there was no way that I was going to pass the test. The rumor around the school is that he was written up in *Life* magazine about fifteen years ago for being one of the best teachers in America; they were supposed to have printed an "honor roll" of the country's finest educators, and Schacht was supposed to have made it, with a picture and everything. The only teacher from Bexley High School on the list.

He was standing by the blackboard in his brown suit when we came into class—he had chalk all over the sleeves, as usual. He was smiling, and he asked us if we'd had a good vacation. We all just sort of mumbled, and then he said he had a surprise for us—he was postponing the test. So the disaster will be delayed.

In study hall the next period Carol Lowenthal sat next to

me; she's one of the very best-looking of the sophomore girls. She said that she heard that Chuck Shenk and I are great dancers; she said, "Next year is really going to be terrific."

Well, first of all I'm not that good a dancer at all. And second of all, I knew what she was getting at. She and her friends—Linda McClure and all the rest of them—are already thinking ahead to next year, when all of the seniors have gone off to college and all of us juniors become the oldest guys in the school. Notice that she didn't say anything about going out with Chuck or me this year; it's next year she has in mind.

Oh, well. It was nice to hear that she was interested, anyway.

After school we had paste-up for our pages in the *Torch* office. I was pasting up page 1—that's the page I'm editor of—and Judy Furman came over and said, "So, did you go out with Lindy New Year's Eve?"

I just looked at her.

I'm listening to "Hootenanny" on WBNS right now. Mom and Dad are in their room watching television; Debby is doing her homework and Timmy's on the phone with one of his friends. I think WBNS realizes that because it refuses to play any rock and roll, it's losing all of its younger listeners to WCOL. WBNS seems to figure that by having "Hootenanny" on the air every night it can get some of us back.

I don't know—I really like folk music, but it gets pretty boring after an hour or so.

TV Guide says that James Dean is on Channel 10 in *East of Eden* at eleven-thirty. If I pull my portable TV close to the bed so the light from the screen doesn't show under the bottom of my bedroom door, and if I keep the sound low enough, Mom and Dad won't know that I've got it on so late. I think I'll stay up and watch.

JANUARY 3

FRENCH quiz this afternoon. I may have flunked it.

Tonight there was a basketball game against Whitehall. All of us (ABCDJ) went to it together.

ABCDJ is what the five of us call each other. We've been best friends all during high school, and I would bet that we remain best friends for the rest of our lives. The letters stand for the first initials of each of our first names.

A is Allen Schulman. His parents' apartment is where the New Year's Eve party was. Besides being the only one of us who doesn't live in a house, Allen is the only one of us who doesn't go to Bexley. He goes to military school down in West Virginia, which is a drag—he's only home during the summer and during school vacations. He's been home for Christmas these last couple of weeks, but in a few days he's going back to his school. I like him as well as anybody in the world, but it's tough having one of your best friends not even be around more than half of the time. It's great when he's here, though—when ABCDJ walked into the school gym tonight, we really felt complete.

B, of course, is me.

C is Chuck Shenk. His father is a big-deal businessman, but the thing I like the most about Chuck is that he doesn't seem to care about anything. You could tell him that the world was going to end at midnight, and he'd probably just toss his head to one side and then say, "Let's go to the Toddle House for cheeseburgers and banana cream pie." A lot of the big athletes in the school don't particularly like Chuck, but I think that's because they don't really understand him. I think he has that problem a lot—my dad, for example, doesn't particularly get along with him, either. People think he's being a wiseass because he's always grinning at what they say, and not saying anything in return. I don't think he's trying to be wise; I just don't think he wastes a lot of time thinking about things one way or the other.

D is Danny Dick. Dan's one of the best tennis players in the state of Ohio—he was one of only three or four guys in our class, in any sport, to letter our freshman year. Sometimes he seems to be living in a world of his own—he talks about an imaginary frog named Reedeep Reeves—but watch him on that tennis court and you've never seen anything like it in your life. Some people rag him because he's short; I think they're just jealous because as big as they are, Dan was the one who was wearing a Bexley letter jacket way before they were. He'll get his revenge on them soon enough; his older brother Dicky Dick is a real big guy, and Dicky grew late, too, so Dan will be catching up. The Dick family has a great-looking gray '56 Thunderbird convertible, which Dan gets to drive all he wants. There's only room for one other person in it, so we can never take it out when we all want to cruise together, but boy, is it beautiful.

J is Jack Roth. He's my oldest friend in the world—we became best friends when we were five years old in kindergarten, which was eleven years ago. His house on Ardmore has a little hill on the street side of the backyard, and when we were kids we used to play Audie Murphy and charge up the hill with toy guns. In a way, Jack seems like the oldest of all of us, even though we're all the same age. His mom died last year, and he's the only one of us who doesn't have both parents alive. It's funny—Jack and I have always been able to talk about just about anything, but we've never talked about that. I've noticed it, though—Jack just seems older now, and I think that's what did it.

So anyway, ABCDJ were all in the stands at the game tonight. We went out into the lobby at half time to get popcorn, and who do we bump into but Lindy and her friends. I immediately felt myself going into a daze; she said something that I couldn't hear, and Allen just walked up to her and told her to go away. That's why I think I like him so much; he knew that if it were up to me I'd stand there and try to talk to her and end up not being cool at all, so he was cool for me.

JANUARY 4

TODAY's Saturday; at noon Dave Frasch and Tim Greiner and I went downtown to the Lazarus department store, and I bought a guitar. It has steel strings and it cost nineteen dollars.

I sat there in the musical instrument department of Lazarus and tried to play it; I have no idea how to play, but Dave already has one, and he said you could learn it pretty easily from a book. So I bought an instruction book; the front half shows you how to make the chords, and the back half has songs that you can play.

Dave and Tim aren't part of ABCDJ; Dave is the quarterback on the football team and Tim is the catcher on the baseball team, so they run with a different crowd—the big athletes. It's funny; I run with my friends, and it's a pretty self-contained group. They run with their friends, the star football and baseball players, and that's a pretty self-contained group, too. The only place that we overlap is with each other—it's like we're each others' only contact with two different parts of the Bexley universe. We sit together whenever we can in classes and pass notes back and forth, and let each other know what's going on with our different groups.

Dave has an idea—if we can all get good enough on our guitars, we'll get a hootenanny group up for the school talent show in the spring. The idea is, we'd be like the Bexley version of the New Christy Minstrels or the Kingston Trio.

We wore our letter jackets downtown. I always like that; when you're walking through Lazarus you see all the guys from the other schools around town—North, East, Arlington, Worthington—and you kind of check them out from the corner of your eye. Our jackets are dark blue, with a white "B" on the front. I lettered in tennis last year, when I was a sophomore; I'm the first to admit that, in the Bexley hierarchy, tennis doesn't rank nearly as high as football or basketball or baseball, but a letter's a letter. You're not supposed to show any emotion about things like that, but the day I got my letter was probably the best day of my life.

JANUARY 5

CHUCK Shenk and I cruised all day; for a few hours this afternoon we watched the Browns and the Packers on TV, but most of the day we just drove around Bexley.

He did a great thing with his car. He got a portable record player, put it on the front seat and somehow ran a wire through the dashboard and connected it to the battery under the hood. We took a copy of "Little Deuce Coupe" with us and played it for four hours straight as we cruised. For the first time, we don't have to listen to what WCOL plays—we can listen to whatever we want to. There's a slight problem in that when Chuck drives fast, the needle skips over the record. But it really is terrific—you can cruise and be your own disc jockey at the same time.

While "Little Deuce Coupe" kept playing, I got silent all of a sudden. Chuck must have been talking to me and I must not have been listening, because finally he said, "Are you in your daze again?" Which meant: "Are you thinking about Lindy again?"

I guess I was. "Little Deuce Coupe" was one of the songs that was on the air all last summer, when Lindy and I were going together. I've got to snap out of this thing, but I can't seem to.

Lindy's three years younger than I am; when we first started going together last June, people thought that the age difference was too much. Me being sixteen, her being thirteen . . . everybody thought it would never work.

We met on the way back from the swimming pool. It was the end of the day, and we were all looking for a ride home, and Denise Blue had a car. Everybody piled in. I was in the back seat, holding my tennis racquet. There were about eight of us in the car, and there really wasn't room, and she ended up sitting on my lap. Lindy Lemmon.

I had known her older brother, Pat—he's on the basketball team—and I guess I knew that Pat had a little sister. I couldn't believe my reaction as we rode in that car. I remember, that song "Harry the Hairy Ape" was playing on the car radio, and Lindy was laughing at it, and I just didn't want the ride to end. Allen Schulman was in the car, and we both got off at his parents' apartment building. The car drove away, and Allen said, "Cute girl." I didn't say anything.

Two nights later we were all hanging around Pongi's front yard, and Lindy and a bunch of her friends came walking by. I would have been too shy to say anything, but she walked right up to me. We talked for about five minutes, and then she said that her parents had a rule—she had to be home by the time the streetlights went on. It was already dusk, so she had to hurry.

The next morning when I woke up, I felt happy. I didn't know what it was; I just felt happy and good and in a hurry for the day to begin. And when I thought about it for a minute, I realized that the reason I was happy was that now I knew Lindy Lemmon.

I guess I still wouldn't have done anything about it, but that night at the dinner table my sister Debby said, "I have a secret I'm not supposed to tell you." Debby is fourteen— two years younger than me but a year older than Lindy. I thought she was just messing around as usual, but then she said it again: "I have a secret."

"What is it?" I said.

"I know someone who has a crush on you," she said.

My mom said, "Who?"

Debby started grinning, and then she began to hum that Peter, Paul, and Mary song, "Lemon Tree." I got it right away, but no one else at the table did; I shot Debby a look that told her to shut up about it.

After dinner Debby and I walked outside and I asked her to tell me what she knew. She said that she and her friends had been over at Johnson's Ice Cream Shop on Main Street, and that Lindy and her friends had been there too, and that Lindy had been asking all kinds of questions about me.

"She got all excited when she realized I was your sister," Debby said.

The next time Lindy and I ran into each other on the street she said, "I talked to your sister the other day." I said, "So I heard," and she blushed, and we started hanging around together all the time.

I'd read things about what it's supposed to feel like when

you fall in love for the first time, but I have to say, I wasn't prepared for it. I was just so . . . happy all the time. A combination of nervous and happy. We would mostly see each other in the daytime; we'd make arrangements to meet on the corner of Bexley Park and Roosevelt; she'd walk from her house and I'd walk from my house and we'd meet and then we'd walk down to this house on Gould, with a big hedge that ran along the street. We'd sit down on the grass next to the hedge, and I'd have my transistor radio, and we'd just sit there and talk all day. Sometimes, if it seemed that no one was around and there weren't any cars coming by, we'd hold hands.

And we'd go driving; I would borrow my mom's station wagon, and we would drive out to the Three-C Highway (it connects Cleveland, Columbus, and Cincinnati) and we'd drive around until dinnertime. Even when we didn't talk, we felt close; that's the first time in my life I've ever had that feeling.

We told ourselves that it would just be for the summer; when the school year started, I'd be a junior at the high school and Lindy would still be going to the junior high school, in the building next door. We knew that wouldn't work. But then, in August, it started to seem not so impossible. For one thing, some of my friends started going out with some of Lindy's friends, girls in her class: Chuck Shenk was seeing Wendy Clowson, and Danny Dick was seeing Janie McKenney. So all of a sudden the age thing seemed to be okay.

Lindy and I would talk on the telephone late every night, after the rest of our families had gone to sleep. We'd say that no matter what happened after school started, we knew that someday we'd be married to each other. Sometimes now, when I'm feeling so bad, I think about those calls.

Anyway . . . school started, and for a few weeks we'd see each other on weekends. At the football games I'd go with my friends, and she'd go with her friends, and we'd catch each other's eyes in the stands.

I can't come up with an exact date when it happened. The weather started to get cold, and summer seemed like it was a long time ago, and when I'd call her on the phone she seemed sort of distant, or she would say that she really couldn't stay on. Sometime in October I asked her if anything was wrong; she said it was too hard, us being in different schools, and she said that we probably would have been better off if we had just broken up at the end of the summer like we had planned.

I never cried. There's not very much about this for me to feel good about, but at least I never cried. I've never felt worse in my life, though. It was like the reverse side of all those mornings when I woke up so happy and ready to jump out of bed. After Lindy and I broke up, I would wake up, and before I even had a chance to think about it I would know that I felt lousy, and that there was no real reason to start the day. It wasn't long before I found out she was going with a boy in her own class; I would start to see them sitting together at football games, and for the first time I felt foolish for being three years older.

When I talk to my friends about it, they say that I'm stupid to still think about her. They say it's bad enough for me to have been dropped, but that for me to keep dwelling on it is really embarrassing. I don't think that any of them have ever been in love, though—I know they haven't, because we've talked about it—so they have no idea how this feels.

Last summer I used to carry a lemon bottle that I found. That's what I called it—a lemon bottle; it was really a little bottle of lemon extract, small enough to fit in my pocket. I dumped all of the juice out of it and carried it for good luck. One night in October, when it was obvious that we really were broken up, I took the lemon bottle and I threw it against the front of Pongi's house. It smashed into dozens of pieces. My friends applauded.

But the next morning I walked back there and picked up some of the pieces. They're dark brown—dark brown glass. I still carry one of those broken pieces with me. It's not for luck anymore; I'm not sure what it's for, and no one else knows about it. But it's in my pocket every day, wherever I go.

JANUARY 6

WE got an Algebra test back that we took before Christmas vacation. I got a 79; the French quiz came back, too, and I got an 81 on that. So I was wrong about flunking it.

I could be doing a lot better in school, though. If I didn't spend so much time thinking about Lindy, I guess I could study better. As it is, I don't care about the grades all that much. Buy my parents are going to go crazy if my grades keep dropping.

After school today I went to Bexley Records and got nylon strings for my guitar. I had been trying to practice, and the steel strings that came with it kept cutting my fingers.

I went to my room and played straight from five o'clock until ten o'clock tonight. The chords are pretty easy; right now I can play fairly decent versions of "Michael, Row the Boat Ashore," "Blow the Man Down," and "Molly Malone." That would be really cool, if we could get a folk music group together.

"Hootenanny" on WBNS was great tonight. They played Joan Baez singing "Copper Kettle"; I think she has the most beautiful voice in the world.

JANUARY 7

WE had an Algebra quiz today, which I ruined. I don't think it will count much; Mr. Schacht came up to me after class and punched me in the stomach—kidding—and said, "I can see by your face that you don't think you did too well."

I said that was right, and he said, "Don't worry. There'll be others." I wonder about him—he's been at Bexley for so long, and he's seen so many people come through the school; I wonder how he makes himself care about what he's doing. He was giving these tests before I was born. Sometimes it seems that he has a private joke going on inside himself that he doesn't share with anyone. That punch in the stomach is as close as he gets to letting it out.

Chuck and I went to Pongi's after school, and we all worked on our guitars. Pongi's house is right in the middle of Bexley; it's about a block from the high school, and it's where everyone hangs out. Pongi's dad is the owner of the RC Cola distributorship in town, so there are always wooden crates of soda pop in their garage. We're not even supposed to ask; we can just take anything we want.

I learned how to play "Down by the Riverside" and "Tom Dooley" today. Dave Frasch came by after basketball practice; he's so good on the guitar that he makes the rest of us look like babies. It must be something, to be like that in everything you do; ever since we were in first grade, Dave has been the one who can step onto the football field or the basketball court and do anything he wants, and now he's the same way with the guitar.

I'm not like that; nothing seems to come that easy for me. The tennis letter, for example; the summer before my sophomore year I played for twelve hours a day, every day, just trying to get good. And when I lettered it was only after sweating it out before every match of the whole season; I never knew when Coach Weis was going to play me and when he wasn't. I would rush to look at the lineup on the locker room bulletin board on the day of every match, hoping to see my name. With Dave it's never been like that; his name has always been at the top of the list. He doesn't even have to look.

And now it's like that with guitars. Chuck and Pongi and I kept checking our fingers against the chord diagrams in the instruction book. Meanwhile Dave just sat there and played anything he wanted to. I guess that's how life goes.

JANUARY 8

NANCY Dartwell got felt up in Florida over Christmas vacation. Dan and I found out in study hall this morning; Nancy was passing a note to someone a couple of tables in back of us, and Dan got the note and we looked at it before we passed it back.

That's amazing. Nancy Dartwell is a friend of my sister Debby's, and she has just about the best body in the school, but there's no chance that anyone around Bexley would ever get a chance to feel her up. She's so pure that there aren't even any rumors about her putting out. But there it was in the note—she said that she met a guy on the beach and they went out that night and he felt her up. And she was on vacation with her parents, on top of everything else.

That's the Bexley quandary, right there. Whenever we go cruising looking for girls, we always go to another suburb; we just assume that we're not going to get anywhere with Bexley girls. I can't count how many nights we've spent at the Whitehall Recreation Center, dancing and standing around and trying to pick up Whitehall girls. Whitehall is only about five miles away from Bexley, but the unwritten rule is that if we're ever going to get lucky, it will be in Whitehall, not Bexley.

Not that any of us has gotten lucky yet. ABCDJ are five virgins—can you use the term virgins to refer to males? Anyway, none of us has ever slept with a girl. If I'm being honest, I have to confess that none of us has ever even been with a girl with any of her clothes off. If it happens, though, we know that it's going to happen someplace other than Bexley.

Except . . . here's Nancy Dartwell passing this note that says she got felt up in Florida. And in the note, she didn't seem embarrassed or ashamed or anything—she was just volunteering the information to her friends. She even seemed kind of proud.

That's the question I have. Here all of us are, driving over to Whitehall on the weekends and hanging around that crummy recreation center in the hopes that some girl will like us and let us put our hand inside her blouse. And here Nancy Dartwell is, going all the way down to Florida before she lets some guy she's never even met put his hand in her blouse.

What a waste of time and travel. It would seem that as long as we want to do it, and as long as the girls in Bexley want to do it, we might as well just stay in Bexley and do it. But it seems like that's never going to happen. Nancy Dartwell didn't know that we saw her note, and after study hall

she just walked past us with a sweet smile on her face and
her nose in the air, like she's been doing for years. To look
at her you'd get the impression that she's in training to be a
nun. And yet it was right down there in black and white,
right in the note: She got felt up in Florida.

Dan says he's going to ask her out.

JANUARY 9

WE had a fraternity league basketball game tonight; the fraternity I'm in, Epsilons, beat Pegasus 62–20. I scored eight
points; Chuck led all scorers with thirty-two. He's really
good; I've always wondered why he never went out for the
varsity at school, but he seems happy playing for Epsilons.

The whole idea of high school fraternities confuses me
sometimes. When I was a freshman I really wanted to get
into Epsilons, but I wasn't asked. Pegasus asked me; I thought
about it, and told them no. I decided I'd rather not be in a
fraternity than be in one I didn't like.

But then last year, after I lettered in tennis, I got asked to
join Epsilons. I suppose I should have said no; after all, I
was the same person they had turned down the year before.
The only difference was that playing on a varsity team had
made them notice me. But I didn't say no; I said yes. And
now I go to the meetings every week and play on the basketball and baseball teams for them—and I guess I feel superior
to the guys in Pegasus.

I'm not exactly proud of all this. My sister Debby behaved
the way I wish I would have behaved. When the girls' sororities were having their rush last summer, Debby decided that
she just didn't like the whole idea—all of the friends she had
made all through elementary school and junior high school
being judged by the upperclass girls, and some being asked
to join while others weren't. So she told them that she wasn't
interested; she didn't want to be considered.

I remember the night that the bids went out for the sororities. All the upperclass girls were driving around Bexley
honking their horns, and the freshman girls who had been

asked to join were running up and down the streets whooping and cheering. Debby stayed in her room; I think I heard her crying. I never talked to her about it, but I thought it was a pretty impressive way for a fourteen-year-old girl to run her life.

Like I say, I suppose my own decision wasn't as impressive. But I can't deny it—when I dress up, I like wearing my blazer with the Epsilons patch on the pocket, and I like it when the big fraternity and sorority dances take place, and my name is listed on the page of the program that we buy. It says "Men of Epsilons" at the top, and then we're all listed; I feel a lot better being on that list than when I wasn't on it.

So we won 62–20 tonight. After the game Chuck and I went to the Ranch Drive-In for dinner, and when I got home, I taught myself to play "500 Miles" on my guitar.

JANUARY 10

WHEN my clock radio woke me up this morning, WCOL was playing a new song called "I Saw Her Standing There." It was by the Beatles, that group from England that got written up in *Time* magazine last year. This was the first I had ever heard them sing. The song sounds like it's going to be a hit.

Tonight there was a Bexley basketball game at Worthington. Chuck, Dan, Jack, and I drove up there to see it—Allen has gone back to military school.

When the game was over we drove back to Bexley and then went to Frisch's Big Boy for some food. Lindy's older sister, Libby Lemmon, was in there with some friends; she's in college now. She said hi to me and was real nice, and it put me right back in the daze. It made me realize that even on days when I'm not thinking about Lindy, I'm thinking about her anyway. If that makes any sense.

While we were at Frisch's Dan kept complaining that there's a lock on the gate to the school tennis courts over on Stanwood—the part of the high school grounds that are closest to his house. It makes him mad because it's really cold out these days, and when the gate is locked he can't cut through on his way to school. Going around the long way takes an extra five minutes.

So after we were finished eating we went back to his house and got a saw. Jack and I stood lookout on either end of Stanwood—Officer Butters from the Bexley police is always cruising at that time of night. And Dan and Chuck cut the lock off.

The thing is, half of the high school will benefit from being able to cut across the tennis courts in the morning. But we're the ones who put ourselves on the line for it, and if we get caught we're the ones who'll be in trouble. So we can't even tell people we did it, and no one will thank us for it.

JANUARY 11

IT turns out that "I Saw Her Standing There" isn't even the good side of the Beatles record. The good side is called "I Want to Hold Your Hand," and WCOL has started to play it about once every hour. "I Saw Her Standing There" is the other side; when I heard it yesterday morning I assumed that it was supposed to be the big hit. This is really unusual— WCOL playing both sides of the same record.

Barry Goldwater came to Port Columbus this morning as part of his campaign for the presidential nomination. Since it's Saturday, and we didn't have anything else to do, Chuck and I drove out there to see him. We only got a glimpse, but at least we can say that we saw someone who's running for president. Not that many nationally famous people come through Columbus.

JANUARY 12

IT'S snowing like crazy; it has been all day. I should have studied Algebra and Chemistry, but a movie called *Beginning of the End*, about giant grasshoppers, was on TV, so I watched that instead. Then I went over to Pongi's house and borrowed his plot summary of *The Scarlet Letter*. I don't know how anyone ever gets through the real books; my concentration starts to go before I can even make it through the Cliffs Notes.

JANUARY 13

No school today! They announced it on WCOL at six forty-five this morning. All the schools in the area are closed because of snow.

Around noon I went to Pongi's. Chuck, Jack, Dave Frasch, Tom Williamson, Gary Herwald, and I were all playing our guitars. I don't know if the others are thinking the same thing I am—but with WCOL playing that Beatles record so often, all of a sudden it seems sort of old-fashioned to be sitting around with wooden guitars singing folks songs. Gary said he read somewhere that the Beatles use electric guitars.

At night I got a call from Judy Morse. I had no idea what she was calling about, but she asked me to Presidential, the big sorority dance on February 8. I hardly even know her, and I'm not very attracted to her, but I guess going with her is better than sitting home. I know it's the same thing that boys go through all the time—asking girls out and then being afraid of being shut down—but I always feel sorry for these girls when the time comes for the turnaround dances, where they have to do the asking. Judy sounded so nervous on the phone—while trying to be cool at the same time—that I just said yes.

I've got to start going out, anyway. I can't spend my whole life sitting around thinking about Lindy.

* * *

The snow has stopped. Being let out of school for a day is such a tease; it just makes you more depressed when you realize that in the morning it all starts over again, and that you'll be sitting in class, and that nothing has changed.

JANUARY 14

THINGS went all right in school today, until sixth-period English class. Mrs. Amos was talking about *The Red Badge of Courage*, and she said that she wanted someone to give a thumbnail sketch of it. All of a sudden she looked at me and called my name. (Actually, she said "Robert." She always calls me Robert.)

I hadn't read the book. I hadn't even read the Cliffs Notes. I considered trying to fake it, but then I realized that would end up as a mess. So I just said, "I haven't read it."

There was total silence in the room. Mrs. Amos stared at me. Then she called on someone else, as if nothing had happened.

Not that I like to disappoint any teachers, but I especially don't like to disappoint Mrs. Amos. She's the adviser for the *Torch*, and she's the one who named me page-one editor of it; it's not much of a secret that she wants me as one of the editors in chief next year. She likes me and treats me almost like I was her son. Maybe grandson; she's a much older woman, and when I take my completed page over to her house for approval one Sunday every month, I feel very much like I feel when I'm visiting one one of my grandmothers. Like I have an obligation to stay and chitchat, but really I'm going crazy waiting to get out of there.

She's a nice lady, though, and I know she doesn't understand it when she finds out that I haven't done the work for her class. She knows that I can do a fairly decent job at something when I'm interested in it; she's never had a single complaint about my work for the *Torch*. It seems to puzzle her that I just don't care about school assignments.

I was afraid that she was going to say something to me after class, but she didn't. It was like when you're in trouble at home, but they go out of their way not to mention it. "I'm not mad at you, I'm just hurt.'' Like that. I'm sorry I make her feel that way, but there's no way I'm going to read *The Red Badge of Courage*. A plot summary before the final, and that's it.

Tonight I had to call Jeff Schmidt and Jennie Beers for the *Torch*. They're nominated for King and Queen of Hearts at the Valentine's dance; one couple is nominated from each class, and they're the senior-class nominees. I have to arrange to get their picture taken for the paper.

Jeff is the star of the basketball team and Jennie is one of the most beautiful of the senior girls. I know Jeff a little bit because he's also number one singles on the tennis team; Jennie I don't know at all. There's a big gap between seniors and the rest of the school, even between them and us juniors.

But it's funny—when I call up and say I'm from the *Torch*, all of a sudden the balance of power changes. If I were to walk up to Jennie Beers in the hallway and try to talk with her, she'd think I was crazy. Who is this guy? She probably wouldn't even know my name.

When I call up and say I'm from the *Torch* and that I want to put her picture in the paper, though, it's different. She was as friendly as can be; so was Jeff when I called him. Very conversational, both of them. Like we were old pals. Just having the ability to put someone in the paper seems to make them much friendlier to you. It's weird.

JANUARY 15

WE took a quiz in Algebra class today and for once I knew what I was doing. I got a 100. Not that it will count for much, but it put me in a good mood. Those quizzes that we hand across the desk to someone else and grade right away in class are sort of like Polaroid pictures; you find out how you did immediately, but there's no suspense.

My good mood only lasted for one period. Our Chemistry test came back and I got a 40 on it. I've flunked them before, but 40 is really pretty bad.

After dinner tonight Jack called me; he said he had ordered

the Beatles' album from Bexley Records, and that they had just phoned him to say it was in. So he picked me up and we drove over there.

We each bought one. Usually I buy singles, and the album was pretty expensive—it was $2.47—but it seemed important to have it. Jack and I brought our albums back to my house, and we went up to my room to play mine.

It's called *Meet the Beatles!* The cover is a black-and-white photograph of them—portraits of their faces. It's really strange to see a formal portrait and then all that hair. WCOL has been playing "I Want to Hold Your Hand" and "I Saw Her Standing There" almost nonstop, but the other songs on the album are just as good. Really amazing. Every time we played the album I would turn the volume on the record player up a little, and finally my father started pounding on the door for me to turn it back down.

Jack went home with his album after a while, but I kept playing mine. "Hootenanny" on WBNS radio was supposed to have a Kingston Trio concert tonight, but I just kept listening to the Beatles.

JANUARY 16

TODAY when I walked to school I went to take the shortcut through the gate to the tennis courts—the place where we'd cut off the lock. This morning there was a new lock in place.

So I walked the long way around the block to the front of the school. We think we can change something about Bexley—even something as small as getting rid of the lock. They just go ahead and put a new lock on. Bexley never changes. The gate hadn't even been open for a week.

I got an 80 on a Chemistry quiz today and an 84 on a History test that we got back. My grades vary so wildly; I'll flunk a quiz and the next time I'll get an A in the same subject and the next time I'll finish in the middle. It doesn't make any sense.

* * *

After school I had to do a lot of work in the *Torch* office. I didn't get done with it until after five o'clock. I walked home and borrowed my mom's station wagon and cruised until dinner.

When I cruise in Bexley it's a little like pacing around the house; if Bexley were covered by a carpet, you could follow my route by the indentations I left. It never varies. I'll head up Roosevelt, past Pongi's, then cut over to Cassady. I'll drive up to Maryland, hang a left, go to Columbia, and drive past Chuck's. His driveway curves behind his house, and sometimes I'll drive in there to see if anyone is around. Then I'll cut down Maryland, go down Cassingham and drive past the school. I'll go around the block, to Ardmore, and go past Jack's. I'll go over to Merkle and see if anyone is home at Dan's. Then I'll start over again.

I'm sure that everyone has their own cruising pattern; when I'm out driving I'll see other guys doing the same thing, and they always seem to be on automatic pilot, just like I am. The one thing I'll never do is drive past Lindy's house; I might go down Powell—the cross street that cuts into her street, Stanwood, half a block from her house—and sneak a sideways look down there. But I won't go by the house itself.

If I did, she or her friends or her brother or her parents would see me, and I can just imagine them saying: "There he goes again." I feel bad enough without them saying stuff like that. I remember the day President Kennedy died last fall; they let us out of school early, and all I could think about was how Lindy was feeling about it. I wanted to walk to her house; I didn't know why, but I just felt that I wanted to be there. So I walked to Powell and Stanwood . . . and I just couldn't make myself walk the last half a block. Here President Kennedy was dead, and I wanted to go to Lindy's, but I thought I'd look stupid standing in front of her house like some idiot. So I walked home instead.

Today I cruised the circuit three or four times, listening to WCOL. Then I went home for dinner. Another big day in Bexley.

Jack, Chuck, and Dan came over after dinner. We went to Super Crust and bought poor boys. That drives my dad crazy; an hour after dinner I walk back into the house with my friends and a bag full of sandwiches.

We went to my room and I started to show them how I could play "Green, Green" on my guitar. Chuck wanted to hear my Beatles album, though—he doesn't have it yet—so I put the guitar away and put the album on for him.

They left. Now I'm watching Yvette Mimieux on *Dr. Kildare*. She looks so good in a bathing suit.

JANUARY 17

I wore my letter sweater to school today. You're supposed to do that on Fridays when there's a game that night. It really makes the day feel special. I remember what it was like before I lettered, coming to school on Fridays and seeing all the lettermen in their sweaters. I never said anything about it—what would I say?—but all I wanted in the world was one of those sweaters. Thank God for tennis.

I think the worst thing about school is constantly having to deal with those tests and quizzes. Today we had a quiz in Algebra; we got a Chemistry quiz back; we took a French test; and we got an English paper back. It's like you're being judged three or four times a day, every day.

I see my dad at the dinner table every night—and I don't care how much pressure he's under at work, it can't be any worse than dealing with all those grades every day. It seems to me that you can deal with it one of two ways. You can become totally obsessed with doing well—in which case you might as well not even be alive, because your whole life is devoted to worrying about school. Or you can be like me and just let it happen.

That sounds good, but when I'm honest with myself I don't quite believe it. When I do well on a test or a paper I feel good; when I do poorly I feel lousy. So obviously I care. It's just that when nighttime comes around I can't deal with any more books; I've seen enough of them in school all day.

Still, even though I manage to rally on the final exams most of the time and do all right on my report cards, I find myself realizing that next year I've got to worry about getting into college. I wonder if I'm going to regret all those nights of cruising and talking on the phone and listening to WCOL.

At the basketball game tonight, Lindy and her friends were sitting in the stands on the other side of the court. She was jumping around like crazy during the game. I kept looking at her.

Once after Bexley had scored a basket she leaped up into the air. She seemed to be looking over at me, so I imitated her. She held up a charm I gave her last summer. I held up my class ring.

At the half we talked out by the Coke counter. She was friendly, but very cool. There was just nothing there. That's the worst thing about this whole situation. If this were in a book or a movie, it would all seem like something tragically romantic, out of the deep past. Something to store in my memory.

But in real life Lindy lives in Bexley and comes to the basketball games and walks down the street. That's so much harder to deal with.

JANUARY 18

I'M grounded for the weekend.

What happened was that this morning I borrowed Mom's car, because we had a Saturday *Torch* production session. When we got done with that I picked Chuck up and we went to Howard Johnson's for lunch. Then we went back to Chuck's and played guitars.

Around dinnertime I realized that I had been supposed to pick my brother Timmy up at one of his friend's. I hurried over there and got him home just a few minutes late for dinner, but Dad blew up and said that I couldn't drive for the rest of the weekend.

So Dan and Pongi brought poor boys over to our house, and we sat around my room and talked and listened to WCOL. "Bobby's Girl" came on the radio, and it reminded me of last summer, so I started to dial for cake.

I forget what "dial for cake" even means—where it came

from. But it's what Lindy and I called it when we would call each other's house, let the phone ring once, then hang up. I'd do it to her house, and she'd do it to my house, and I'd do it to her house again, and finally one of us would stay on the line and talk. It used to drive our parents crazy. My dad would say, "Who's calling all the time and then hanging up?" And I'd say, "I don't know. Probably the cake dialers."

So I heard "Bobby's Girl" on the radio, and I thought that maybe Lindy was listening to WCOL, too, and maybe she was hearing the song and thinking about last summer. I told Dan and Pongi that I had to go somewhere for a minute. I left them in my room, and I went down the hall to my sister Debby's room—she was out with her friends.

I locked the door and rang Lindy's phone once. A few minutes later our phone rang once. It made my heart leap. I called again and she answered.

"Was that you?" she said. I said that is was; she said that it had been a long time since anyone had dialed for cake at her house. She sounded kind of bored; it wasn't any better than at the basketball game. The only time she sounded excited at all was when she said she had a crush on Sonny Dargusch.

Jack came over later and joined us in my room. He asked me what was wrong but I didn't say anything.

January 19

There's a new Beatles record on WCOL—"She Loves You." Tonight I hooked up our family's Wollensak tape recorder and sat by the radio for two hours waiting for it to come on. It finally did, and I got it on tape. I've been playing it over and over all evening.

JANUARY 20

GREAT news! Jack and I went over to Steve Pariser's house tonight, and he arranged it so that we're going to meet the Beatles!

Steve's a senior; he has an uncle who has a friend who works at a ticket agency downtown. Steve called his uncle right in front of us, and his uncle said that if the Beatles come to Columbus for a concert, he'll get us backstage so that we can do an interview for the *Torch*.

At first I didn't believe it, but Steve's uncle said that his friend at the ticket agency knows all of the people who run the Veterans Memorial Auditorium, where all the musical acts play when they come through Columbus. He said that the Beatles should be more than glad to give us an interview, because it would be a good way to get publicity at Bexley High School, and that the Beatles are aware that kids buy all the records.

Now all we have to wait for is the announcement of whether or not the Beatles will come to Columbus. The paper said that they're coming to America next month to be on television in New York; New York is only an hour or so away on an airplane, so it would make sense for them to come here.

Jack and I already started writing down questions to ask them.

JANUARY 21

FINALS begin tomorrow. Twice a year, this happens; the semester ends, and I realize that all the nights of not doing homework have finally caught up with me. There's nowhere to run. It's the scariest part of the year.

I walked home right after school and went to my room and came up with a strategy. I'd spend all afternoon and all night on Algebra and French; I wouldn't even bother with History, because I know that better than the other two, and I think I'll do as well as I can on that one anyway. Those are the three tests I have tomorrow.

Pretty soon I realized that I couldn't stay in my room; with my guitar and the radio and the portable TV, there were too many potential distractions. So I went down to the basement; the only things down there are a mat where our dog, Nippy, sleeps, and an old couch with a lamp next to it. I lay down on the couch and started reading the Algebra.

After a few hours I realized that there was some stuff I just couldn't figure out by myself. I called Marc Gertner and Larry Solove on the phone—they know everything in Algebra—and they helped me out. It seems so simple when they explain it.

Then I worked on the French for six hours straight. It gives me a headache, going over and over that stuff. I know that I wouldn't have to do this if I would just spend a decent amount of time every night on the homework. But knowing that doesn't help me on the night before finals.

When I went upstairs to bed, everyone was asleep. Mom and Dad were in their room with the lights out; Debby was in her room with the lights out; Timmy was in his room with the lights out. I remembered that I had forgotten to let Nippy in, so I went back downstairs and opened the back door. He came trotting inside, and I opened the basement door and he went down there.

I can't sleep.

JANUARY 22

IT wasn't as bad as I thought. Algebra went all right—I could have gotten a B, I could have gotten a D. French was surprisingly easy—I think I may have gotten a B at the worst. History was hard, but I knew the stuff.

Tomorrow are the finals in Chemistry and English. The other Chemistry classes had their test today, and the word is that it was easy. That means that ours will be hard.

The new WCOL survey came out today. "She Loves You" just made the list—number forty. "I Want to Hold Your Hand" is number one. *Meet the Beatles* is the featured album. All right!

I sit here listening to the radio all evening. Why aren't I studying Chemo?

Someone just dialed for cake. I rang Lindy's back, with no response.

JANUARY 23

THE Chemistry and English finals were both okay—I think I did as well as could be expected. We already got the Algebra finals back. I got a 76, which may even be a B if the scale is low enough.

I think of Mr. Schacht sitting there in his house last night, grading all of the Algebra tests so we would have them back the day after we took them. What a way to live. I wonder what he thinks about.

We had an Epsilons basketball game tonight. I played great—we won 47–45, and I won the game with a layup in the last two seconds. Something like that makes me feel so good, and then I try to put it in perspective. Not only is it just one little basketball game here in Bexley, but it's not even varsity—it's just fraternity league. Still, though, it's better than losing.

After the game we cruised in Pongi's car with the top down and the radio turned up loud. It felt weird being in the convertible in January—we were still sweating from the game, and the air was cold and it made me shiver to sit in the wind like that. It was fun, though—everybody on Main Street and Broad Street stared at us.

But then Pongi went honking past Lindy's house a couple of times. I put my head down by the seat and tried to hide. I wish he wouldn't do that.

I'm glad this semester is over. Halfway to summer.

JANUARY 24

I'M feeling the sickest I've felt in a long time.

After school I went downtown with Chuck. In the record department on the fifth floor of Lazarus, they had this thing where you could join the Beatle Boosters Club. Chuck and I signed up, and we each got a button and a newsletter. I'm a little confused—either the button or the newsletter has the identifications wrong. On the button it says that one guy is Paul McCartney, but in the newsletter the same guy is identified as John Lennon. I thought I had them straight from the album cover, but now I'm not sure.

We went to the Bexley basketball game tonight, and afterwards we went over to Steve Pariser's house to hang out with the seniors. The seniors were all smoking pipes.

We cruised in Gary Robins' car, and they lent us their pipes. I smoked one with some cherry-flavored tobacco. I didn't know you weren't supposed to inhale it, so I just kept sucking it in and not saying anything, and I felt my head getting dizzier and dizzier. No one else seemed to be affected by it, though, so I just kept it up. Everyone in the car had pipes in their mouths, and the whole inside of the car was filled with smoke. You could hardly breathe.

By the time they dropped me at home I felt like I was about to pass out. All I could feel was that burning cherry flavor in my throat and this hot sickness in my stomach. I've just thrown up twice; Mom knocked on my door to ask if I was all right—I guess she heard me in the bathroom. Never again.

JANUARY 25

I was still dizzy when I woke up this morning. If it wasn't a Saturday I would have thought about staying home, but I didn't want to waste a weekend day. I went downtown again with Chuck and Pongi, and then we just cruised for rest of the afternoon.

At night we went over to Whitehall to look for girls at the recreation center. Some Whitehall guys tried to pick a fight with us; one of them said to me, "Why don't you get a shovel and pick your nose?"

That used to really bother me when I was a freshman and a sophomore. When people used to say I had a big nose and make fun of me, I would really feel terrible. That's one of the things that Lindy changed; when we started going together, I stopped caring so much if someone knocked my nose. I just figured that I was past that.

So the guy said it, and I was wondering what to do about it, but then Pongi backed him down and we left. We went to a pay phone; last night the seniors said that we ought to quit going to Whitehall to look for girls, and we should concentrate more on the girls who are younger than us at Bexley. They said that we should come on really strong to the Bexley girls and let them think we're getting a lot of action. Then they'd want to be with us.

So from the pay phone in Whitehall we called Robyne Finke's house, where a lot of the freshman girls were hanging out. Dan got on the phone and said, "Hey, baby, where's the action?" Robyne said, "I don't know, you tell me." Dan didn't know what to say, so he just said, "The action's right here, baby," and then he handed the phone to me.

I started to say something, but Robyne had handed the phone to someone else—to my sister Debby. So there I was, with Debby on the other end of the line. I hung up and we went to Rubino's for a pizza and then went home.

JANUARY 26

I hate Sundays. Nothing to do. This afternoon Chuck and I drove over to Alum Creek and watched some guys play hockey. Then we went to the Pancake House. Dee, this cute waitress, was real nice to me; she came around to our side of the counter and sat next to me.

When I got home my brother Timmy had had a fight with Mom and Dad; he ended up locking himself in his room.

Timmy's only ten; I feel sorry for him, still having all this stuff to live through. I think of what the last six years have been like for me, and then I think that he hasn't even started growing up yet.

Sometimes I feel like sitting down and telling him what to expect, but I never do. Part of it is because no one ever sat me down and told me what to expect; but most of it is because I would have no idea where to start. How do you tell a ten-year-old kid what's going on inside of you? Most of the time I'm not even sure myself.

I knocked on his door, but he just yelled for me to go away.

JANUARY 27

AT dinner tonight Dad said that I had to get a haircut. Chuck's dad has been telling him the same thing. They both say that we're trying to look like the Beatles, which I guess is true. I don't know how I'm going to get around it.

JANUARY 28

THERE was a fight today after school. In the morning the word was going around that Pete Snyder was after Mike Talis. By third period everyone was talking about it in the hallways.

At noon the gym teacher, Mr. DeJong, and some of the other teachers said that they didn't want Snyder and Talis to have a street fight. They said they'd fix it up so that the two of them could fight with boxing gloves after school.

The fight was supposed to be on the Shelf—this balcony above the basketball court. DeJong said that no students other than Snyder and Talis could be up there. So we just waited around down below on the court; we couldn't see anything, because the bleachers up on the Shelf hid it, but we could hear everything that was going on up there.

It seemed like every male teacher in the school was up on the Shelf. You could tell right away that Talis was getting killed. We knew he was going to be no match for Snyder. I don't know—it seemed to me that for the teachers it was all one big spectator sport. I mean, they could have stopped the fight before it even started, if they'd wanted to. All they would have had to do is sit Snyder and Talis down together and talk to them.

But they didn't—it's almost as if the teachers were promoting the fight. I kept thinking about it, and all I could figure out is that the teachers must get as bored around here as we do. The fight seemed to pick up their day.

When Talis came down he was really beaten up. He was bleeding and his eyes were puffy. The teachers made a big deal out of having Snyder and Talis shake hands in front of all of us. I still think that if they'd really cared, they could have made sure that there wasn't any fight in the first place.

JANUARY 29

THE week's WCOL survey came out. "I Want to Hold Your Hand" is still number one; "She Loves You" moved all the way up to number eight. Pongi said he picked up WBZ in Boston on his car radio, and that he heard an even newer Beatles record—it's called "Please Please Me."

We got our semester grade cards today, too. I ended up with a 3.0 for the semester, with the help of two incredibly lucky breaks on the final exams. I credit it to carrying the piece of the lemon bottle in my pocket during finals.

Dad said that I have to get a haircut tomorrow with no excuses or I'm grounded again.

JANUARY 30

GOT a really crappy haircut after school. It depressed me. At dinner I asked Dad if it made him happy, and he said that it was still too long to suit him.

We had a fraternity league basketball game tonight. I played badly; we lost 38–30, and I only scored two points—a nothing shot from right under the basket in the first minute of play. Every time I would see my reflection with this dumb haircut, I would feel like hiding.

JANUARY 31

NUTTY day. I wore my letter sweater to school this morning, because it's Friday; as I was standing by my locker Judy Morse came up to me and started talking.

I really haven't talked to Judy since she asked me to the Presidential sorority dance that's being held next month. We've passed each other in the hallways a lot of times, and we always smile and say hi, but she's acted a little embarrassed.

But today she came right up and started a conversation. She said that her parents were going to be out tonight, and that if I wanted to come over and watch TV I could.

I didn't think I was going to do it; I was over at Chuck's tonight with Jack and Dan, but then I got real bored and I thought, why not? I had Mom's station wagon, and I didn't have to be home early. So I called Judy from Chuck's and asked if the invitation was still on, and she said to come on over.

When I got there she was in the den watching television. She got us Cokes and potato chips; first I sat in a chair and she sat on the couch, and then when she went off to go to the bathroom I moved over to the couch, and when she came back she sat on the chair. So I didn't do anything—but then in a little while I left the room to go to the bathroom, and when I came back she was on the couch again.

I sat down next to her on the couch and we watched the television set and didn't say too much. I wanted to put my arm around her, but I didn't know what she'd do if I did. About twenty times I started to do it, but I kept backing off. Finally I told myself that I'd count to a hundred in my head, and when I reached a hundred I'd just put my arm over her shoulders and see what happened.

I started counting, and neither of us was saying anything, and finally I got to a hundred and I moved my arm and put it over her shoulder. I was ready to yank it back if she seemed not to like it, but she responded right away; she slid over next to me and put her head on my shoulder. Neither of us said anything; we both pretended like we were interested in what was on the TV.

She kept moving closer to me and snuggling up against me. At one point I moved my arm, and my hand ended up on the front of her shirt. She didn't say anything or move my hand, so I kept it there.

It was really weird. For about an hour I sat there like that—with my hand on her chest—and it was okay with her. But a couple of times I tried to kiss her, and she didn't want to. She turned her head, or said "Unh-unh." But my hand being there seemed to be perfectly all right.

I don't even know why I was doing it. I kept wondering whether Lindy would be jealous if she knew about it. Around twelve-thirty we heard a noise at the door; it was Judy's parents coming home. We quickly moved apart from each other on the couch, and when her mom and dad came in I stood up and she introduced me and we all shook hands.

When they went upstairs to go to bed I told Judy that I should probably go home. She said she was looking forward to Presidential, and I didn't know what to say so I said that I was, too.

I was confused as I drove home. I wish I knew what girls wanted.

FEBRUARY 1

I was in my room playing my guitar tonight when Dad tried to walk in. I had the door locked. He started shaking the door, and when I opened it he said, "Why do you always lock this? What are you trying to hide?"

I don't know why I do it. I've been doing it for years. It seems to be the only privacy I have in the world—Timmy's room is right across the hall from me, and Debby's is right next door, and Mom and Dad's is right across from hers. It's like we're right on top of each other all the time, and the only way I can have a place that's mine is to lock the door.

I don't think that's such an irrational idea. I guess if I had tried to explain it that way to Dad, he might have understood. But I just said, "I'm not trying to hide anything."

He looked around the room and shook his head. Then he walked out; he left the door open a few inches. When I was sure he'd gone downstairs, I closed it all the way and locked it again.

FEBRUARY 2

I slept until eleven-thirty this morning; Sundays may be a drag, but at least I don't have to get up while it's still dark. It was really warm for this time of year, so I went over to Chuck's house, and he and Jack and Dan and I played two-on-two basketball on his driveway.

At night Jimmy Crum called. Mom and Dad were out; Debby

was playing records real loud, and Timmy was running around with one of his friends screaming, and I couldn't hear what Jimmy was saying. I told Debby and Timmy who it was, but they thought I was kidding; they didn't believe me.

Back in eighth grade, Mom and Dad gave me a present of season tickets to the Ohio State basketball games. That was when they had the great team—Jerry Lucas, John Havlicek, Larry Siegfried. It turned out that my seat at St. John Arena was close to the spot where Channel 4 broadcast the games.

Jimmy Crum has been the Channel 4 play-by-play man for years. He has an assistant named Gary Taylor, who keeps the statistics for him during the game, and hands him notes telling him who's scored how many points, who has how many rebounds, etc. I got to talking with Gary Taylor, and one game he let me try keeping the statistics for the visiting team while he concentrated on the Ohio State statistics. I guess he liked the way it worked out, because from that time on, we did it every game. He kept Ohio State's numbers, I kept the visitors' numbers. I never got paid for it, but after a while Gary told Jimmy Crum that I was a big help, and Jimmy started mentioning my name on the air.

It was great—Jimmy would say, "Now it's time for our half-time statistics, so we'll turn to our men with the pencils, Gary Taylor and Bobby Greene, and find out how the teams are doing." I never got my picture or my voice on TV, but everyone in Columbus watches the Ohio State games on Channel 4, and the next day everyone in school would say that they'd heard Jimmy say my name. It must be sort of what it feels like to be famous.

The next year Mom and Dad gave me tickets as a present again, but they weren't near Jimmy Crum and Gary Taylor. But Jimmy asked me for my phone number, and a couple of times since then when Gary hasn't been able to make it to the game, Jimmy has called and asked me to fill in.

That's what he was doing tonight. I could hardly hear a word he was saying because of Debby's records and Timmy's yelling. But he said that Gary Taylor had a kidney stone, and could I work at the Ohio State–Michigan game tomorrow night? He said he'd leave a pass for me at the box office.

I said I'd be glad to do it. After we had hung up I went to

my room and learned to play the Kingston Trio's ''M.T.A.''
from a guitar songbook I just bought.

FEBRUARY 3

CHUCK got a white '64 Impala convertible. He drove it to school
today. That would really be something—to have your own car.
He says I can drive it sometime, but that's not the same.

The Ohio State game was great tonight. I had to do the
statistics for both teams—Ohio State and Michigan—and it
was really hard; I had to be writing stuff down every second,
because as soon as one team got done shooting at their end
of the court, I'd have to switch pieces of paper and do the
other team at their end of the court.

Jimmy Crum said my name a lot. It's the strangest feeling;
I sat there handing him the numbers, and he would say my
name, and the reality of it was that we were just two people
sitting on chairs next to each other. But I knew that every
time he said it, the whole town was hearing it. Very bizarre.

Ohio State won, and Jimmy didn't ask me to give him the
pass back, so maybe it will be good to get me in at other
games the rest of the season. It's funny—when the game was
over and everyone was leaving St. John Arena, I felt real low.
Like the excitement was gone, and I was already missing it.
I've felt that way before, usually after I've had an especially
good time, and I don't really understand it. Just empty. I sat
there next to Jimmy, and he signed a few autographs, and
then I noticed that the arena was almost deserted, so I left to
go home. I wanted the game to still be going and the people
to still be yelling and Jimmy to still be saying my name into
his microphone.

FEBRUARY 4

YESTERDAY we had an Algebra quiz; today we got it back. I got a 30. Mr. Schacht asked me to stay after class.

I waited by his desk, and when everyone had left he said, "I was watching the Ohio State basketball game last night. Was that you that Jimmy Crum kept mentioning?"

I said that it was.

"You kept the statistics for both teams?" he said.

I said that I had.

He began to shake his head. "You know," he said, "I don't think I have too many students who could do that. Keeping statistics under that kind of pressure is very hard. Most people would clutch. But obviously you can do it. And yet here's your quiz—what did you get on it, a 40?"

"Thirty," I said.

He shook his head again. "I can't understand it," he said. "Can you explain it to me?"

"Not really," I said. "It's just that keeping the statistics at the basketball game is fun, and taking Algebra quizzes in here isn't fun."

I thought I saw him begin to smile, but then he said, "See if Seth Hock will let you take his quiz home with you. He got a 100 on it; study it and see what you can learn."

I walked out of the room. When I got to the hallway I looked back inside. Mr. Schacht was bent over his desk, grading papers.

I saw Judy Morse in the hallway after school. She asked me if I knew who we were doubling with for Presidential next weekend, and I told her probably with Pongi and his date. She didn't say anything about the other night at her house.

Worked on "The Sloop John B." and "Don't Think Twice, It's All Right" on the guitar after school.

Candy Grossman and Robyne Finke were over visiting Debby at our house this afternoon. I went into Debby's room and talked for a few minutes; when I walked out I didn't go down the hall to my own room right away. I stood outside Debby's door and listened to see if they said anything about me.

Debby said something bad about me. Robyne said, "Oh, I think he's cool."

It's funny how something like that can affect you. Debby can be expected to crack on me like that, because she's my sister. But if Robyne would have agreed with her, it would have put me in a bad mood all night. Because she said what she did, I felt great.

FEBRUARY 5

BILL Reilly, this sophomore who is an epileptic, went into a kind of spell second period. He gets them sometimes. It's not like a real seizure; it's sort of like he's in a trance—asleep on his feet. I heard once it was from his medication.

These guys were making fun of him. I couldn't believe it—they were gathering around him and saying stuff to him and laughing. Chuck and I saw what was going on, and we took him and walked him down to the nurse's office. The nurse called his mom and his doctor.

After school I ran into David Brown in the parking lot. He and some of his friends are supposed to be running around with Lindy and her friends, and the word has been spreading that they want to fight us.

He was with Janie McKenney, one of Lindy's best friends. Janie said hi to me, but David just stared. I stared back.

Finally he said, "Hard guy," and walked on.

I think we'll have to fight them eventually.

New survey day on WCOL. "She Loves You" is up to number one. "I Want to Hold Your Hand" drops to number two. "Please Please Me" is number thirty-one. There are two great non-Beatles songs, too: "California Sun," by some group whose name I don't know, is number twenty, and the pick hit is "Fun, Fun, Fun" by the Beach Boys. It's about a girl who takes her father's Thunderbird—it's great to listen to while you drive around.

FEBRUARY 6

NANA, my grandmother, came home from a trip. She brought me a "surf shirt" and a madras cap. There's no way I'll wear that creepy stuff, but she'll be watching to see if I do. Grandmothers.

FEBRUARY 7

IT'S Friday, and there was a Bexley basketball game at Whitehall tonight. We drove over in Chuck's new car.

Lindy and her friends were there and they were talking with David Brown and the guys he runs around with. At halftime we all went out to the lobby, and David Brown walked past me as if he didn't see me, but just as we were passing he rammed his shoulder into me. He looked back and smiled.

The Beatles are in New York. They're supposed to be on "The Ed Sullivan Show" on Sunday.

FEBRUARY 8

CHUCK and Dan and I played ice hockey on Alum Creek this afternoon. We didn't have any of the right equipment, so we used tennis racquets and tennis balls.

Presidential was tonight. Pongi picked me up, and then we picked his date up, and then we went to pick up Judy Morse.

You're supposed to send flowers for big dances like this one, so I'd sent her a wrist corsage, which she was wearing.

The dance was at Winding Hollow Country Club, and when we got there I noticed that Judy was wearing a dress you could look right down. Every time we'd get out on the dance floor and she'd start moving, you could see her bra. Girls must know it when they dress like that.

The dance was all right; everyone was there. Afterwards we went to Howard Johnson's for food, and she sat real close to me in the back seat of Pongi's car. When I went to kiss her, though, she didn't let me; it was just like that night at her house.

We all had desserts at HoJo's, and then Pongi drove to Judy's house and I walked her to the door. I planned on just getting out of there; I told her that it had been a nice evening, and she put her key in the door and went inside.

So I was walking back to Pongi's car, making my way through the snow on her driveway, and she came flying back out of the front door. She called my name, and I turned around, and she said, "Come here." I walked back up to her door, and she flew on me—started kissing me like crazy. She said that her parents might go out of town next week, and if they did she wanted me to come over.

I got into Pongi's car and he said, "What was that all about?"

I told him that I had no idea, and I don't.

FEBRUARY 9

THE Beatles were on "Ed Sullivan." They are simply the greatest thing ever to hit America. I thought I was impressed with them because of their records on the radio and their pictures in the paper, but that was nothing compared to seeing them on TV.

Before they even came on, the girls were going nuts. Then Ed Sullivan said, "And now . . . the Beatles!" They were standing there like they were nervous, and then Paul McCartney leaned into his microphone and started "All My Loving": "Close your eyes and I'll kiss you . . ."

It was like there was a riot in the studio. In addition to

"All My Loving," they sang four other songs: "Till There
Was You," "She Loves You," "I Saw Her Standing There,"
and "I Want to Hold Your Hand." They seemed to lose their
nervousness after the first song, and on the rest of the songs
they really seemed to be enjoying themselves. Sometimes you
could hardly hear them because of the screaming—especially
when two of them would lean into one microphone together
and harmonize.

Next week they're supposed to be on from Miami, and the
week after that on tape. Right after the show ended, my phone
started ringing. In the first fifteen minutes after "Ed Sullivan" went off the air, I talked to Dave, Chuck, Dan, Jack,
and Pongi's little sister Terri. It was as if everyone had to call
their friends to talk about what they'd just seen on TV.

Even Dad seemed to think they were all right. I remember
when Elvis Presley was first on "Ed Sullivan"; I was only
nine at the time, but I still remember how angry it made him.
He just hated the very sight of Elvis. Tonight with the Beatles
he didn't go so far as to say that he liked them—but he didn't
say that he hated them, either. He made some comments
about their hair, of course, but I expected that. I turned around
during one of their songs, and he was actually looking at the
screen and smiling.

FEBRUARY 10

THIS morning right before the bell to start homeroom I went
into the boys' locker room. About twelve guys were all standing in front of the big mirror, trying to comb the front of
their hair down on their foreheads.

The only thing people are talking about is the Beatles. All
during the last month there have been some of us who have
liked their music, but the "Ed Sullivan" appearance changed
everything. Now virtually everyone in the school is Beatles-
crazy. It was funny to see guys with crew cuts and flattops
standing in front of that mirror, trying to make their hair look
like Paul McCartney's.

* * *

There's word around the school that there may be something going on between Judy Morse and me. Pongi must have told people about her running out of her house Saturday night and calling me back to kiss her. I may have to cool it with her. I don't want people thinking that we're going together.

I went to Rogers' Drugstore on Main Street after dinner and got the new issue of *Hootenanny* magazine. After all these weeks of trying to learn folk songs on my guitar, the hootenanny stuff all of a sudden seems less exciting. I guess it's because of the Beatles; after seeing them sing last night, the stories and pictures of folk groups don't do as much for me. And now the idea of all of us getting a folk group together for the school talent show seems kind of dumb.

FEBRUARY 11

DAD was in a bad mood at dinner tonight. I guess he had a bad day at the office or something; he snapped at me and then he got mad at Timmy and sent him upstairs before dessert.

Dad is vice-president of the Bron-Shoe Company, which is the company that bronzes baby shoes. They do other kinds of plating, too; every year he'll get to gold-plate a baseball that was used to win the World Series, or a football that was used in the Rose Bowl, and stuff like that. I remember once at dinner he pulled a golf ball out of his pocket and asked me if I knew what it was; he handed it to me and told me that it was the ball that Arnold Palmer had used to win the Masters.

He doesn't talk about business problems much at home. When we were little kids he used to take us down to his office on holidays when there were parades in Columbus, and we would watch the parades from his window. He'd always try to make the same joke; we'd get dressed and go downtown, and we would be early, so he would sit us up on his windowsill and there would be nothing going on down on the street. So he'd say. "Ooops! We're late! We missed it!" And then a few minutes later the parade would come marching down the street.

That seems like a long time ago. At dinner he and Mom talked about some people at his office whose names I didn't recognize. Apparently someone had screwed up a big shipment, and Dad had to get things straightened out. I excused myself from the table early and took Mom's car and cruised a while.

FEBRUARY 12

WE had a *Torch* meeting after school tonight that lasted all the way to dinnertime. That's taking up more and more of my time; I really like being on the newspaper, but I can't wait for tennis to start again.

There's something about playing on a varsity team that nothing else can touch; on the days of matches, when the cheerleaders put paper tennis racquets on the lockers of the varsity players, with our names written on them in Magic Marker, that's the best feeling in the world. Everyone who walks past your locker that day knows that in a few hours you'll be representing Bexley against another school.

I remember when I was a freshman, seeing those paper things on the lockers. The cheerleaders put them up there for every sport—football, basketball, baseball, track, all the rest. I used to think that was an unreachable goal—to have one of those things on my locker. And then there it was. I kept making excuses to walk by my locker all that day, just to look at it.

I have tests in Chemistry and History tomorrow, so tonight Chuck and I went to the Bexley Public Library to study. On the way over there we started talking about David Brown and Chet Crosby. Now the word is that not only is Brown looking for a fight with me; Crosby's looking for a fight with Chuck, too. Brown and Crosby are best friends.

I told Chuck that we should just walk into Rubino's Pizzeria Friday night and fight them. I'm sick of hearing all this talk about it; I told him that we should just do it and get it over with.

He says he's not sure. Actually, it's easier for me to talk about it than it would be to do it; Brown's much bigger than I am, and I have no idea how I would do against him. But I'm tired of all the stares, and of the muttering every time I

walk past him. The weird thing is that I don't even really
know him; we probably haven't said twenty words to each
other in our lives. But once the word starts that someone
wants to fight you, you're in each other's lives.

FEBRUARY 13

WHAT a bad day. The Chemo test was hard, and the History
test was unbelievable. Then at night we lost a fraternity league
basketball game 35–30. I played terrible—only two points.

And then Dan and I were cruising in his T-Bird, and we
were driving down Cassingham and we got barraged by
snowballs. Dan slammed on the brakes and we jumped out
of the car to go after whoever did it, and there was no one
there. I don't know if they were hiding, or they ran away, or
what—but there we were, standing in the middle of the street
pissed off, and there was no one in sight. If they were watching us, they had to be laughing.

FEBRUARY 14

TONIGHT was the night I thought we were going to fight David Brown and Chet Crosby. There was a Bexley basketball
game; I wore my letter sweater. We were sitting on one side
of the court—and Lindy and her friends were sitting in their
usual spot on the other side.

She was with Janie McKenney and Wendy Clowson. Midway through the second quarter, Brown and Crosby sat down
with them. Lindy, that wiseass, started waving at me. She
knew what she was doing—she wanted a fight.

So Chuck and Dan and Jack and I walked out to get Cokes
at half time, and Brown walked by Chuck and nudged him,
but didn't say anything.

When the second half started we went back to our seats. I
said to Chuck that this was getting ridiculous; we had to fight

them. They were pushing us too far. So we decided to go to the hangouts after the game and see what happened.

We went to Super Crust first, and they weren't there. Then we went to Rubino's, and they weren't there, either. We ended up at Pongi's house, playing guitars and listening to records.

FEBRUARY 15

I'M awfully lucky to be around to write this tonight.

Today was one of those long Saturdays with nothing to do, so early in the afternoon we decided we'd drive to Dayton. Pongi drove his car; Jack, Chuck, Dan, and I went along.

Pongi and Dan told their parents they were going, but Jack, Chuck, and I didn't have permission. In Dayton we saw some guys we met last summer—Bart Weppern, Gary Snyder. Jack had gone out with a girl from Dayton, Joyce Burick, and we went to her house for a while. Then we cruised around Dayton—this hard-looking guy in a 409 started chasing us for no reason, but we lost him.

It was a pretty good day, and right after dinnertime we started back for Columbus. About halfway there it started to snow, and it kept getting worse. The road was completely icy.

Pongi was driving, and I was next to him in the front seat. Jack and Chuck and Dan were in the back. Pongi's usually a fast driver, but he was being really careful this time; the road was totally slick, and you could hardly see out the front windshield because of the snow.

All of a sudden, on the highway about ten miles outside of Columbus, we hit a bad patch of ice. It was like it was happening in slow motion. First we swerved over into the lane of oncoming traffic. Pongi was fighting the wheel the best he could, and he got us to swerve back into our own lane. But all that did was make us swerve even more; I could see him trying to turn the wheel, but this time we slid even farther into the oncoming lane. Any car that was coming the other way would have slammed right into the front of ours.

Nobody was saying anything. "I Want to Hold Your Hand" was playing on the radio—that was the only sound in the car.

We swerved a total of four times. It was like we were just waiting for a car going the other way to hit us. Finally we were swerving all the way across the other side of the road, and then all the way back. Pongi said, "Here we go."

We crashed through a guardrail and went flying over an embarkment. I never thought about what it would feel like to die, but this was it. I just knew that these were going to be the last seconds I was alive. I was calm, but I felt sad. It was like being aware that your life was ending, and not being able to do anything about it.

We hit three times, each time harder. Finally we came to a rest in a ditch. I knew I wasn't dead because "I Want to Hold Your Hand" was still playing. Pongi said, "Is everybody all right?" I looked around into the back seat, and Jack and Chuck and Dan were just sitting there. We climbed out of the car; it was still snowing hard.

A car behind us had stopped, and the driver got out to see if we were okay. A few minutes passed; someone in a nearby house must have called the operator, because within ten minuted there were two ambulances and a cop and a tow truck.

We just walked around in the snow. Pretty soon a Channel 10 car arrived; they must listen to the police radio or something. A guy with a camera got out and aimed it at us. That's all we needed—for our parents to see us on the eleven o'clock news. But Dan got a great idea. He gave the finger to the camera, and everywhere the cameraman went, Dan stood in front of him giving him the finger. There's no way they were going to be able to use any of it on the news.

The tow truck pulled Pongi's car out of the ditch; it was pretty banged up, but he was still able to drive it. We went the rest of the way into Columbus. I'm not going to tell my parents about it. Chuck and I finished the evening watching TV with Candy Grossman and Robyne Finke at Robyne's house.

FEBRUARY 16

IT felt good to wake up alive this morning. I had breakfast and immediately went over to Pongi's. Jack and Dan and Chuck were there, too; we talked to Pongi's parents about what had happened, and they weren't mad. Pongi had to tell them about it, because the car was so messed up. We sort of asked them not to mention to our parents that we had gone to Dayton.

Then we drove back out to the scene of the crash. We wanted souvenirs. We picked up pieces of the guardrail, and branches from these little trees the car had knocked over. Being there in the daytime was eerie; it brought back how awful it had been last night, but somehow in the light of day it seemed different— like seeing a newspaper picture of it or something.

We went back to Bexley, and we saw Jay Maupin cruising with Susie Sloan. They've started going out together; it's big news in the school, because he's the best athlete in the senior class and she's the sexiest of the sophomore girls. We followed them for a while, and then he figured out what we were doing and he circled around and chased us. Then we went home.

It's funny—this afternoon, on our way back out to the scene of the crash, we passed the Park towers, the apartment building where Allen Schulman lives.

When Allen's in town, he's a big part of our lives—ABCDJ wouldn't exist without him. But now that he's back at military school, sometimes it feels as if he doesn't exist. During the summer and during school vacations we spend most of our time up in his parents' apartment. But now there are weeks that go by when I have to admit that I don't even think about him.

Looking at his apartment building, I was thinking how tough that must be for him—being down there at military school, knowing that the people he's closest to are living out their lives without him. Like last night—as terrible as it was, it seemed that Allen should have been there. As it is, he doesn't even know about it.

The Beatles were on ''Ed Sullivan'' again tonight. It was sort of disappointing. The show was broadcast from Miami; the audience was pseudo-sophisticated—they just sat there and watched, and hardly screamed at all. That took a lot away from it.

The Beatles sang ''She Loves You,'' ''This Boy,'' ''All My Loving,'' ''I Saw Her Standing There,'' ''From Me to You,'' and ''I Want to Hold Your Hand.'' I got mad, watching those people in the audience just staring at the stage and not doing anything. It wasn't even that they were old; the camera kept showing the people in the seats, and there were a lot of kids. But they were all dressed up, and mostly they watched the Beatles like it was a movie or something. Maybe people are like that in Miami.

FEBRUARY 17

SECOND period today I told Dianne Kushner about the accident. She was impressed. Everyone is.

The Beatles were on the cover of *Newsweek* today. Great article.

It's funny how, after you hear a song on TV, it keeps going through your head—much more than after you've heard it on the radio. All day long in school I kept thinking of "From Me to You," because the Beatles sang it on "Ed Sullivan" last night. Mr. Millard would be talking in History class, and all I could hear was that song.

Tonight Jack and I went to Bexley Records and we each bought the single of it. It's not on their album. "Please Please Me" is on the other side.

FEBRUARY 18

OUR accident is still the main topic of conversation. Today in the hallway I saw Coach Weis, and I asked him if he knew when tennis practice was going to start.

He smiled. "There'll be a note posted in the boys' locker room, Crash," he said.

I didn't even know the teachers knew about it.

It was embarrassing after school. The bell had rung, and most people had gotten all of their stuff out of their lockers and gone home. Chuck and Dan and I were still hanging around in the hallway outside Mrs. Amos' room.

Chuck was kidding Dan about something, and Dan—joking—said, "You fucker." Right at that moment Mrs. Amos came out of her room. She heard it.

We didn't know what to do. Dan turned red, and Chuck started to laugh, and I turned away. Mrs. Amos just looked at us, pretended she hadn't heard, and walked back into her room.

FEBRUARY 19

DAD got a new '64 Thunderbird today. He drove it home from his office after work. It's a beige convertible; it's really beautiful. It's a lot different from Dan's family's '56 T-Bird; a lot bigger and more modern.

After dinner we all went out for a ride in it. Dad and Mom were in the front seat, and Debby, Timmy, and I were in back. We drove all over Bexley and halfway downtown. I asked Dad if I could drive it some day; he said maybe. For now, I guess I'll still be driving Mom's station wagon.

FEBRUARY 20

MRS. Amos called me aside today and told me that the *Torch* had been named an all-American school newspaper. That makes me feel good; I would guess that the reason she is telling me all this is that she's going to choose me to be one of the main editors for next year. Which makes me a little nervous; I don't know how I'm going to go to tennis practice every day and put the paper out, too.

Chuck's hair is getting pretty long; at the basketball game the other night a girl called him "Beatle." But there's a problem; today in the hallway C.W. Jones, our principal, grabbed

Chuck by the shirt and said, "Get a haircut." Chuck's really depressed about it, but he'll probably have to do it.

Had a fraternity league basketball game tonight, and I played great. It was like I was hypnotized; everything I threw into the air was going in. I only played three quarters and scored eleven points—and I didn't even shoot that much.

Afterwards Jack and I went to Howard Johnson's East for dinner. I love fried clam night at HoJo's; it's all you can eat, and Jack and I each had three plates.

FEBRUARY 21

AFTER school today Chuck and I went downtown to Lazarus; they got a Beatles guitar chord book in stock, so I bought one. It'll be great, playing Beatles songs instead of that folk stuff. I bought the single of "Fun, Fun, Fun," too.

At night we all went over to Nancy Dartwell's house; there were a lot of people there. I don't know what's wrong with us; everyone was in a bad mood and snapped at each other. First Chuck wanted to fight Jack, which I broke up. Then he wanted to fight me.

We're so screwed up. We're each other's best friends in the whole world, but things get so boring around here that we start picking on each other. I just wish it was summer and I was in love with Lindy and she loved me and we roamed all day and walked in the sun and went to the pool and were happy in the truest sense.

FEBRUARY 22

I woke up at eleven-thirty this morning; it's Saturday. Mom said she wanted me to go get some groceries for her. I asked if I could drive Dad's Thunderbird, but he said no.

So I took the station wagon; I picked up Jack, and we each

bought a pair of Weejuns. Then I went to the grocery to get the stuff for Mom. Jack and Chuck have dates tonight, but I don't.

In the afternoon we went to the district wrestling matches, which were being held at Bexley. I helped sell popcorn in the lobby. About midway through the match Lindy's older sister Libby came in, and I immediately went into a daze. Just seeing Libby made me start thinking about Lindy again.

At night I stayed home. I played "Fun, Fun, Fun" on the hi-fi in the living room about twenty times, and then I dialed for a cake with no results.

I sat down and figured it out. It's been 258 days since I first met Lindy. I think that I'll always be different than before because of it.

FEBRUARY 23

THIS morning Jack and I went over to Chuck's. They didn't get anything on their dates last night. At least they went out. I hate staying home on weekend nights. Maybe I'll go to Judy Morse's again after all.

Dan and I went to the school courts this afternoon and played some tennis. It was really cold; even snowing a little. But it felt great to have a racquet in my hand. I can't wait for the season to start.

The Beatles were on "Ed Sullivan" again. Terrific as usual.

The National Honor Society assembly is coming up on Thursday. It's a big secret; if you make it they tell your parents beforehand so that the parents can be at the assembly, but you don't find out yourself until you're tapped. The parents aren't supposed to tell you that they've been called. Both juniors and seniors are eligible; the really good thing is to make it your junior year. I sure hope I have a chance, but I guess I really don't. It would make my parents feel so good if I made it.

FEBRUARY 24

HAD an impossible Algebra test this morning. After school, I called Tom Keys, the sports editor of the *Columbus Citizen-Journal*. I had called him before about a summer copyboy job, and he said he'd talk to me about it. Today he said I could come down to see him tomorrow afternoon. That would be something—a job at a real newspaper.

FEBRUARY 25

CASSIUS Clay beat Sonny Liston! I listened to the fight tonight on the radio in my room. This is one of the most amazing things that's happened in a long time. Sonny couldn't answer the bell after Round 6. They're saying he might have a broken shoulder. At the beginning of Round 4 Clay claimed that Liston had something on his glove, and that he couldn't see because of it. But he won anyway. I can't believe it!

After school I walked past Mark Engelman and some of the other seniors. Engelman stuck out his hand for me to shake, and said, "Congratulations. I hear you made National Honor Society." I didn't know what to say, but then he started laughing. He was just joking.

I went down to the *Citizen-Journal* for my job interview. It was really something—they all work in this one big room, and there's a lot of noise, and it feels very exciting.

I sat next to Tom Keys' desk in the sports department and talked to him. He was in the middle of writing tomorrow's column. I couldn't believe I was talking to him just like he was a regular guy—I've been reading his column for years. As we talked some of the other sports writers whose names I know—Kaye Kessler, Tom Pastorius—were working on their stories, too.

Mr. Keys said that I was a little young to be hired, even for the summer. He said that they usually hire journalism students from Ohio State. But he had me fill out an application, and he said that if anything opened up, he'd let me know.

I hated to leave. I can't imagine a better job—all those people were putting together the news we'll be reading tomorrow morning. It didn't look like a business office; they were talking back and forth and wandering around and laughing and drinking coffee. It seemed like it must be more fun than work.

FEBRUARY 26

I didn't make National Honor Society. The assembly's not until tomorrow, but Mom told me at dinner tonight.

We were all at the table, and Dad was cutting the meat, and Mom looked over at me and said, "Well, I didn't receive any phone calls." I knew what she meant—if I'd made it, the school would have called Mom and Dad to tell them to be there.

She smiled and said, "There's always next year." Meaning that I can make it when I'm a senior.

"It doesn't matter," I said.

But I was going crazy inside. Part of me was really resentful—I was thinking of reasons why they didn't accept me. Stuff like just because I've never believed in combing my hair back like Jim Guthrie, or laughing at teachers' jokes like Joe Doylston, or making pointless comments in class like Jon Rinkler, I didn't get into their little club. It was like I was making a speech in my head: "Well, they'll just have to get along without me." I didn't say anything out loud, though.

Most of all I was upset for Mom and Dad. It would have really made them proud to be able to come to the school tomorrow and to see me get initiated. My Mom deserves something like that.

The principal and the faculty select the National Honor Society members. In my head, I was still making my speech: "If I don't fit the perfect image of C.W. Jones and his teacher puppets, I guess that's the way it is." But I just kept sitting there, saying nothing.

When I get angry, I can't sit still. I feel like doing two things right now—fighting David Brown and Chet Crosby (which we had a chance to do after school today), and getting Lindy back (which I'll probably never get a chance to do).

I took the station wagon after dinner, went over to Luke's Shell Station and put a dollar's worth of gas in it, and cruised for two hours. I didn't stop anywhere and I didn't say a word to anybody.

FEBRUARY 27

THE assembly was today. I didn't feel all that bad, considering. I got most of it out of my system last night.

All the people you would expect to make it made it. It's funny—when the senior members went out into the audience to tap the new members, I kept thinking that maybe I'd get tapped after all. I thought that maybe Mom and Dad had been pulling something on me last night. But of course they hadn't been.

There were some people who made it who I know had worse grade points than I do. I guess I can understand why I didn't make it—it's fairly common knowledge that I don't study, and that I have to salvage things every six weeks on the final exams. That's just not the way National Honor Society members operate. Still, it would have been nice.

As I was walking out of the assembly, I passed all of the parents of the new members, who had been standing out of sight at the back of the auditorium. Mr. Schacht was walking next to me. He must have been reading my mind. He said to me, "Don't worry about it. It's a farce." I think he was just trying to make me feel a little better; if he was, it worked.

It looks like we won't be interviewing the Beatles. I've been bugging Steve Pariser to talk to his uncle about it; ever since his uncle said he'd be able to fix it up, I've been thinking about it.

Today Steve said that the Beatles probably won't even be coming to Columbus. Columbus is too small a city for them, he said; his uncle said that there's a chance the Beatles will do a closed-circuit concert for the whole country, but not a concert just for Columbus.

FEBRUARY 28

THERE was an afternoon Bexley basketball game today right after school. Lindy was there with David Brown, which put me in a bad mood. I was feeling depressed at night, so I called Judy Morse, and she said to come on over. Her parents were out.

We watched TV and had some Cokes. She put a Four Seasons album on, and she leaned against me while we were pretending to watch the show on the TV, which had the sound turned down. I started to kiss her, and she let me, and she let me put my hand over her blouse again, too.

It was weird—even though it was supposed to be this romantic scene, the whole thing felt like I was watching it from the outside. Almost like I was standing outside her house, looking in a window. It felt good, what we were doing, and Judy is a nice enough girl, but I just didn't feel anything for her. I was hearing the Four Seasons album, and when we would stop kissing for a moment I would see the TV show, and I could hear their grandfather clock ticking. Judy's family has a dog, and the dog kept bumping up against my legs, and I was noticing that all the time, too.

I got the impression that she was feeling the same way. I don't really think she likes me that much; the fact is that I don't have a girlfriend and she doesn't have a boyfriend, so there we were. But I didn't really want to be there all that much; we don't mean anything to each other, and we were pretending that we did. Every time we would stop kissing we would look at each other, but neither of us could think of anything we wanted to say. So we would start kissing again, because we didn't know what else to do.

I suppose it was better than the last time I was at her house—when she wouldn't let me kiss her at all. But mainly I kept thinking of getting out of there, and finally I did. I drove past Candy Grossman's house. Dan's Thunderbird was in front, so I went in. There were a lot of people over there; Dan and I left and went cruising in his car.

I tried to explain to him what I was feeling. I told him that I'm still in love with Lindy, and that the good feeling of just being around her could never be replaced by my hand on some girl's front.

"Yeah, but you've got to get over that," Dan said.

I said I knew it, and we went to Rubino's for a pizza.

FEBRUARY 29

PONGI raced Bob Peterson in their cars tonight. Then we went to Melanie Frank's house; there were a lot of people there, but it was really boring, and I said so to Jack. Melanie overheard me and got mad; she said that if I didn't like her party, I could leave. So I did. I went home and learned how to play "Blowin' in the Wind" on my guitar.

MARCH 1

WHAT a day. It's Sunday, so Dave Frasch, Mike Melton, Dan, and I went over to the school tennis courts and played doubles for about two hours. We finished at about 2:45 P.M., and Pongi cruised by. Dan, Mark Smilack, Mark Smilack's little sister Marcia, Melanie Frank, and I started riding around in Pongi's car.

We passed Chet Crosby on Roosevelt, and he saw Dan and me and gave us the finger. Then we saw Lindy's mother, Barbara Lemmon, driving her car—with Lindy and Wendy Clowson in there with her.

I've always really liked Mrs. Lemmon—she's much easier to talk to than most mothers; she even asks me to call her Barb-I. So we honked at her—and she started to chase us! Pongi was trying to lose her, and she was following his car all over Bexley! Right on his tail! We couldn't believe it.

Pongi drove up Bryden Road to my house and pulled into my driveway—and Barb-I pulled in right behind us! She was honking, and Lindy had the radio turned up real loud. My dad was in the front yard, and he had no idea what was coming off.

Barb-I backed out of the driveway, and then we chased her. We finally stopped around four o'clock, and we went to Pongi's. I was happy, but very confused. If Lindy doesn't care about me at all, why would she let her mom chase us? It would have been just as easy to tell her mom to take a turn at some street; but they willingly stayed on our tail. Does it mean I have a chance to get her back again? Was she being purposely mean? Did she just have nothing else to do? I have no idea.

I got home a little after six o'clock, and I could see right away that Dad was furious. At first I thought it was because of the cars chasing up into our driveway. But then he said: "Didn't you forget something today?"

I had promised him that I would wash his new car. In the excitement of being chased by Barb-I, I had completely forgotten it.

"I waited around all afternoon for you," Dad said. "I wanted to take the car out, but I was waiting for you to wash it. Do you call that responsibility?"

I didn't want to argue, so I just started to walk away. But I guess he took that as being insolent, because he said, real loud:

"Your seventeenth birthday is coming up, and there *was* going to be a car in your future."

I turned around. Mom was standing there, and she looked so sad. Apparently he wasn't kidding; my birthday is March 10th, and apparently he had been planning to surprise me with some kind of car of my own.

Once Dad says something, he never goes back on it. So I knew right away that there was no way I was going to get the car.

If he just wouldn't have said anything, he might have cooled down by tomorrow. But because he said it, I know that there's no chance I'll get one. Damn. Why couldn't I have remembered to wash his car?

MARCH 2

FULL day in school. First we had an assembly about the atom, and then I had a French quiz and a History test. Both were hard.

I was almost late because Dad blew up at me again this morning. He came down to breakfast, and I was eating a Swanson Turkey TV Dinner for my breakfast. He said that was the stupidest thing he had ever seen—he said that no one in his right mind would eat a turkey dinner for breakfast. I said it tasted great. At first I thought he was kidding about being upset, but he wasn't. Obviously something's bugging him lately.

So when he got home from work tonight I washed his car for him like I was supposed to do yesterday. I hope that calms him down.

WCOL has a new thing at night. It's called "Hotline Hitline"—it's like an instant survey, so you don't have to wait a week to find out what the top songs are. For an hour before it goes on the air, people call up to vote for their favorite songs, and then Bob Harrington counts them down. Tonight there were ten Beatles songs on Hotline Hitline, plus "We Love You Beatles."

I got a new mattress. Boy, it's firm.

MARCH 3

AFTER school today Dan and Dave Frasch and Mike Melton and I played doubles. Mike was my doubles partner when we lettered as sophomores last spring; we really play well together.

There's something about being on that tennis court that makes me feel better than anything else. As soon as I step onto the court I feel different; I walk between the white lines, and it's like I'm in a place where I know I'm good and I know I can handle anything. Whatever problems I have just go away.

I was feeling that way while we were playing. David Brown and Chet Crosby were running on the track, and when they passed our court they whistled—making fun of tennis. But I don't care. When I'm on the court it doesn't seem that anything else matters.

MARCH 4

FRATERNITY meeting tonight. The seniors are concerned that their references to Epsilons in their senior sketches in the yearbook have been edited out. In the *Bexleo* every year, every senior gets to write a paragraph of little items next to his or her picture. In the past, the members of Epsilons have always included a line that says "Men of Epsilons." But C.W. Jones doesn't approve of high school fraternities, and the rumor is that he had the adviser of the *Bexleo* go through the galley proofs and take all the fraternity references out.

MARCH 5

Two bad tests today. Everyone screwed up on the Algebra—we graded them in class. Mr. Schacht said that he was giving up on all of us. And Chemo was just as hard.

Tonight after dinner I walked over to Main Street and just wandered around. I went into Rogers' Drugstore and looked at the new magazines. Then I went over to the Eskimo Queen for a chocolate soda. Then I went down to Rubino's and sat in a booth to see if anyone I knew would come in for a pizza.

No one did, so I went to Jack's house. We said that we were going to study French together, but we ended up talking. I didn't get home until eleven-thirty. Mom was waiting up—she said that eleven-thirty is too late for a school night. I don't know. I was just in a weird sort of mood.

MARCH 6

LAST night I dreamed I beat up David Brown and Chet Crosby.

* * *

We played Turn The Crank, a kind of poker, at Pongi's tonight. I ended up losing a dollar, which bothered me—but when you think about it, whatever else I would have done for three or four hours would have cost me that much, anyway.

The SAT tests are tomorrow morning. I'm kind of nervous about them, but there's really nothing you can study for. Not only are they supposed to be hard tests, but they completely disrupt your Saturday.

I just dialed for cake. It worked—two minutes after I rang Lindy's phone once, our phone rang once and then stopped. I can go to sleep now.

MARCH 7

TOOK the SATs today. They were held at the Columbus School for Girls; we all had to be there before eight o'clock in the morning. I didn't think they were all that hard, but it was really interesting to watch people react.

I sat next to Jeff Schmidt, for example. He's a senior—blond, great-looking, the star of the basketball team, number one singles on the tennis team—and I've never seen him be anything but loose and funny in school. But today he was like everyone else; he knew that if he screwed up on the SATs, he'd be in trouble getting into college. He was visibly nervous, and I'd never seen him like that before. We talked just before the tests started, and he was totally serious.

The tests took three hours; we sat at tables in the CSG cafeteria and marked the answer sheets. The thing I noticed as I looked around the room was that no one was smiling or laughing or fooling around. No one. From the outside it might have looked like a study hall, but a study hall where everyone had just learned that a friend had died.

We went to Pongi's after the SATs. He got a pipe—a GBD—and he was smoking it in his room.

* * *

Our family went to dinner at Keunning's. I told Dad about Pongi's pipe and he laughed. On the way home he stopped the car at Rogers' Drugstore and went inside. When he came out he handed me a paper sack.

Inside it was a corncob pipe—one of those dumb-looking kinds that farmers smoke; the kind you buy for twenty-nine cents.

"There," he said. "Now you have a pipe, too."

I guess he's in a better mood.

MARCH 8

WENT to Chuck's to work on Algebra homework this afternoon. We had both washed our hair this morning; it's really getting long. Chuck's older brother Bill went to Rubino's and brought home pizzas for all of us. Chet Crosby's picture was in the *Sunday Dispatch* sports section for track; we cut it out and burned it.

Tonight on "Ed Sullivan" the Dave Clark Five were on. They were pretty cool, but they're definitely not the Beatles. They sang "Glad All Over"; after the show ended I taught myself how to play it on my guitar.

MARCH 9

TOMORROW'S my birthday, but we had my birthday dinner tonight. Mom and Dad gave me a new wooden guitar that's a lot better than the one I have; Nana gave me a sweater; Debby gave me the second Beatles album; Tim gave me a pouch of cherry tobacco for my corncob pipe.

Those are nice presents, but I really wanted that car. I kept thinking all week that maybe Dad would surprise me by going back on what he said and giving me a car anyway. I kept watching out the window for him to come home from work, thinking he might be driving a car for me. But when he came in the driveway it was just him in his Thunderbird.

It would have been so great to have my own car. Just to go anywhere I wanted, whenever I wanted.

It's raining like crazy tonight. The radio says that some parts of town are flooded.

I'm sitting in my room smoking a bowl of tobacco in my pipe. I've got to cut that out; it's a bad habit to get into.

MARCH 10

MY birthday. Seventeen years old. Dianne Kushner wished me happy birthday in school; she is so cool.

After school Dan and I went to Cochran's Drugstore because I wanted to get another pipe. I figured that as long as I was smoking in my room, I ought to have something better than that corncob thing.

I was afraid that the girl behind the counter wasn't going to sell it to me because I was too young to smoke. But she gave it to me right away—a Yello-Bole, for $1.95.

Dan started talking to her about buying tobacco, and she told him that he looked thirteen. He gave her the finger and then we left.

Invitations came out for Cynthia Blatt's sweet sixteen party. I'm paired up with Melanie Frank; Jack is with Marcia Smilack; Chuck is with Sue Young; Pongi is with Linda Paine. I haven't really said much to Melanie since she told me to leave her house when she had all those people over and I was knocking it. So I have no idea how she'll react to being paired up with me.

After school I called the *Citizen-Journal* to see how things looked for a summer job.

"We've still got your application," Tom Keys said. "But right now we're full up with Ohio State students. We've got your number, though, and we'll call you if anything changes.''

I could hear the typewriters pounding in the background, and people calling across the room to each other. It sure would be something to work at a newspaper.

MARCH 11

ACTION. Tonight there was the athletic banquet at school, to honor the winter sports teams. The dinner was held down in the gym; Chuck, Dan, and I went up onto the Shelf to look down and watch.

Lindy was in the crowd. Her brother Pat was getting an award. She looked up at the Shelf and saw that I was there. She held up her charm bracelet and showed me the charm I had given her. Why does she do that?

As the banquet ended we went back downstairs. Lindy walked out—with another girl and David Brown. Brown jammed his shoulder into me as he walked past me.

It took me about fifteen seconds to react. I walked out into the school lounge; Brown and Lindy and the other girl were standing by the apple machine.

I said, "Listen, Brown, if you're looking for trouble you know where you can get it."

"Any time," he said.

We stood there staring at each other, and then Lindy pulled on his sleeve and they walked away.

I can't believe how many people are talking about the Dave Clark Five. It's like they have no loyalty and no taste. The Dave Clark Five can't compare to the Beatles; but just because they were on "Ed Sullivan," and just because they're from England and they have long hair, people at school think they're great. Today someone even asked me if I thought they would overtake the Beatles. Unbelievable.

MARCH 12

I got an appointment card from Northwestern University in the mail today. I'm supposed to visit their campus in Evanston, Illinois, and be interviewed by an admissions officer on March 24. Dad is going to take me there.

Worked on the *Torch* from the end of school until dinnertime, and then for two hours tonight. I'm spending more time on that than I am on my schoolwork.

MARCH 13

DIANNE Kushner was teasing me in English today. She's the best-looking girl in our junior class; she's on the cheerleading squad, and will probably be head cheerleader next year. I was talking about going to Northwestern for the admissions interview, and she said that she'd like to go with me.

Judy Furman overheard her, and said, "Why would you want to go along?"

Dianne said, "For sex."

I knew she was only kidding, but it drove me crazy just thinking about it. Later on Judy said to her, "Why do you really want to go on that trip with Bobby and his dad?" And Dianne said, "It would be just like a honeymoon."

I wish.

MARCH 14

HAD my first beer.

It was a typical Saturday; I slept late and hung around Pongi's during the afternoon. At night Dan and I went to the school play; I was driving Mom's station wagon. After the play was over we got back in the car and were cruising, when all of a sudden there was this loud yelling from the back. Tim Greiner, Ed Weston, and Leon Friedland had gotten into the car during the play and had hidden back there. It was pretty funny, but I'm glad we weren't talking about them.

We dropped them off, and then went to a party at Gregg and Gary Robins' house. The Robins twins are seniors, and their dad owns a beer distributorship in town. Chuck and Jack were there, and then Dan and I got there; the four of us were the only juniors.

The seniors were all drinking beer—Gregg and Gary's parents weren't home—and they were making fun of us because we'd never tried it. So we said we would. The Robins twins went to a refrigerator in their garage and gave us a six-pack of Old Dutch.

It was sort of embarrassing—Chuck and Jack and Dan and I were sitting there with the six-pack in front of us, and all the seniors were just staring. None of us knew what to do. So Dan took one of the cans out of the six-pack and said real loud, "Does anybody have a church key?" The seniors laughed, but they gave him an opener, and Dan opened a can and took a big gulp.

The rest of us opened cans, too, and started to drink. It didn't taste all that bad, but it was kind of hard to swallow all at once; Chuck and Dan were trying to tip it right back into their throats, but Jack and I were going more slowly. It was mostly hard to get used to; I can't really believe that so many people think it tastes great.

The seniors got tired of watching us and went back to their own conversations. Chuck and Jack and Dan and I sat there with our four beers, and Dan started to act like he was a little drunk. Chuck said that his parents were in Cincinnati, and asked us if we all wanted to sleep over at his house, and we said yes.

We asked the Robins twins if we could have the other two cans of beer from the six-pack, and they said to go ahead. I drove Mom's car home and ran in to ask Mom and Dad if I could sleep out; I was careful to talk slowly and not to breathe in their faces so they wouldn't figure out what I had been doing. They said I could go to Chuck's; Jack had followed me home in his dad's car, so I went outside and got in and all four of us went to Chuck's.

He had forgotten his house key, and his brother Bill was up at Ohio State. So we had to wait in the car in his driveway until Bill got home. We passed the two cans of beer back and forth; we started singing the Old Dutch theme song real loud: "A beer is just a beer unless it's Old Dutch . . ."

I'm not sure if I was drunk or not; I felt sort of funny, but it may just have been that I was tired. The beer was 3.2; in Ohio you can buy beer with 3.2 percent alcohol when you're eighteen, and beer with 6 percent alcohol when you're twenty-one. I wonder if you can feel the difference when you're drinking 6 percent?

When we had finished the beer we went across the street to Charlie Hoffhine's house and hid the empty cans in his garbage can, so that no one would know. Then we went back to the car and all fell asleep. Bill Shenk finally pulled in at five o'clock in the morning; he acted like we were crazy, sleeping out in the car. It was really cold by that time. He let us into the house and we all found beds and went to sleep for good.

MARCH 15

WE all woke up about ten o'clock and had a big breakfast in Chuck's kitchen. Then we went over to Mark Smilack's house, where a bunch of guys were playing basketball in his driveway. We divided up into teams and had a tournament all afternoon.

Pongi got mad at Chuck and started tearing the engine out of his car. It was really weird; Pongi just popped open Chuck's hood and started ripping the motor out piece by piece. Chuck tried to stop him, but Pongi kept tossing pieces of the motor onto the street.

Finally Chuck's older brother Bill came driving by and said, "What the hell are you doing?" Pongi wasn't going to wise off to Bill, so he started putting the parts back in the car. We all worked at it, and when we were done the car ran as well as it had before.

Pongi apologized to Chuck; they shook hands and we all drove to the Toddle House for banana cream pie.

MARCH 16

I'M really sore tonight; Dave Frasch and I ran around the track all afternoon in preparation for the tennis season. That's the greatest feeling—being so tired and worn out that it physically hurts, but knowing that you're in better shape because of it. My lungs felt like they were on fire.

Chet Crosby was running at the same time we were. We exchanged a couple of looks, but no words.

WCOL had to discontinue Hotline Hitline. Too many people were calling, and the phone company said it was breaking down their lines every night.

MARCH 17

WE had our first tennis meeting today. Coach Weis said that we all had to run six-minute miles, which shouldn't be too tough. I can't wait for the season to start.

Then after the tennis meeting Mrs. Amos took all of the juniors on the *Torch* staff out for ice-cream sundaes. I had a banana royale. She said that she was going to name the editors for next year soon, and that we should be thinking about what we want to do on the paper.

At night Dan and I went to the Science Fair. We were wandering around the school building, looking at the exhibits, and I walked into one of the rooms and there was Lindy.

She looked beautiful. I don't know if she was wearing makeup, or whether she was tan, or what, but seeing her made my heart stop. Because she still goes to school in the junior high school building, I don't see her up close very often. And now we were standing face-to-face.

"Do you hate me?" she said.

I didn't say anything.

"Can't we be friends?" she said.

"As soon as you grow up," I said. I didn't mean it as bad as it sounded, but I didn't know what else to say and I couldn't say what I was really thinking.

"Okay," she said, and she smiled. "I'm grown-up."

Her mom and dad walked up, and we said hello, and then Dan and I left the room.

I guess I was being silent, because Dan said, "You're back in the daze again, aren't you?"

"Let's go to Rubino's," I said. I just had to get out of the building.

MARCH 18

MR. Millard gave us a multiple-choice test in History today, and for one of the answers he put "I.P. Daly." It cracked the whole class up.

MARCH 19

MR. Schacht caught me in a daze during Algebra class this morning, and spent five minutes calling me a moron in front of the rest of the class. But on my way out of the room he winked at me to show he hadn't really meant it.

Allen's coming home from military school for spring vacation tomorrow. For the first time since winter ABCDJ will be complete again.

MARCH 20

It's great having Allen home. It's Friday, so after school we went over to Jack's to wait for Allen to arrive, but he was late. So I went home for dinner, and about seven o'clock they all showed up at my house—Allen and Chuck and Dan and Jack.

We tried to fill him in on everything that's happened since he went back to school—we told him about crashing through the guardrail, and about our drinking the beer, etc. It's funny—he never tells us too much about what he's been doing at military school. He seems much more interested in what's going on in Bexley. I really don't think he likes it there.

We all went over to Mark Smilack's house, where there was a party going on. I think Allen likes Mark's younger sister Marcia. He has an advantage over us when it comes to girls—because he's not here most of the year, they think he's a little mysterious. Us, they see every day.

MARCH 21

What an amazing night. Dave Frasch, Kenny Stone, Leon Friedland, and I had tickets to see Peter, Paul, and Mary at Veterans Memorial. We had great seats, in the third row; the concert was terrific. They sang for hours, but the concert went by like it was twenty minutes.

After the show they stayed out on the stage and let the people come up for autographs. So we climbed up there and got them to sign our programs, and I told Peter that we worked for our high school paper. Actually, I'm the only one on the *Torch*, but I didn't want to screw the other guys. I said that we'd like to interview them.

Peter said to wait over by the side of the stage, and that if they had time they'd talk to us. We waited for about forty-five minutes, and then Paul walked over and said, "Are you the guys who want the interview?"

We said yes, and he motioned us into a little dressing room. "Ask away," he said, and we just stood there saying nothing—we didn't know what to ask. So I asked him how the group had gotten started, and he told us; we kept asking about their songs, and he kept answering—it was great!

Peter joined us after a few minutes, and I asked him what he thought of the Beatles. He said, "The Beatles are like ice cream and balloons and summertime and Pepsi-Cola. They're new and they're fresh and they're fun, and you have to love them." Peter and Paul were both such intelligent guys, and I didn't get the impression that they were trying to talk down to us. What a perfect end to the concert.

After a while they said that they had to change their clothes and get back to their hotel; they shook hands with each of us. On the way out we were just staring at each other; we couldn't believe we had really met them.

The only disappointment was that we didn't get to interview Mary. She never came into the room. We talked about why that might have been, and Leon said that she was probably having her period.

MARCH 22

MOM woke me up early, and said that even though it was Sunday, she wanted me to get up. She said that she wanted me to go down to Hideaway Hills with her and Dad to help clean the cottage up.

Hideaway Hills is this place near Lancaster, about an hour south of Columbus, and Mom and Dad have a cottage there that they go to on weekends in the summer. I don't like it much; all there is down there is a bunch of dirt roads, and I'd rather be home with my friends. Plus, I like it during the summer when Mom and Dad and Debby and Timmy are down there, and they leave our real house for me.

This winter, though, I've been asking them if ABCDJ can go down to the cottage alone sometime. This morning Mom said that my friends and I could go down there, but only if I went today and helped them get the cottage ready for spring and summer.

So I called Dan, and he and I rode down there with Mom and Dad. A water pipe had busted over the winter, and we helped fix it. Two girls named Carol Tinapple and Susie Schmidt were down there at their own cottages with their parents, and they came over and were real friendly with Dan and me. If they have some friends, that's a possibility if ABCDJ come down sometime.

At the end of the day Dad said, "There, that wasn't so bad, was it?"

I said it was okay. But when I'm with Mom and Dad at Hideaway Hills I feel like a little kid on a camping trip with his parents. It would be great to be down there alone with my friends.

When we got back to Bexley Dan said that Nancy Dartwell had invited him over tonight. She has a friend, Donna Trell, who I've danced with at some open houses, and Dan said that Nancy and Donna wanted me to come, too.

So we went to Nancy's, and we were sitting in her den. There were two couches; Dan and Nancy were on one couch, and Donna and I were on the other. Dan and Nancy really started going to town; the lights were off, but I could see them out of the corner of my eye. I didn't know what to do. A Johnny Mathis album was playing, and they were going at it, and Donna and I were just sitting there.

So I started to kiss her. She let me do it, but didn't do anything herself; she didn't pull away, but she didn't even kiss me back. I felt like I was kissing a marionette.

Finally I asked her if anything was wrong. She said, "Everybody knows you still like Lindy. You're just trying to use me. I'm not a cheap tramp."

I didn't know what to say, so I just sat there and listened to the music. Dan and Nancy were going crazy on the other couch, so in a few minutes I started to kiss Donna again. Same story; she didn't pull away, but she didn't get into it, either. She just sat there like a rock and let me kiss her.

On the way home I thought about what she said. She has a point. But I sure was jealous of Dan.

MARCH 23

I love spring vacation. Slept late, then Dan and I went over to the school and played a little singles tennis. We went to his house and each took a beer out of the refrigerator; we took the beers into his room. I only had about a fourth of mine.

Allen and Chuck and Jack came over, and we went to the outdoor basketball courts at the junior high school and started shooting around. Chet Crosby came up with some guys and said, "Can we play you?" So we did. We won; Crosby had to taste defeat, and that made me feel so good. Lindy was around, which made it even better.

Dad told me I had to get a haircut; that kills me. So I did; I got it all cut off. It looks horrible. I swear, this is the last time I'm doing it.

After my haircut we went to the basketball courts and played some more. When it got dark we decided we wanted to drink some beer, but we didn't have anybody to get us any. So we went into Pongi's garage, where his parents had some stored, and we each took a can.

We ran into some girls on Main Street and tried to be cool for them, but they wanted nothing to do with us. I think it was probably because my haircut is so creepy.

MARCH 24

DAD and I flew to Chicago this afternoon. My interview at Northwestern is early tomorrow morning, so we had to be here the day before.

Chicago is really scary. Dad rented a car at the airport to drive us downtown; the freeway isn't anything like in Columbus. It's packed solid and all of the cars seem like they're going a hundred miles an hour. Dad wasn't saying anything as he drove, but I could tell that the traffic was making him nervous; he wasn't used to it.

We checked into the Oxford House hotel downtown, which is where Dad stays when he comes to Chicago for business. We're sharing a room. It's really an odd feeling; Dad and I don't spend all that much time together, and now here we were sharing a hotel room. There were a lot of silences; I didn't know what to talk about most of the time.

We went to the hotel restaurant for dinner, and then Dad asked if I wanted to see a movie. I said sure, so we walked into the Loop. All of the Chicago newspapers were displayed in boxes with big headlines saying that General MacArthur is near death; it's really something to see four newspapers in one city. All those headlines made the news seem so important; I wasn't even aware that General MacArthur was sick.

We went to see *Seven Days in May*; the theater was pretty crowded, mostly with businessmen. I was one of the few kids. It was a good movie, and I tried to pay attention, but I just kept thinking of how weird it was to be sitting in a movie theater in Chicago with my father. I wondered what my friends were doing back home.

When the movie let out we walked some more through the Loop. Dad asked me if I wanted to stop somewhere and get a soda or some ice cream, but I just wanted to get back to the hotel. I don't know what it was—it just felt funny walking around this busy downtown area I knew nothing about late at night.

So we went back to our room. Dad bought a paper on the way up and read it in bed; then he turned the lights out and said that we had to be up early tomorrow morning. He fell asleep right away; I heard him snoring, but I also heard all the traffic on the streets down below, and I couldn't get to sleep for a long time.

MARCH 25

WE drove up to Evanston early this morning. A student guide took Dad and me on a tour of the campus. I think Dad was getting a little upset that I wasn't asking the guide more questions. We walked through some dorms, and the library, and the journalism school, and I mostly just listened. At one point the guide ran off to get a drink of water, and Dad said, "Aren't you interested at all?"

The fact is, it was making me kind of sad. All I could think about was that in just over a year I'll be getting ready to leave Bexley to go to college—and I sure don't feel like doing that. Here we were, walking all over this beautiful campus, and all I wanted to do was be cruising the streets of Bexley with my friends. The guide was very enthusiastic about what a good school Northwestern is—but everything he said just made me realize all over again that my days in Bexley are numbered.

I couldn't explain that to Dad, though, so I just followed along on the tour. I had my interview with an admissions officer; it felt like it went pretty well. He seemed impressed that I was an editor of the *Torch*, and he told me how good Northwestern's journalism program is, which I already knew.

Dad wasn't allowed in the room for the interview, and the second I came out he started saying, "How did it go?" I just shrugged and said, "Okay."

He said, "Is that all you can tell me? That it went 'okay'?"

"It was fine," I said.

He started shaking his head. "First you don't say a word the whole time that young man was showing us the campus," he said. "Then you can't tell me how the interview went. I'm really glad we took the trouble to come up here."

"I told you, it was fine," I said. My thoughts were still in Bexley.

We flew back to Columbus in the early afternoon, and I met up with Dan and Allen. We rode around for most of the day.

At night there was an open house, and Dan and Nancy Dartwell were dancing. She told him something that made me crazy when he repeated it to me.

She said that Donna Trell has been making fun of me since the other night—Donna has been saying that I'm "too slow."

I can't believe it. There I had been, thinking that she didn't want to go any farther; there she had been, sitting right there on Nancy's parents' couch accusing me of trying to use her and of still liking Lindy and of trying to treat her like a tramp; and now she's going around saying that I'm too slow.

When Dan told me, I said, "Look, you were there. You were on the other couch. How could she say that?"

"I don't know, Greene," Dan said. "I know you must have tried like hell. But that's what she told Nancy."

Every time I think I understand girls, I find out all over again that I don't know anything.

MARCH 26

DENNIS MacNeil screwed a girl. He told us today.

We don't really run around too much with Dennis—he's a junior just like us, and he's on the swimming team, but we hang out in different crowds. Last night there were some rumors at the open house that he'd gotten a screw, and today Dan and Allen and Chuck and Jack and I were sitting on the sidewalk outside Pongi's house and Dennis came by. So Chuck asked him if it was true.

Dennis said it was. He said he had gone up to Cleveland, and it had happened with a girl he met there.

I don't know why, but I definitely got the impression he was telling the truth. Maybe it was because he was being so calm about it—he didn't seem like he was out to impress us. He was just saying it like it was a matter of fact.

We were trying not to act too excited, but what he was saying is really something. I've never known anyone who that's happened to. It just seems like something out of another world—a girl actually allowing a guy to do that. I can hardly even imagine it.

And here Dennis was—a junior from Bexley, just like us—and it had happened to him. He already seemed different than he ever did before. He seemed a little older, and a little farther along. Like he had left the rest of us behind.

When he had left, we kept talking about it.

"I wonder how he talked her into it?" Chuck said.

"I wonder how he knew it was okay to keep going?" Allen said.

"I wonder what he felt like with all of his clothes off in front of a girl?" Jack said.

It's all we could talk about all afternoon. It's not quite the same thing as if it had happened to one of us in ABCDJ. But still, it's someone we know. I can't quit thinking about it.

MARCH 27

ALL day long my friends ragged me about "forty-nine per-cent." They were saying it because Donna Trell supposedly told some people that I "wasn't half the man" that Calvin Lucas is. Calvin's the guy she used to go out with.

It really started to bug me. We went to the Eskimo Queen for chocolate sodas, and it was "forty-nine percent." We went to school to shoot baskets, and it was "forty-nine per-cent." They just wouldn't lay off.

Jack and I drove downtown to O.P. Gallo's Formalwear to reserve rented tuxes for a dance that's coming up. I ordered one with a blue-and-white pin-striped jacket, and Jack or-dered one with a madras jacket. But when I got home Dad said I had to change my order—he said that no one with any sense wore anything but a black jacket with a tuxedo. Really made me mad.

Then later on I saw Lindy and Janie McKenney riding around in a car with some guys from Columbus Academy. Academy is the private school in town—we call them the Tweeds, and we hate them. I couldn't take seeing that—Lindy with David Brown and Chet Crosby is one thing, but Tweeds is too much.

After dinner Dad let me drive his Thunderbird for the first time. He only let me take it for five minutes, but it was great. Smooth and easy.

I was still not happy about that "forty-nine percent" stuff, and later on Dan picked me up and we drove around. We saw Nancy Dartwell's car in front of Donna Trell's house, and we went up to the door, and they invited us in.

Donna's parents were out for the night, so we went into the den and started playing some records. I played it cool; I didn't say a thing to her about the "forty-nine percent" stories. I pretended like I hadn't heard anything.

But then we started making out, and I was going like crazy. We made out for about forty minutes, and this time she wasn't holding back. For a lot of the time she let me put my hand over her blouse. I looked out of the corner of my eye at one point when my hand was on her blouse, and Dan was on the other couch with Nancy, looking over at me.

Finally Donna pushed my hand off her blouse and said, "I still think you may be using me." I could have said something about what I'd heard, but I didn't.

After a while Donna's parents came home; when we heard them come in the door, we turned the lights back on and switched couches so that the girls were on one couch and Dan and I were on the other. Dan and I took off, and when we got into his car I said, "A hundred and one percent."

We started laughing and cruised down Roosevelt.

MARCH 28

JACK and Dan and Allen and I went to Hideaway Hills this afternoon; it's Allen's last day home before he goes back to military school, so we wanted to do something special. Mom and Dad gave me the keys to the cottage and said to be careful.

We got down there, and the three of them said they were going to drive into Lancaster and see if they could find a store that would sell them some beer. I waited in the cottage; Carol Tinapple came over and said hello, and we sat out on the porch and talked.

They came back—and they had two six-packs! We started drinking, but I felt guilty because Mom and Dad were trusting me to be in charge. So I only had one bottle. The other guys were drinking like mad, though; they got drunk. They were talking loud and laughing a lot. I felt left out.

We went up to the lodge for dinner—they tried to talk real slow so that no one would know they had been drinking. Then after dinner we went back to the cottage and they drank some more. When they were really drunk we went walking around the hills. We were up by the tennis courts, and Dan started laughing and saying that he was going to roll down the hill to our cottage. He plopped himself onto the ground and just started rolling!

The hill is really steep, and it was dark out. Just as Dan got near the dirt road at the bottom of the hill, some headlights started coming up the road. Dan rolled onto the road, and the car saw him and stopped.

It was a Jeep driven by one of the rangers that patrol Hideaway Hills. The ranger got out of the Jeep and looked down at Dan. Dan was flat on his back on the road. He looked up, smiled, waved, and said, "Hiya, Ranger Joe!"

I hustled everybody into the cottage. Dan and Allen fell asleep right away, and Jack and I sat up and talked. There was a knock on the door—the ranger wanted to see if everything was in order. I stood at the door and talked to him there—I didn't want to let him inside, because there were beer bottles all over.

I was hoping that maybe Carol Tinapple would come by again, but she never did, so I went to bed, too. The hills are really relaxing.

MARCH 29

WE woke up about ten o'clock this morning; the cottage smelled like a brewery. We opened up all the doors and windows to air the place out, and then we made breakfast.

Jack and I put all of the beer bottles in a paper bag and walked to one of the neighboring cabins to use their garbage can. I don't know how often the garbage is picked up at Hideaway Hills, and if Dad came up and found beer bottles in our garbage can he'd go nuts.

We drove back to Columbus and went to Chuck's and Pongi's. We told Chuck about drinking the beer last night, and he was mad that he hadn't come with us. It started snowing late this afternoon, which is weird for this time of the year.

We drove Allen down to his parents' apartment and said

good-bye to him until the summer. He leaves for military school tonight.

"Only two more months," Chuck said to him, and we all stood around looking at each other and not knowing what to say. It's tough every time he has to go back there.

This is the last day of spring vacation; school starts again tomorrow. Tennis practice, too.

At dinner Dad asked what we had done at Hideaway Hills. I didn't even want to hint about the beer, so I said, "Carol Tinapple came over for a while."

"Now I can't allow that," Dad said. "There are to be no girls in that cottage when your mother and I aren't there."

I nodded.

"Is that understood?" he said.

I said yes. If he knew about the beer, he'd never let me go down there without him and Mom again.

At night I studied Algebra. I wish I had some idea of how to do it.

MARCH 30

SCHOOL wasn't so bad, considering that we had to be back. Got my page proof for the *Torch*—it was really screwed up. I'm going to have to go down to the printer's while they make the corrections.

Tennis practice after school. I was late—I was fooling around with the *Torch* page, and I apologized to Coach Weis, but he wasn't too pleased.

At night Dave Frasch and I went to the library and did poem analyses for English. They're supposed to have some books up at the Ohio State library that analyze the poems for you, but you need an OSU fee card to get in there. I called Ron Clowson—he's the older brother of Wendy Clowson, Lindy's friend, and he goes to Ohio State. He said he'd lend me his fee card; I'll probably pick it up tomorrow.

MARCH 31

THE day went fast in school again. The Michigan State University glee club was on a tour of Ohio and they sang at an assembly in the morning, so all of the other classes were shortened. Then in the afternoon French and English and even History seemed to fly by. In History Mr. Millard was talking about George Lincoln Rockwell, the American Nazi Party leader, and he called him "Rockhead."

I went to the printer's after school and fixed my *Torch* page up. Then tonight I went to pick up Ron Clowson's fee card. Wendy was running around in a nightgown you could see right through—you could see her bra perfectly.

I did five more poem analyses in my room. I hadn't listened to "Hootenanny" on WBNS for months, so I turned it on. "Autumn to May" was playing, and it reminded me of Lindy and last summer. I could have turned it off but I let it play.

APRIL 1

TENNIS practice after school was hard—Coach Weis ran us around the track so many times that I thought my chest was going to explode. David Brown and Chet Crosby were hanging around giving the stare.

APRIL 2

BACK in the damn daze. In school today Mrs. Amos asked Judy Furman and me to stay after English class. When the rest of the class had left, she said that she wanted us to be co-editors of the *Torch* for next year. That feels pretty good.

After school we had an unbelievably hard practice—if you pushed me now I'd fall right over. David Brown was hanging around again, and we stared at each other again.

After dinner I had to walk over to Main Street to get some note cards. I walked up to Rogers' Drugstore, and there was Lindy's mother's car—I recognized the B-2-L license plates half a block before I got there.

So I walked into the store—and there was Lindy. We just stood there face-to-face. She was wearing her summer jeans, and she looked beautiful.

She spoke first. She said, "Will you mind if Wendy and I come to see you play on Tuesday?" Tuesday is our first varsity tennis match of the season, against Chillicothe.

"No, I wouldn't mind," I said.

People were walking past us in and out of the store. She said, "Someone rang our phone last night, and I called to see if it was you, but your sister answered, so I hung up."

"Yeah, Debby said that someone hung up," I said.

"Do you still hate me?" Lindy said.

"Hate you?" I said. "No, I don't hate you."

"Are we good friends?" she said.

"Lindy, I don't know," I said.

We walked out of the drugstore together. Mrs. Lemmon was sitting in the car, and she motioned me over.

"Hi, Barb-I," I said.

"Lindy said that you have a tennis match next week," she said. "May I come and watch?"

"Sure," I said. "You can come."

Lindy got into the car and they drove away. It's midnight now, and I'm still awake thinking about her.

APRIL 3

TODAY was the day.

School was average. We had an Algebra quiz, and then second period I answered some questions right in Chemo. I handed in a paper in English.

After school we were supposed to have tennis practice, but it was raining. So Coach Weis pulled the divider across the basketball court, and we practiced indoors. We were supposed to hit against the divider wall.

I was walking up to the wall to pick up a ball that had rolled over there; I picked it up and turned around to walk back—just as Dan was leaning into a forehand. He was only a few feet away from me; the ball smashed full-speed into the middle of my face. My nose started bleeding like crazy; there was blood all over the place. I had to go into the locker room and lie down on a bench; it took about half an hour for it to stop.

Dan came in and kept apologizing; I told him it wasn't his fault. I got dressed and went home and had dinner, and after

dinner, Dan called again to say he was sorry. I told him not
to worry about it, and we said we'd meet later on.

After dark Pongi picked me up. Dan and Chuck were in
the car, too, and we cruised around Bexley. We were driving
down Powell when, at the corner of Dale, we saw Lindy and
Wendy Clowson and Janie McKenney standing with some
other girls and talking under a streetlight.

We kept driving. Dan said, "Greene's in his daze." We
drove around the block, and they came up with a plan. It
wouldn't be cool for me just to get out of the car and start
talking to Lindy. So they said they'd make it look like they
were pushing me out. That's what they did; we circled the
block, and when we got back to Powell and Dale, Pongi
stopped the car, and Chuck opened the door, and they all
pushed me out.

I pretended that I didn't want them to do it, and after they'd
driven away I turned around to talk to Lindy.

Except that the girls weren't the only people there.

David Brown was standing with them.

We were under the streetlight, and the girls weren't saying
anything, and Brown and I were looking at each other.

"Any time," he said.

I thought that this had gone on long enough. "How about
right now," I said.

We weren't going to fight with the girls standing right next
to us, so we crossed Powell and stood in somebody's front
yard. The girls were still under the streetlight, looking at us.

For a moment it seemed that we might not fight. We were
just standing in the yard, and it didn't seem that either of us
was going to do anything.

But then Brown said, "Pussy."

I moved toward him, and he threw the first punch. It landed
on my cheek. I threw a punch at his face, and it connected.
Then he landed a solid punch right on my nose, and I started
spurting blood.

I don't think it would have been so bad if that thing hadn't
happened at tennis practice. But I had bled so much in the
afternoon, and all it took was that one punch to start it again.
I was spouting blood like a fountain.

It was strange; it didn't hurt very much, and even though
Brown is bigger than I am, I didn't feel like I was being

swarmed over. We kept hitting each other, and I got him good once—his nose started bleeding, too, and pretty soon both of our shirts were covered with blood. I could hear the girls screaming across the street.

He started fighting pretty dirty—he was kicking and choking. I'd say it was about a tie, although I looked much worse because of all the blood. Then all of a sudden Pongi's car came driving up Powell. Pongi saw what was going on, took a hard left onto Dale, threw the gearshift into "Park" and came flying out of the driver's side of the car. His engine was still running.

"Come on, Brown!" he said. His fists were up.

I pushed him away. "It's my fight," I said.

"Come on, Brown!" Pongi said again. He really wanted him.

By this time the girls were coming across the street. I was completely covered with blood, and Brown was almost as bad. I had swallowed a lot of my own blood, and I could taste it. We were both breathing hard. I wasn't real anxious to continue, and I could tell that he wasn't, either.

Dan came out of Pongi's car. "It's over," he said. "That's it. It's over."

Brown and I looked at each other one more time. Then he walked back across Powell, and I walked to Pongi's car. I got in and we drove away.

"Are you okay?" Chuck said.

"I'm fine," I said. "If I hadn't bled so much this afternoon at tennis, I wouldn't look nearly this bad."

They drove me home. Luckily, Mom and Dad were out for the evening. I rang the front door and Debby answered. When she saw me she started crying.

"Cut it out," I said. "It looks much worse than it is."

I went upstairs into the bathroom. I could see why Debby had been scared; my whole face was caked with blood. I changed clothes. Timmy came across the hall from his room and said he'd wash the clothes out so that Mom wouldn't see the blood. I told him that if he couldn't get the blood out, he should just throw the shirt away.

Chuck and Dan and Pongi were waiting for me downstairs. We got back in the car and drove off. "Well, at least that's over," I said. Pongi's parents had some beer in their garage, and we each had a bottle.

APRIL 4

THE phone was ringing at nine o'clock this morning. I was hoping to sleep late, because it's Saturday, but I picked the phone up and it was Lindy.

"Are you all right?" she said.

"I'm fine," I said.

She said she was calling from Wendy's house. "I was so worried about you," she said. "Later on last night a bunch of guys said that you were knocked out and had to be taken to the hospital."

"Lindy, you saw me walk to Pongi's car and leave," I said.

"I know," she said. "But everyone was saying you were in the hospital."

My mom picked up the other line. "It's for me," I said. "I'm on this phone." I waited until she hung up before I continued talking.

"It looked a lot worse than it was," I said, and I explained about bleeding at tennis practice.

Lindy said, "I went home and got my lemon bottle and carried it the rest of the night wishing you good luck." Last summer, after I started carrying a lemon bottle, she started carrying one, too.

"Well, I'm okay," I said. We talked for a minute or so more and then hung up.

We had a Saturday tennis practice this afternoon; I played with Dan and Dave Frasch and Eddie Weston and Gary Herwald. A lot of people were kidding me about the fight, but it was good-natured, and I didn't mind it. Lindy came walking by the courts twice. I thought about her carrying the lemon bottle and wondered if it meant anything.

APRIL 5

DAD let me drive his Thunderbird all afternoon today! I picked up Chuck and Pongi, and we cruised around Bexley for hours. I'm real nervous driving that car; I keep thinking what Dad would do if I banged it up. But I love being in it.

The Searchers were on "Ed Sullivan." They sang "Needles and Pins"—really great.

Late tonight the cake dialers hit our phone twice in a row. I thought it might be Lindy, but Debby said that everybody's saying that Lindy loves Chet Crosby.

The more I think about it, the more I think that Lindy really must have been worried about me after the fight. The fact that she called me up and talked—she never has done that. She always dials for cake and waits for me to call back.

APRIL 6

COACH Weis teamed me with Jon Kaplan at tennis practice after school; we beat Herwald and Weston 6-4. The lineup for tomorrow's match with Chillicothe doesn't go up until after lunch tomorrow; I'm nervous to see where I'll be on it.

After practice today I was walking back toward the locker room, and there was David Brown on the track. We were walking right toward each other. Everybody stopped to watch—they all know about the fight.

As we passed each other David looked at me and said, "Hi, Bob."

"Hi, David," I said.

Just like that. All those months of stare-downs and insults; all that thinking about a fight. And now, just because we hit each other for a few minutes, we're suddenly friendly.

I sort of understand it—it has something to do with the fact that he and I were involved in something that nobody else was a part of, and that binds us together in a funny kind of way. Because we fought, we're now in a club that no one else belongs to. Something like that.

Still . . . it doesn't make a lot of sense. But all of a sudden it's obvious that we aren't going to fight again. That's over; I think we both knew it the moment we spoke today.

APRIL 7

SIXTH period the lineup went up in the boys' locker room; Kaplan and I were listed as playing second doubles. That's the bottom slot on the lineup—there are first, second, and third singles, and first and second doubles. Still, I was glad to be playing.

After school Coach Weis handed our uniforms out. That's one of the greatest things about playing varsity—wearing the Bexley uniform. The shirt is all right—it's a regular white tennis shirt with "Bexley Tennis" in blue on one side of the chest. But it's the warm-up jackets that everyone loves.

The warm-up jackets are white and are made of this soft, fuzzy material—everyone calls them "white fuzzies." To walk out of the locker room and onto the courts with everyone looking, wearing your white fuzzy—it's the best feeling I know of.

In fact, the only time Coach Weis lost his temper at me was last year, after an away match with Worthington. The two doubles teams—Dave Frasch and Dan Dick, and Mike Melton and me—were riding back to Bexley in Coach Weis' car. We had won the match, so we stopped at the Dairy Queen and bought sodas for everyone.

We got back into his car. Coach Weis was driving, and Dave was in the front seat with him. Mike and Dan and I were in back. I had a chocolate soda, and I was leaning forward to talk to Coach Weis and Dave. Dave leaned forward in the front seat to change channels on the radio. From the back seat, I leaned forward, too. I was saying something, and—not on purpose—I held my paper cup with the soda in it over the front seat, in back of Dave. Dave sat back real quickly—and smashed the soda cup. The chocolate stuff and the ice cream got all over the front seat of Coach Weis' car—and, more importantly, all over Dave's white fuzzy.

Coach Weis slammed on the brakes and started screaming at me. Dave took off his white fuzzy—it was completely soaked with my soda. I felt terrible. Coach Weis said that I was going to have to pay for the laundry bill, and I said I'd be glad to.

He never charged me for it; once he cooled down he forgot all about it. But that just shows how important those uniforms are. And when I got mine this afternoon and put it on, it was the first time I had felt exactly that way since last year's tennis season ended.

So we walked out to the courts, and there was a pretty good crowd there. Tennis doesn't draw anywhere near the crowds that sports like football and basketball and baseball do, of course, but there were people sitting by all the courts waiting to watch. We started our match, and I saw Lindy and Wendy Clowsom walk up and join the people at our court.

I glanced over at her, and she flashed her lemon bottle at me. That made me play great; we won easily, 6-1; 6-1. The team won, too.

Lindy left as soon as the match ended, but tonight she dialed for cake at my house and I called her back. She told me that for good luck she had put a note in the bottle; the note had said, "I know you will win, Bobby. Love ya, Lindy."

There it is, right there. Not "Love, Lindy." But "Love ya, Lindy." "Love, Lindy" is what someone would sign if she really meant it. "Love ya, Lindy" is what you sign in someone's yearbook, just to be polite.

APRIL 8

DURING Algebra class first period, Mr. Schacht started talking about the English Co-op tests that everyone in the junior class took a few months ago. The results came back, and the teachers have seen them, but we haven't.

"You know," Mr. Schacht said, "there was one person who got the highest possible score on those tests. The highest you can get—the 99th percentile. But that person is in one of my classes, and that person usually does miserably in here. I just don't understand it. Usually if a person does well in the English Co-ops, he'll do well throughout school. But if I hadn't seen this person's score with my own eyes, I wouldn't have believed it."

The next period I had study hall. I got a rest room pass, and I was on my way to the boys' room when I heard a voice call my name. It was Mr. Schacht. I walked over to him and we stood by the stairwell.

"You know who I was talking about, don't you?" he said.

"Who?" I said.

"You," he said.

"Oh," I said. I guess it made sense.

"I really don't understand it, Bob," he said. "If you can do so well on that test, why don't you do better in my class?"

"I don't know," I said.

"No, I'm really curious," he said. "What do you think the reason is?"

I didn't know what to say. He had asked me the same kind of thing before, after he had heard that I was the statistician for Jimmy Crum at the Ohio State basketball game. I got the impression that my bad work in Algebra really disappointed him.

"Well," I said, "I like to write. That kind of thing comes easy to me. When I write something, I feel like I've done something that no one else has done before. The words are mine; they didn't exist before I wrote them, and now they do exist."

I hesitated. I thought I might be sounding dumb. But Mr. Schacht nodded for me to go on.

"Math's not like that," I said. "Even if I do everything exactly right, what's the result? I'll come out with the same answer as everyone else in the class."

"And that doesn't satisfy you?" Mr. Schacht said.

"I guess not," I said. "I mean, I feel bad when I screw up, and I don't get the answer. But getting the answer right— I don't know, it must not appeal to me that much, because I avoid working on my Math homework as much as I can. You must know that.''

"Is it hard for you?'' he said.

"Yeah, it's very hard for me,'' I said.

"And writing isn't hard?'' he said.

"Writing's different,'' I said. "It's just different.''

He smiled. He patted me on the back, which surprised me. He doesn't do that much.

"Do me a favor,'' he said. "Just try a little bit harder. You only have until the end of the semester, and then you're done with Math.''

"Yeah, but there's Physics next year,'' I said.

He laughed. "Worry about that when you get to it,'' he said. He looked at me. He was still smiling, and then he walked away.

APRIL 9

AT practice after school Mike Melton and I were teamed against Weston and Herwald. We won the first set 6-3 and were ahead 4-2 in the second when Coach Weis ended practice. That means that we'll play first doubles tomorrow against Portsmouth.

Lindy walked by the fence next to the court where we were playing and said, "Those shorts.'' I was wearing the shorts that I used to wear all the time last summer when we were together. Melton looked over at me and just shook his head.

APRIL 10

ALL day long in school all I could think about was the match. The weather forecast said rain, so I kept looking out the window for clouds. It was still clear at noon; Dan came over to my house for lunch.

It rained sixth period, but seventh period the sun came out

and dried the courts. Melton and I played first doubles; we lost our match 6–4, 3–6, 6–8. The team won 3-2.

Mike and I used to be such a good doubles team; now we play so bad together. He really doesn't want to be my partner anymore, anyway; he's a lot better than I am, and he wants to play singles.

Lindy and Wendy Clowson were at the match, but they left around five forty-five, right before we lost the third set. Lindy dialed for cake tonight at ten-fifty; I called her back and we talked until eleven-forty. She said that Chet Crosby had told her not to come watch me play, but that she had come anyway, against his wishes.

I hate losing matches.

APRIL 11

SATURDAY. Dan and Jack and I went downtown; at Lazarus I bought two records—"The New Girl in School" by Jan and Dean, and "I Am the Greatest" by Cassius Clay. We cruised most of the afternoon.

At night some seniors bought us some beer; we each had about three. Then we went to Wendy Clowson's; people knew we had been drinking. Wendy had some notes that Lindy had sent her in school; she had signed them "Lindy Crosby"— as in Chet. Seeing those words on the note paper made me feel awful. I had been feeling pretty high from the beer, but seeing that turned everything around. I went home soon after.

APRIL 12

WE had weekend tennis practice today. I played Herwald in singles; beat him 6–3, 6–3. Jack had hidden the empty beer bottles from last night, so we put them in a bag and took them and got rid of them.

APRIL 13

WHEN I got to school this morning someone had put a "Boozer Bob" sign on my locker. I heard it was Tim Greiner and some other guys who had heard about us drinking Saturday night. I took the sign down right away; the last thing I need is for Coach Weis to see it.

After school we had practice, and then Dan and I went to the Eskimo Queen. At night I got hit by the cake dialers twice; so I called Lindy, who denied doing it.

It was a pretty disappointing conversation. She kept mentioning Chet Crosby, and at one point she said that Chet called her mother "Barb-I," just like I do. That made me feel terrible.

Then her mom got on the phone. Knowing that Chet called her that, I just couldn't say it. So I said, "How are you doing, Mrs. Lemmon?"

She said, "If you call me Mrs. Lemmon, I'll just have to call you Tennis Player. Lots of luck, Tennis Player."

I said I had to get off. I was playing the radio, switching the dial around, and the Beatles' new song, "Can't Buy Me Love," was playing at the same time on WCOL and on WBZ in Boston, which I can pick up.

Sometimes it seems that everything that happened last summer never really happened. The idea that Lindy could have cared for me so much—it seems impossible now.

I've got to stop dialing for cake so much. I vow not to do it anymore, unless she makes it necessary.

APRIL 14

I had to read a chapter from *The Scarlet Letter* by Nathaniel Hawthorne for English homework, so I went to the Bexley Public Library tonight. It's not as bad doing homework when there are a lot of other people around.

The library is on Main Street. Just about everything that

matters in Bexley, except for the houses, is on Main Street. The library is at the far west end, along with Cochran's Drugstore and Wentz's Pharmacy. Then a little bit farther to the east is Bexley Records and Kroger's grocery and the Toddle House. Then comes Luke's Shell Station and Rubino's, and after that Rogers' Drugstore and Johnson's Ice Cream and Super Crust and the Eskimo Queen. Right over the Bexley line is the Pancake House.

It's really not that long a strip, but everything you need is right there. Sometimes when I'm cruising I'll drive all the way down Main Street and back, just to see who's hanging out. When you go to the library you park in the lot in front of Cochran's, if there's a space. There was tonight, so I lucked out.

When I got home, Debby told me the cake dialers had hit a few times. Then the phone rang again. I picked it up on the first ring, but Dad had already picked it up. He hates the cake dialers—he just goes nuts when people ring our phone and hang up. This time it was Dianne Kushner, who wanted to talk to me about a *Torch* assignment. But before I could say anything, Dad said it was too late to be calling our house, and that she couldn't talk to me, and that she'd have to discuss it with me in school tomorrow. She said okay and hung up, and I sat there listening to a dial tone.

APRIL 15

AT practice today I was paired with Jon Kaplan again. We beat Weston and Herwald 7–5, 6–4, which means we'll play in the away match with Delaware tomorrow. But this is starting to bother me; it's like I have to earn my way onto the team every match—if Weston and Herwald would have beaten us today, they would have played tomorrow and I wouldn't. And Kaplan and I play lousy together.

Last year at this time Melton and I were solid on the varsity. It was just taken for granted we'd be playing every match. Now I feel real uncertain. Word is that Melton is going to get his wish and play singles, and Frasch and Dick will play

first doubles. Which means that I'll be competing for second
doubles every match. I don't like this.

APRIL 16

WE got out of school early today to make the trip to Delaware. Kaplan and I won our match, 6-1, 6-2, and the team
won 3-2. So our win was the margin of victory.

Nothing makes me feel better than that. I'm standing on
the court, and the whole team is counting on me, and at least
for that one moment I *am* Bexley—I'm the person representing Bexley High School. It's hard to explain how important
that is, but I don't get that feeling at any other time, and I
love it.

Pongi's little sister Terri made cheerleader for next year.
She's a nice kid, and I feel happy for her. For a girl, being a
cheerleader must be the same feeling as playing a varsity
sport is for a guy.

I was reading some *Scarlet Letter* in my room tonight when
the phone rang, and it was Lindy. I just get dizzy when I talk
to her. We were on the phone for over an hour.

At one point, testing her, I said, "Why don't you get off
and call Chet Crosby?"

She said, "This might sound dumb, but I think I dropped
him two weeks ago."

I asked her why everyone was saying they were going together.

"I have to go with him to prove I'm not fickle," she said.

I didn't know what to say to that. We talked until her mom
got on their phone and told her to get off.

APRIL 17

IN the hallway this morning Mr. Millard came up to me and said, "How'd you make out in the match yesterday?" I told him.

That's another thing about playing varsity—the men teachers treat you like a real person. Mr. Millard was the captain of the Ohio State basketball team when he was in college, and when he asks me about the match, it's like he's acknowledging that, in a small way, we have had the same kind of experience. I didn't even notice that kind of thing before I lettered, but last year, when I made the varsity, all of a sudden I could feel the change in how the men teachers acted toward me.

I got out of school second period to go downtown and have Dr. Basch drill a filling. It's weird being in downtown Columbus on a weekday—there are no kids around. Just businessmen and women shoppers. It makes me feel like getting back to school.

I worked on *Torch* from the end of school until dinnertime, and then at home all evening. I still didn't finish; tomorrow we have Saturday tennis practice at 10 A.M., but I'm going to have to go to school even earlier to finish up the *Torch* stuff. Pongi and the boys came by in the middle of the evening, but I said I couldn't go out; I had to work on the newspaper.

APRIL 18

WHAT a rotten day. I got to the school building at eight-thirty this morning, and had to knock on a window to get a janitor to let me in, because the doors are locked on Saturdays. I finished up my pages for the *Torch*.

Then I went straight to tennis practice. Kaplan and I lost to Chet Weld and Steve Grossman—6–0 in the third set.

Damn! That means that I won't be in the lineup when we play Upper Arlington on Monday. This will be the first time in two years that I sit out a varsity match.

We drove around most of the afternoon. Mom and Dad and Debby and Timmy are at Hideaway Hills for the weekend; we got some of the seniors to get us two eight-packs of Carling Black Label. We stopped at the TAT carryout and got poor boys, and then we took the beer and the sandwiches back to my house. I was still feeling terrible about the tennis thing, but I had three beers and started to feel a little better.

For some reason, with the beers in me, I thought that if I called Lindy I could straighten everything out. I called her at Wendy Clowson's, but she knew something was different about me. I was feeling so loose because of the beer; I kept trying to get her to be in the same frame of mind I was. But the more I talked, the more distant she got. She said that people were telling her that she was leading me on.

As we talked and I could tell that she wasn't interested, the beer began to wear off. Wendy got on the phone and said, "Lindy really wants to be good friends with you. Do you think that could ever happen?" I said no. Jack and Chuck were standing right behind me, trying to hear what was going on.

After I had hung up I felt stupid. The rest of them kept drinking beer, but I stopped. It didn't taste good anymore.

APRIL 19

JACK slept over last night; we got up at about eleven this morning and took the beer bottles down to the rain sewer at the end of my block and dumped them. Then we went to the Toddle House for breakfast.

The seniors were there, too. I guess they had a pretty wild evening; they had girls over at Mark Engelman's house, and they drank a pony keg of beer—that's the equivalent of forty-eight bottles.

We drove around with them in the afternoon. Engleman said something really interesting.

He said, "A year ago I was looking at Diane Baker at open houses, and thinking how beautiful she was—I would have been happy just to touch her. Last night, as I was sitting there kissing her, I thought how far you could go with just a good line. The novelty of a cool car wears off, but they never get tired of your talk."

I think he has a good point.

I'm really down tonight. I need Lindy, but now I have to stay away from her because I made such an ass of myself on the phone last night. And the Upper Arlington match is tomorrow—I just hope it rains, so it's called off.

APRIL 20

I kept looking out the window all morning during classes. I was trying to make it rain. Third period the skies opened up and it began to pour. By noon they had announced that the Upper Arlington match would be postponed.

That made me feel good for a moment, and then I thought about it. Here I was, taking consolation in the fact that a match I wasn't playing in was called off. That's pretty pathetic. Last year I remember looking out the window on the day of every match, hoping so hard that it *wouldn't* rain so that we would be able to play. I just couldn't wait to get into uniform and get onto the court.

Now here I was, breathing a sigh of relief because the match was rained out. I have to get back in the lineup.

We had an Epsilons meeting tonight, and when I got home the cake dialers hit. I rang Lindy's phone once; someone again rang ours once. I called her house and let it ring and she answered in a tired voice. She said it hadn't been her. So I said goodbye and hung up.

APRIL 21

HAD an Algebra quiz, and got our unknowns to analyze in Chemo. The STP sorority is having girls from Louisville and Dayton come in this weekend, and there's a big dance. I got the name of the girl I'm fixed up with—hope she's cool.

APRIL 22

AT practice after school today, Herwald and Weston beat Weld and Grossman. Since Weld and Grossman had beaten Kaplan and me, that means that Herwald and Weston will play in the match with Columbus Academy tomorrow.

Chet Weld came up to me and said, "The way I figure it, that puts you at fourth doubles now." I felt like smacking him, but the thing is, he's right—I'm down to fourth doubles, and only first and second doubles get to play in varsity matches. This is getting very bad.

Dan and I were talking about rubbers, and we dared each other to try and buy some.

So after school we walked to Rogers' Drugstore. I've been in that store a million times in my life, but as soon as we walked in I felt like everyone in the place knew exactly what was on our minds.

JoAnn, the lady who works there, kept hanging around behind the pharmacy counter. Finally she walked to the front of the store, and Jack, the pharamcist, was back there alone.

Dan and I walked up and started looking at aspirins and stuff.

"Hi, Bob," Jack said. "Hi, Dan." He's an older man; he has known our families for years.

We kept looking at the pills.

"Is there something I can help you with?" he said.

Dan and I just stood there.

Finally I mumbled:

"Prophylactics."

Jack said, "Pardon me?"

"Prophylactics," I said, this time louder.

He started to smile. "Is there any particular brand you'd like?" he said.

Dan and I looked at each other.

"What do you recommend?" Dan said.

"Well, most people buy Trojans, but the Cadillac of prophylactics is called Fourex," Jack said. He reached behind the counter and came out with a little cardboard box. He pulled it open and pulled out a blue plastic capsule.

"Each comes in its own little container, with a lubricant inside," he said. "They're more expensive than the others, but they're supposed to be the best."

"How much are they?" Dan asked.

"A dollar eighty for a pack of three," Jack said. "Sixty cents apiece."

Dan looked at me. "What do you think?" he said.

"Let's get 'em and get out of here," I said to him. I was getting nervous.

"A pack for each of us," Dan said.

Jack put two packs of Fourexes into two small paper sacks. He handed them to us.

We looked toward the front of the store, where JoAnn was waiting at the cash register.

"Do you think we could pay you here?" I said.

Jack grinned. "Sure," he said, and took our money.

As we were walking out of the store, JoAnn said, "Aren't you boys going to buy anything today?"

We clutched our paper sacks close to our sides so she wouldn't see them. "Not today," I said. "Bye, JoAnn."

So now we have rubbers. The next thing is to use them.

APRIL 23

THE last thing I did before I went to bed last night was to hide the rubbers. I can't let Mom find them in my room.

At first I put them in my top dresser drawer, under all the

underwear and socks. But then I figured that was stupid; when Mom brings the laundry up, it would be too easy for her to find them there.

Plus, Dad always puts his copies of *Playboy* under his shirts in his shirt drawer; he started doing it when we were little kids, so we couldn't find them and look at them. We always did, though. Anyway, the point is that our family has kind of a tradition of hiding things in clothes drawers. So I had to think of somewhere else.

I finally came up with the answer: my *Sports Illustrated* drawer. I have a desk in my room, and there is a deep drawer on the bottom right side where I keep all my old copies of *Sports Illustrated*. I took about half of them out of the drawer, then put the pack of rubbers in, then put the magazines back. No one will look there.

We lost to Academy today, 3–2. There was a big gallery; Herwald and Weston, who played second doubles in my place, lost their match 10–8 in the third set, which was the deciding factor.

I stood there and watched. I hate it when Bexley loses. I especially hate losing to Tweeds. But most of all I hate not playing.

Kaplan and I are supposed to play Herwald and Weston on Saturday. That should decide whether we get back into the lineup.

APRIL 24

I had to get my *Torch* pages done after school, so I was late to tennis practice. Coach Weis looked at me and shook his head. He is not pleased.

We went to Putt-Putt this afternoon, after tennis practice. Putt-Putt is a miniature golf course out on Hamilton Road; it's part of a national chain, and they even have a Putt-Putt professional putters tour that has its own weekly TV show.

There are different colored balls. There are also different

colored light bulbs mounted on the shed where you get your clubs and balls. If you're putting with a blue ball, and the blue light is on, and you're the first putter on the course to get a hole in one with a blue ball after they make an announcement, then you get a free game. You go and turn your blue ball in, and they give you your free pass, and they also give you an orange ball for you to use for the rest of your round. When you're playing with an orange ball you can't get a free game; the orange ball is to prevent you from trying to win twice during the same round.

Dan's really good at Putt-Putt; it seems like he's always playing with an orange ball. Putt-Putt is closed during the winter months, but it opened up again this week, and it felt good to be back. The opening and closing of Putt-Putt is kind of like the changing of the seasons.

Tonight was an open house in preparation for tomorrow night's STP sorority party. We all met the girls we're fixed up with. Mine is named Debbie. She's kind of short and cute, but she talks about a boyfriend in Louisville.

I got home at one-thirty. A few minutes later Chuck and Jack barged in; they said they wanted to sleep over, so I said okay. And then a few minutes after that Mom and Dad came home from a party. They were drunk, and they stayed up talking to us and joking with us. It was really a riot.

APRIL 25

WE lost to Herwald and Weston—7–5 in the third set. All during the match I was completely nervous; I realized how important it was to win. I felt tight on all my shots—I couldn't play my regular game. I just kept thinking: If I blow this shot, it could mean that I won't letter.

To letter, you have to play in at least half the varsity matches. I can't even think of a person who has lettered one year and then has failed to letter again the next. If I don't letter, I'll be the laughingstock of the school.

We have Sunday practice tomorrow, but today's match was

the important one. It was like I was watching myself play, but I couldn't do anything about it. I am so down.

The STP party was tonight. This girl Debbie has been going with her boyfriend for *six years*! So there wasn't much I could do; we just danced a lot and made polite conversation. I didn't feel much like being at a party anyway, because of the tennis.

APRIL 26

I got up around eleven o'clock this morning, had lunch, and then went over to school for practice. Kaplan and I were supposed to play Pongi and Mark Rinkov. We won, 6–1, 6–4, but it doesn't matter; Pongi and Rinkov are several rungs below us on the ladder, so it doesn't help us at all.

When I was walking back to the locker room Coach Weis came up beside me. I asked him if we had any chance of playing in the next few matches.

"Not the way you've been playing," he said. He looked at his clipboard. "You're all the way down to fifth doubles."

I just sat in my room tonight, thinking about it. I even prayed about it: Please, God, help me get back to my old position. I need that letter. Without it, I'm just nothing again.

APRIL 27

PRETTY good day. The Chemo test wasn't bad at all; I got the vocabulary words right in French; the English essay test was easy. After school I checked page proofs for the *Torch*, and everything looked real good.

Then tonight we had an Epsilons meeting, and after it was over Harry Post, the adult adviser, asked Joel Seiferas and me to stay and talk. He said that we would make good officers for next year, and that we should think about running.

Boy, would that be great. To be an Epsilons officer would make my high school career complete. I was just floating, thinking about it.

Later on I went over to Chuck's house to borrow his Cliffs Notes for *Moby Dick*. We were both hungry, so we got some pizzas from Rubino's and ate them in his family's kitchen while we talked.

APRIL 28

AT practice after school Coach Weis had me play Chet Weld in singles. I can't figure out what it's for—the singles positions on the team are already solidly held by people, and my only chance of lettering is to do it in doubles.

Weld won the first set 8–6; I won the second set 9–7. We're supposed to finish the match tomorrow.

APRIL 29

TODAY was the day we had pictures taken for the yearbook. I wore a coat and tie to school for the picture of the *Torch* staff.

Then, at tennis practice, I finished my match with Weld. Just as we were getting started Nick Briscoe, a Tweed, drove past the courts in his car.

Weld called across the net to me, ''Isn't that Lindy with Nick?''

If he was trying to psych me out, it backfired. It just made me so mad that I immediately went ahead 4–0, and ended up beating him 6–3. I should have beaten him even worse.

At the end of practice we had the tennis team picture taken. Every year the top players get to wear uniforms in the picture, and the rest of the team has to wear their own shorts and shirts. So Coach Weis was handing the uniforms out, and he called my name and handed me a white fuzzy. He said, ''You get to wear it in the picture because you're a returning letterman. That can be your one consolation.''

Doesn't sound good.

APRIL 30

USUAL boring day in school. The finished *Torch*es came back; they look great. They'll be passed out in homerooms tomorrow morning.

I went to Jack's after dinner; we shot baskets, and then we got poor boys. After I finished mine I went home. The cake dialers hit, and when I called Lindy back she said it had been her.

She said, "When we went together last summer, it was good but it wasn't *good*, not right. When I go with you, I want everything to be right." But then in the next sentence she said she couldn't be sure if we could ever go together again.

It was warm out and I couldn't sleep, so I went out and sat on the front stoop for a while. Bexley is really quiet late at night.

MAY 1

I took a long walk tonight and thought about things.

After school Kaplan and I had played Chet Weld and Mike Luby, and we got killed. Lettering again is looking less and less realistic. There's still an outside chance, but it's getting dimmer.

At dinner Dad asked me how practice had gone. I didn't say much; it would embarrass me to tell the truth. I excused myself early and then went out to walk around Bexley.

I decided that if I don't letter, it's not the end of everything. It's awful, but life will go on. The way lettering works is, the first year you letter, you get the letter itself. The second year you get a Bexley belt buckle. The third year you get a trophy. The fourth year—although there aren't many people who letter four years—you get a bigger trophy.

So technically, all that not lettering would mean is that I wouldn't get a belt buckle. I still lettered last year, and no one can take that away from me. I know people will be talking behind my back because I failed to make the grade this year. But I've got to live here, and I've got to go to school all next year, so all I can do if it happens—if I don't letter—is hold my head up.

I thought about Lindy, too. On the phone yesterday she said, "I was thinking in bed the other night—of all the boys I've ever known, who I would like to live with the most when we grow up. Do I have to say who?" When she says something like that my heart almost melts. But it's pretty obvious that she doesn't really feel about me like I feel about her. If I was smart I'd just make myself forget about her. But I can't.

I walked up to Broad Street, and then back to Main Street, and then I went home again.

MAY 2

CHUCK and Jack drove up to Cleveland this morning. It's Saturday; last night they talked to Dennis MacNeil, and he told them the name of the girl he screwed in Cleveland. One thing led to another, and Dennis called her long-distance and told her that he had some friends coming to Cleveland, and she agreed to get a friend and to go out with Chuck and Jack.

So they drove up there in Chuck's car. It's eleven-thirty now; I'm about to watch *The Wild One* with Marlon Brando on the Channel 10 movie. I keep thinking about Chuck and Jack; they could be doing it right this minute.

MAY 3

CHUCK and Jack barged into my house about ten-thirty this morning. They had just gotten back from Cleveland. They were pretty excited.

They drove up there late yesterday afternoon and went to see the girl Dennis MacNeil had called. Her name is Pat Simley; they said she's real tall. She had a friend with her, and they went out for hamburgers. Chuck and Jack had a couple of six-packs of beer in the trunk; they parked with the girls and started drinking the beer.

They started making out. To make a long story short, Pat let Jack put his hand in her pants, and the other girl let Chuck unhook her bra and put his hand under it. So Chuck and Jack didn't actually screw anybody, but they got farther than they'd ever gotten before.

They kept telling me the story in all the details. Finally I said, "Didn't the girl feel bad that she'd gotten screwed by

Dennis MacNeil, and that he'd obviously told you about it, and that you were after the same thing?''

''We were worried about that,'' Jack said. ''But she didn't seem to mind at all. She seemed to like doing that kind of thing.''

''God, that's amazing,'' I said. ''A lot different from Bexley girls.''

''I know,'' Chuck said. ''She was asking us how Dennis was getting along. Just like he was an old friend or something, and like there was no big deal.''

They said that they slept in Chuck's car after they dropped the girls home, and then had breakfast in Cleveland and drove back here.

I'm so jealous. Those guys now have nothing to look forward to for a while.

MAY 4

I got out of school this morning to go to this Mental Health Conference downtown at the YMCA; the school sent me because I'm an editor of the *Torch*.

It wasn't much; just a lot of students from all the schools around Columbus sitting around a room listening to experts talking about the importance of mental health.

There was this really cool girl, though; she kept staring at me, and I couldn't help but notice. Finally there was a five-minute break, and she came over to where I was sitting.

She said, ''Didn't you get your picture in the *Dispatch* for looking like Ringo Starr?''

I thought she was making fun of my nose, so I just mumbled something and turned the other way.

At tennis practice I played Gary Herwald in singles. I won the first set 6-4, and we were tied 10-10 in the second set when time ran out. We're supposed to continue it.

After practice Dan and I talked about Chuck and Jack's trip to Cleveland. We're both going crazy with envy. We decided that we're going to go up to Cleveland this weekend and try to get together with the same girls Chuck and Jack were with.

Our parents would never let us go if we told them why we're going, of course. Plus, if they found out that we had nowhere to stay, they'd never let us out of the house. So Dan's going to tell his parents that we're staying with relatives of mine; I'm going to tell my parents that we're staying with relatives of Dan's. Then one of us will borrow one of our parents' cars, and we'll just sleep in the car like Chuck and Jack did.

I can't wait.

MAY 5

SCHOOL drove me crazy today. First we had a hard Algebra test, and then we had lab in Chemo—I had no idea what my unknown was. Then we had a pop quiz in French. A day like today makes you feel like you're getting beaten up every period.

After school I played Herwald again. He won the second set, 14–12, so we're even—we play the third set tomorrow. I just have to beat him to save any chance of lettering.

Dan and I continued to work on our Cleveland plan. We've both told our parents the stories about staying with each other's relatives. Now all we have to do is get a car, and then sneak out of school early on Friday.

The big news tonight is that Todd Laffman, who's a guy in our class, broke his father's rib. Apparently Laffman got a bad grade on an Algebra paper, and his dad started bawling him out. So they were in the kitchen of their house, and his dad kept it up—and Laffman hit him! His dad flew backwards and started clutching his side; he went to the hospital, and they told him the rib was broken.

People can't believe it—punching your own father, and breaking his rib on top of that! I got three calls tonight from people asking me if I'd heard. Laffman supposedly has no idea what's going to happen to him. Grounding seems way too mild for something like this.

MAY 6

I may have had a worse day in my life, but I don't know when. First at practice after school Coach Weis had Kaplan and me play Weston and Herwald. We lost. Then there was still time at the end of practice, so I played my third set of singles with Herwald. He beat me. I can't see any way of lettering now.

When I got home at dinnertime, Mom and Dad were sitting there glaring at me. It seems that they had called Dan's parents about our trip to Cleveland—and had found out that we had made up the stories about where we were staying.

"I never ask you about what you do," Mom said. "But I don't expect you to lie to me when you tell me something."

I sat there.

"I don't even know what the big deal about Cleveland is anyway," Dad said. "Why do you feel you have to go up there?"

"Just to get out of here for a few days," I said. I couldn't very well tell him about wanting to screw Pat Simley.

"Where did you and Danny think you were going to stay if you didn't have a house to sleep in?" Mom said.

"We were just going to find a place," I said.

Dad was shaking his head. "I don't know what's wrong with you lately," he said. "Most of the time you don't say a word to us. And now when you do tell us something, it turns out you're lying."

"I can't tell you how disappointed we are in you," Mom said. "And Danny Dick's parents feel the same way about him."

We ate in silence; after dinner I drove over to Dan's house. He was hanging out in his front yard. He got in the car and we cruised.

Tomorrow's Thursday. We have just one day to calm our parents down and still get up to Cleveland for the weekend.

* * *

I lay in bed tonight thinking about how screwed up things have gotten. The tennis thing just tears me up. We all used to talk about how we'd rather not have a sports letter than to get one as a gift—once in a while a coach will give a guy a letter who doesn't really deserve one, and everyone's aware of it. We always used to say that a gift letter was worse than no letter at all.

But now I'd even take a gift. If Coach Weis wanted to give me a gift letter, I'd accept it.

I thought about wanting to die.

MAY 7

THE tennis team beat Upper Arlington 3–2 today. I sat and watched. I wanted to be out on the court so badly.

Dan and I talked our parents into letting us go to Cleveland. I have an aunt and uncle up there—Aunt Sue and Uncle Ben—and Mom called them and asked if it would be okay for Dan and me to say with them. They said yes.

It's sort of creepy—having your mom call to get you a place to stay. But it was the only alternative we had. We don't get a car—we're riding the train up there after school tomorrow. Our parents are treating us like little kids, but at least we get to go.

Dennis MacNeil said he wouldn't call Pat Simley for us—he said that enough was enough, and that if he kept sending guys up there to screw her then she'd never be with him again. He did give us the name of another guy in Cleveland—Howie Talford—and he said that Howie Talford would be the go-between. Talford knows Pat Simley, too, and would introduce us to her.

So tonight I called Howie Talford in Cleveland. He seemed to be a pretty nice guy. He said to give him a call when we got in tomorrow night, and he'd take care of everything.

MAY 8

WE had an essay quiz in History this afternoon. I couldn't concentrate at all—all I could think about was getting out of school and going to Cleveland.

Finally the bell rang. I hurried home and got my suitcase; Mom drove Dan and me down to Union Station to get the train. It was weird—talking to her about what we were going to do in Cleveland, and knowing what we really wanted to do.

"If you'd like, I bet Uncle Ben and Aunt Sue would take you to an Indians game," Mom said.

"That sounds great," I said. I looked out of the corner of my eye at Dan.

"And you boys really should have packed your tennis racquets," Mom said. "I'm sure there are a lot of good courts up there."

"Maybe we can borrow some racquets, Mrs. Greene," Dan said.

We got to the station. Mom kissed me goodbye and told us to be careful. We got onto the train. On the way up there we ate in the diner and talked about what to expect.

"You're probably going to have to be with Pat," Dan said. "Everyone says she's real tall." Dan is always pissed off about being so short.

"I'm sure she has lots of friends," I said. "She did when Chuck and Jack were there."

When we got into the station in Cleveland we shifted to a Rapid Transit train, and rode it out to Uncle Ben and Aunt Sue's house. They had saved dinner for us, but we told them that we had eaten on the train. We had to sit around and talk to them for a long time.

Finally I said that I'd like to use the phone. I called Howie Talford's number, but a girl—it must have been his sister—said that he was out at a party. I said that it was important that I get hold of him, and she gave me the number of the party.

I called; there was a lot of music and noise in the background. Howie Talford came to the phone, and I told him that Dan and I had arrived in Cleveland. He said that Pat Simley wasn't at the party—but that he had talked to her during the day, and she knew that some guys from Columbus were coming up. He said that he would be playing baseball tomorrow morning at a playground—he gave me directions how to get there. He said to meet him there, and he would tell us how to hook up with Pat Simley and her friends.

So we were in Cleveland with nothing to do. We walked around the neighborhood for a while, and then we went up to the guest bedroom. We were in our beds talking, and there was a knock on the door.

It was my cousin Carol. I had never met her before—she's Uncle Ben and Aunt Sue's daughter, and she's our age. She had been out all evening, and she wanted to introduce herself.

She was really cool. She was wearing a nightgown, and she came in and sat and talked with us. After a while she asked us if we drank beer, and we said we did; she said she did too, although her parents didn't know about it. She said if she was real quiet she could go down to the kitchen and get a bottle out of the refrigerator.

When she came back she had one. We passed it back and forth, splitting it three ways. Carol was so easy to talk to— we must have talked for three hours. I could tell that she was curious about the real reason we were in Cleveland, but we didn't tell her, and she didn't press us on it. Finally she went to her bedroom. It's nice to have a cool cousin.

MAY 9

WE were up early. We had breakfast with Uncle Ben, Aunt Sue, and Carol; they asked us what we were going to do today.

"I guess we'll go over to the playground and play base-ball," I said.

So we walked over to the junior high school playground, following the instructions that Howie Talford had given me on the phone last night. When we got there, there was a ball game going on; Dan and I sat on the sidelines and watched, and when the team that was out in the field came in to bat, some guy said to me, "You Greene?"

It was Howie Talford. He said that he'd call Pat Simley for us as soon as the game was over. So Dan and I sat there, not saying much, and finally the game ended. Howie Talford said to follow him, and he walked to a pay phone and called Pat Simley.

He told her that the guys from Columbus were in town. They talked for a few minutes. Then he hung up, and he said, "Pat and her friends are going to be at Euclid Beach at three o'clock. You're supposed to meet them by the Ferris wheel."

He said that Euclid Beach was an amusement park that was right next to the beach. It was a long way away, in a different part of Cleveland; he wrote down instructions on what buses to take. Dan and I went back to Uncle Ben and Aunt Sue's, and just hung around the house until it was time to leave.

We went down to the bus stop and waited for the right one to come. We had to transfer once; it was hot on the buses, and we rode through some pretty bad areas of Cleveland. It seemed like we were on the buses for hours, and the temperature kept going up; I was sweating. But finally we got to Euclid Beach. We were about half an hour early.

We wandered around the amusement park, and then we went to the Ferris wheel. No one was there. So we just stood there—all these little kids kept pushing past us to get on the ride. Finally, at about three-fifteen, four girls walked up.

They looked at us. We looked at them. Finally Dan said, "Is one of you Pat?"

This tall girl, kind of pretty, nodded her head.

"I'm Dan," Dan said.

"I'm Bob," I said.

"I guess we were supposed to meet you," Dan said.

The other girls introduced themselves. For the life of me I couldn't figure out how we were supposed to go from standing there to having sex with these girls. But it didn't really matter, because the next thing the girls said was that they had to go.

Just like that. Pat Simley said, "We have to meet some other people," and she turned and walked away, and the other girls went with her. It was obvious that she couldn't stand the sight of us. We come all the way to Cleveland, and they walk away after thirty seconds.

I looked at Dan and he looked at me. Then he yelled, "Hey!" One of the girls, who had introduced herself as Ann, turned around. Dan walked up to her and threw his arm over her shoulder, and the two of them walked away together.

I felt miserable. I stood there by the Ferris wheel, watching Dan and Ann walking in one direction, and Pat Simley and the other girls walking in another direction. When they were out of sight I didn't know what else to do, so I started walking around the amusement park.

This was terrible. I didn't even know how I was going to get back to Uncle Ben and Aunt Sue's; I wasn't sure I could figure the buses out without Dan. I thought that he and that Ann girl had probably gone somewhere, and were making out right that minute.

I walked around Euclid Beach for about half an hour, and then, as I was stopping to get a Sno-Kone, I looked over— and there was Dan.

"What are you doing?" I said.

"I've been looking for you," he said.

"What about Ann?" I said.

"She left me five minutes after I met her," Dan said. "She didn't want anything to do with me."

We looked at each other and shook our heads. We went to a pay phone and called Howie Talford. He told us how to get to his house on the bus, and we went to the bus stop and headed that way.

When we got there his parents weren't home. We went down to the basement; it was dark and cool down there, and his parents had a bar set up. Howie gave each of us a beer. The radio was on to KYW, and a song by a new group called Gerry and the Pacemakers was playing. The song was called "Don't Let the Sun Catch You Crying"—it was real sad, which fit our moods.

We had three or four beers each, and we were feeling a little bit courageous, so we decided to call the girls. We were going to ask them if they wanted to meet us somewhere and have some beers. Dan dialed Pat Simley's number; I got on the other phone. As soon as we said who we were, they said they had to go, and hung up.

"I don't know what to tell you guys," Howie Talford said. "Sometimes you win, sometimes you lose." He was trying to cheer us up, but we didn't want to hear it.

So we went back to Uncle Ben and Aunt Sue's. "What do you think is wrong with us?" I said to Dan.

"They hated us," he said. "They hated us!"

Carol was out, so we killed time all evening and then cussed ourselves to sleep.

MAY 10

UNCLE Ben and Aunt Sue had a huge Sunday breakfast for us. Dan and I didn't say much about yesterday; they asked us if we'd had a good time in Cleveland, and we said yes. Carol said she wished she would have known that we didn't have anything to do last night; she would have stayed home and hung out with us.

We were taking a two o'clock Greyhound bus back to Columbus; so we caught the noon Rapid Transit near Uncle Ben and Aunt Sue's house, and got to the bus station in plenty of time. Dan and I walked all the way back to the rear of the bus, and sat on the big bench seat that ran the entire width of the bus.

We started rolling to Columbus right on time. "I wonder why it's so easy to talk to someone like my cousin Carol, and it's impossible to talk to a girl you want to go to bed with?" I said.

"Yeah, I know," Dan said. "Carol was great. But I felt like a goon around those girls at Euclid Beach."

"It's like as soon as they know you want to go to bed with them, all the power is in their court," I said.

The bus wasn't very crowded. At one point Dan said, "You know, we have a problem."

"What's that?" I said.

"What do we tell Jack and Chuck?" he said. "And everybody else in Bexley who knew we were coming up here? We can't just say that we got shut down. Especially since Jack and Chuck did so well with the same girls."

I thought about it. "What do you suggest?" I said.

"Well," Dan said, "why don't you say that you got a dry fuck, and I'll say that I got bare tit."

"Okay," I said.

I waited a few seconds.

"What's a dry fuck?" I said.

"I'm not sure exactly," Dan said. "I heard some seniors say it once."

"Where are we supposed to say this happened?" I said.

"On the beach," Dan said. "We'll say that we took the girls from the amusement park right onto the beach."

"In the middle of the day?" I said.

"We don't have to go into details," Dan said.

"I hate lying to those guys," I said.

"Me, too," Dan said. "But the truth is so embarrassing."

We sat and thought for a while as the countryside went by outside the windows of the bus.

"Boy," I said. "It sure is hard to get a screw."

"We got screwed all right," Dan said. "But not in the way we were hoping for."

All of a sudden, just as if we had planned it, we both started singing our own words to the tune of this new Beatles song called "P.S. I Love You":

"P.S., we got screwed . . ."

We looked at each other and burst out laughing. We started singing again:

"P.S., we got screwed—screwed, screwed, screwed . . ."

Dan's father picked us up at the Greyhound station in Columbus. "So how was Cleveland?" he said.

"Real good," Dan said.

"Great, Mr. Dick," I said.

We rode from downtown Columbus toward Bexley in his car. The radio was turned to WCOL. Just as we were crossing Parkview the Beatles came on, singing "P.S. I Love You." Dan made a sound like he was spitting, but managed to control it.

MAY 11

AFTER first period in school this morning, Jack and Chuck were waiting in the hallway for Dan and me.

"So how was it?" Chuck said.

"Great," Dan and I said at the same time.

"Did you meet the girls?" Jack said.

"Yeah," I said.

"And?" Chuck said.

We didn't say anything.

"And?" Jack said.

"What do you mean?" I said.

"Well, how did you do?" Chuck said.

This was going to be harder than I thought. I felt ridiculous telling them the lie.

"We did pretty good," Dan said.

"How good?" Jack said.

I could feel the seconds ticking by. I was thinking about telling them the truth, but finally Dan broke the silence by saying, "Bare tit."

Chuck and Jack looked at me. I didn't say anything.

"Well?" Jack said.

"Dry fuck," I said.

They looked at me for a moment.

"What's a dry fuck?" Jack said.

"What, you don't know?" I said. The bell rang and we went to our second-period classes.

After school the tennis team played Columbus Academy and won 5–0. I didn't play.

Tonight Jack called me at home. "Tell me the truth," he said. "You guys didn't really do anything with those girls in Cleveland, did you?"

He wasn't teasing me. Of all my friends, I feel the closest to Jack. I think he felt bad that we would lie to him.

"Jack, do me a favor," I said. "Just don't ask about Cleveland."

"Okay," he said. "But I think I know. Nothing happened."

"Just let it go," I said.

"I know you too well," he said.

"Please," I said. "Just let it go."

"Okay," he said.

MAY 12

I'M so fed up about tennis. Before school today, Dave Frasch said that Coach Weis wasn't going to play the top four guys in tonight's match, because it was supposed to be an easy match. That got my hopes up—if everybody moved up four notches, then maybe I'd play.

The list went up in the middle of the day. The top four guys didn't play—and I *still* wasn't on the list.

This is driving me crazy. Tomorrow I'm going to tell Coach Weis to do me one favor this year—not to mention my name at all at the letter assembly.

MAY 13

HAD two Algebra tests today—both bitches. Plus I got called on in class in Chemo, and we had a History quiz.

I saw Coach Weis in the hallway and told him that I thought he was screwing me. He said he wasn't. He said, "What could I have done for you that I haven't already done?" I said, "I guess nothing."

I walked away, but then I thought about it and went back to him. I said, "If you wanted to help me, you could play me singles in the last few matches of the season. The matches aren't that important anyway, and if you combine them with the matches I played at the beginning of the season, that might be enough to letter."

He didn't say anything, but I can tell he's thinking about it.

Tonight we decided to call girls for each other.

It's always hard to call girls and ask them out, in case you get shut down. So Jack said that he'd call Linda Pendleton and say he was me, and ask her out. I said I'd call Linda Loeffler and say I was Chuck, and ask her out.

That way at least when you get shut down, you don't have to hear it yourself.

I called Linda Loeffler's house. Her mother answered, and I said, "Is Linda there?" She asked who was calling, and I said, "Chuck Shenk." She said that Linda wasn't home.

Then Jack called Linda Pendleton's house and said he was me, but she wasn't home either.

At least it seemed like a good idea.

"P.S. I Love You" is number one on the new WCOL survey.

MAY 14

IN Chemistry lab today I turned my back, and I heard Dan laughing. He had poured nitric acid and sulfuric acid on my lab book, and it was eating its way through the cover.

We played Grandview at home after school—and Coach Weis had me play second singles! I won 6–2, 6–1, and the team won 5–0. It felt so good to play again—I had almost forgotten how much I love playing in varsity matches.

After the match Dan and I went in to take our showers, and in this little room next to the locker room were all these boxes filled with fried chicken from the Willard Restaurant. When we got done with our showers, the chicken was still there. It smelled great.

I turned out that it was for the Latin Club banquet tonight. We looked at each other—there were so many boxes of chicken, and we were so hungry after the match, and finally we each took a box and went behind some lockers and ate the chicken and the cole slaw. We left for home before the Latin Club people arrived.

I had to do *Torch* pages at Mrs. Amos' house tonight—and she kept me there until ten o'clock! I didn't know how to get out of there. Tonight was a night that I was really going to study Chemo, but when I got home I just went to sleep.

MAY 15

TROUBLE. I got to school this morning, and in homeroom there was an announcement on the PA system that if anyone knew anything about fried chicken being stolen from the Latin Club banquet, to report immediately to C.W. Jones' office.

It seems that there were exactly enough boxes of chicken to feed the people who had signed up for the Latin Club banquet. They had all paid for the chicken in advance. When the banquet started, they came up two boxes of chicken short, so two people didn't get to eat.

Miss Wylie, the Latin teacher and Latin Club adviser, was beside herself. At first she was blaming the Willard for delivering too few boxes of chicken—but then someone went into the boys' locker room and saw the two empty boxes of chicken, with the empty cole slaw containers and the used plastic forks, in one of the big wastebaskets, where Dan and I had left them.

So now there's a major investigation. I found Dan in the hallway between classes, and we decided not to say anything for the time being.

It's Friday night. Chuck and I cruised around for most of the evening, and at eleven-thirty I dialed for cake and Lindy called back and invited us over.

We went. Lindy and her mother were in their living room watching TV, and we all sat around and talked. Then Chuck asked if anyone felt like some food, and Barb-I said that she would, but she didn't feel like going out. So Chuck and Lindy

and I went to Main Street and ate at the Pancake House, and
we got some pancakes to go for Barb-I.

We brought them back to her, and when we got there,
Lindy's older sister Libby had come home. Libby knows
Chuck's older brother Bill, and she kept making a big deal
over the fact that she couldn't believe that Chuck was old
enough to drive now.

We all went up to Lindy's room. I had never seen it before.
There was a poster that she had made by cutting letters out
of headlines in magazines—it spelled out "Chet Crosby." I
pretended like I didn't notice.

In the car on the way back from the Pancake House, Chuck
had been driving, and Lindy and I had been in the front seat,
too. She had kind of laid her hand next to mine. I didn't hold
it. But our hands were touching for the whole ride.

MAY 16

SLEPT late, then drove up to Ohio State to watch Dan play in
the district tennis matches. He lost. When I got home Dad
made me mow the lawn—first time this year, but it won't be
the last.

At night we cruised, and ended up going to Wendy Clowson's house. Lindy was there, and she and I were sitting in
the Clowsons' TV room talking. Who walks in but David
Brown.

We've been pretty friendly to each other since our fight.
When I saw him I raised my hand, and he said, "Hi, Bob."
But then he looked at Lindy and said that he didn't think Chet
Crosby would like her being there with me. David had about
four guys with him, and they were standing there the whole
time.

David and his friends walked out, and Lindy said that she
didn't want to "get into trouble" with Chet, so she walked
out, too. And I just sat there. I ended up talking to Wendy.

Lindy, how can you do it? Last night at your house you
play all our songs on the record player; tonight you do this.

MAY 17

WE had Sunday tennis practice today. Kaplan and I lost to Luby and Smilack. The word is that C.W. Jones has been asking around about the Latin Club chicken incident, and that he knows that Dan and I did it. Tomorrow should tell.

MAY 18

DAMN. What a born loser. In homeroom this morning, the PA announcement said, "Will the following people please report to the principal's office: Dan Dick. Bob Greene."

I walked down the empty hallway, and I saw Dan coming from the other direction. We just shook our heads. C.W. Jones was sitting there behind his desk; up on the wall was a big black-and-white picture of the ship he had commanded in the Navy. He said, "As you know, some chicken dinners were stolen from last week's Latin Club banquet . . ."

I figure it would only get worse if I let him go on, so I said, "We did it."

"I know you did it," C.W. said

We tried to explain that we didn't mean anything by it; Dan said, "There was all this chicken, and we didn't even know whose it was."

"Is that how you usually do things?" C.W. said. "If you see something and you want it, you just take it, because you don't know whose it is?"

"We're really sorry," I said.

"We really are," Dan said.

"I'm afraid that's not quite good enough," C.W. said. "As you know, Miss Wylie is very upset about this happening. She worked all spring to have a successful Latin Club banquet, and you two pretty well ruined it."

"We'll pay her back," I said.

"Oh, you'll pay her back, all right," C.W. said. "Making up the money is the least you can do. But both of you are going to have to serve detentions all this week, too."

I let out a breath.

"All five days?" I said.

"All five days," C.W. said. "Both of you."

He had to know what that meant—that if I had detentions all five days this week, there was no way that I could play in the last two tennis matches. Even if Coach Weis had wanted to let me play singles so that I'd have a shot at lettering, now I'd have no chance. The detentions wouldn't affect Dan; he's played every match this year, and his letter is all set.

"I know this is unpleasant," C.W. said. "But you should have thought of the consequences before you stole the chicken."

We left his office and went to first-period classes. Everyone was asking why Jones had wanted us in his office, and by second period the story was all around the school.

At lunch Chuck said he had seen Coach Weis in the hallway, and Coach Weis had said, "This was the straw that broke Greene's back."

There was a match with Delaware after school. I hoped for rain, but it was a hot, sunny day. Dan and I sat in C.W.'s outer office until five o'clock, and then we went home.

MAY 19

AT noon today the tennis team met, and we voted for next year's captain. I voted for Dan.

It was another beautiful, sunny day, and there was another match after school. Dan and I sat in C.W.'s office, watching the clock.

MAY 20

IN sixth-period English class Mrs. Amos moved me away from Dianne Kushner, because she had heard Dianne calling me "honey." She must have thought Dianne was being serious. I only wish.

We served another detention, and then I had to go down to the *Torch* office for paste-up. C.W. Jones appeared in the doorway and called me outside. He said that he had the list of lettermen for spring sports—the names that will be announced at tomorrow's assembly. He also had the list of captains for next year. He had to give them to me so that we could make deadline for the paper; if we waited until tomorrow the names wouldn't make the next issue.

"I just want you to know," C.W. said, "that the incident with the Latin Club chicken had no bearing on the letter list."

I didn't say anything. I just took the envelope from him.

After he'd left I opened it up. It was tough seeing it in black and white: there were all the lettermen for this year, and my name wasn't on the list. In a way it was better seeing it before the assembly—at least I won't be sitting there in the auditorium tomorrow hoping that a miracle happens.

Dan was voted tennis captain, too, which is nice.

I got out of there about six-twenty, and went over to Jack's house to shoot baskets. We were playing one-on-one when I heard a voice call my name. I looked over; it was Lindy, standing in Jack's garage. She was wearing shorts and a sweater. Janie McKenney was with her.

"It's the twentieth," Lindy said.

As if I didn't know. June 20 was the day we met last year, and I'm aware of our anniversary every month. We stood there and talked for a few minutes, and then she said she had to go home.

After I was done at Jack's I picked Dan up and we went to Wentz's Pharmacy for sodas. He knew that C.W. had given me the letter list and the list of captains; he kept asking me whether he was tennis captain or not, and I kept telling him that I couldn't say, because I had given my word to C.W. to keep it a secret until after the assembly. I don't know why that should matter to me; C.W. hasn't been doing me any favors lately. But somehow it feels important—because I'm one of the editors of the *Torch*, I get to know things that no one else knows, and I feel that that's a big responsibility. If Dan wouldn't have been elected, maybe I would have told him, to help ease the letdown. But as it stands, he's going to feel great tomorrow when he finds out. That's lot better than I'm going to feel.

I dialed for cake when I got home, and Lindy called back. We wished each other happy anniversay and then I went to bed.

MAY 21

I washed my hair this morning and combed it down over my forehead; I wore my white Levi's which are starting to turn green. I looked like a damn Beatle, but I didn't care. I was just daring C.W. to throw me out of school before the letter assembly.

I saw him in the hallway, but he didn't say anything. I felt awful at the assembly. When they read the names of the tennis lettermen, I felt as if everyone in the auditorium was staring at me. I just looked at the stage and didn't look around. It was like time was going in slow motion.

Tonight Dan was supposed to pick me up, but he called and said he had smacked his family's Buick over on Dawson; he pulled past a stop sign and someone skidded into him. So we just walked around. They're decorating the high school gym for the prom; neither of us have dates for it, but we went over and watched.

About eight-thirty we walked past Lindy's house on Stanwood. She saw us through the front window and ran upstairs so she could talk to us from her own window. She congratulated Dan for being captain, and then she invited us in. Her dad and her brother Pat were home. It was real awkward; I can tell that she really doesn't care for me at all. God, what can I do?

MAY 22

DAN and I had our last detention after school today. It's Friday, and tonight we asked the seniors to get us some beer. They got us two sixpacks. We took the beer to Chuck's, because his parents weren't home.

I didn't get too drunk, but Chuck and Dan were really on their asses. We went over to the gym to watch them working on prom decorations again. Some people knew we were drunk. Jack was there working on the decorations, and he told us that we'd better get out of there before someone got us in trouble.

Chuck and I started leaving—but Dan started running around like a crazy man. Part of the prom scenery was this cardboard park, and Dan went over and sat in it and started yelling and singing. Someone said that Office Butters was coming by every hour or so just to check on things. We had to literally chase Dan around, but we finally got him out of the school before anyone could do anything.

We went to an open house, where Steve O'Grady had a fight with a guy from another school. There was this kid there who had a bottle of Canoe cologne that he had gotten for his birthday; for some reason I thought I had to have it, and I paid him five bucks for it. When I got home Debby told me that Mom and Dad knew I had been drinking, and that they were furious and wanted to talk to me about it in the morning. Great. I was still carrying the bottle of Canoe around.

MAY 23

I woke up at ten-thirty, and thought that was a good sign. I figured if Mom and Dad were really that mad, they would have woken me up earlier.

But Dad was working a Saturday half day, and Mom was waiting for him to get home. He walked in a little after noon, and he was really burned. Some people had seen us last night

and had told Mom and Dad that we had been drinking beer.
I don't know how they knew; probably because of what happened at the gym.

"You are seventeen years old," Dad said. "You are not
old enough to drink. If this ever happens again—*ever*—you
will never drive the car again, and you will spend all your
evenings at home."

Mom just stood there, looking at me like she was disappointed.

We had lunch and didn't talk much, and then Dan and
Pongi and I met up and walked around. We walked by Lindy's, and she was out in her driveway in a bathing suit. Just
then it started to rain, and she joined us and we all walked
around Bexley in the downpour stomping in puddles and stuff.
When we got back to her house we were all soaked; she took
out a plastic comb and combed my hair.

MAY 24

WOKE up late and called Jack, Dan, Chuck, and Pongi, but
everyone was still sleeping. Jack finally called at noon. He
said he had made out with Marcia Stewart last night.

In the afternoon we had our first Epsilons softball game of
the season, over on the diamond behind Montrose Elementary School. We played two games against Pegasus; we won
one, they won one. I played second base. I only got one hit,
but I was connecting with the ball pretty good, and I handled
everything that was hit near me in the field. We were hungry
after the games, and went to Javan's to get ribs for dinner.
There's something that always feels great after you've played
ball on a warm day.

MAY 25

I'M president of Epsilons. It came as a complete surprise. We had our usual meeting tonight, and Harry Post, the adult adviser, said it was time to elect new officers. They opened the floor for nominations, and Joel Seiferas and I were nominated. The two of us were told to leave the room.

They debated for about half an hour, and then they had the vote and I won. I can't believe it. This almost makes up for the tennis and everything. Being president of Epsilons is just as good as being a returning letterman in tennis. Chuck and Jack are officers, too—Chuck is vice president and Jack is pledge master.

After I got home the phone started ringing with people congratulating me. The word spreads around the school pretty fast.

MAY 26

I knew I spoke too fast.

Last night was the spring sports banquet, and a lot of guys from Epsilons who lettered on spring sports teams were there. They're pissed off that the election was held on a night they weren't at the fraternity meeting. Some of them want to be officers, and they're saying that a new election has to be held.

Isn't that typical? I finally get something that I want a lot, and the next day people try to take it away. After school we had a meeting of the new officers; if there's still grumbling by Friday, we're going to have a meeting of the whole fraternity at Chuck's house.

MAY 27

WHAT a riot. This morning C.W. Jones came up to me in the hallway and said, "You have a driver's license, don't you?"

I didn't know what he was getting at. I said that I did.

"I have something that I want you to do," he said.

He told me that he had forgotten to get his own driver's license renewed, and that it had expired. So he was without a license, and he had to get a temporary one. The law said that he couldn't drive a car until he had the temporary.

"I want you to drive me out to the testing center," he said.

I almost laughed out loud. Me driving the principal to get his temporary! But we walked out to his car, and I got behind the wheel, and we drove out Broad Street.

C.W. didn't say anything; I could tell he felt a little embarrassed. I kept hoping that people would see us—what would they think? Me driving C.W. Jones' car!

We got to the testing station, and I sat in one of the chairs where parents usually sit while their sixteen-year-old kids are taking their temporary tests. The test is all a written one; the driving part of the test comes after you've had your temporary for a while. I sat there watching C.W. with his white crewcut, standing at a table filling out his test, and I could feel myself grinning.

Finally he came back and sat down next to me, and we waited while the test was graded. He still didn't say anything.

Then one of the test givers came out, looked down at the form, and said in a loud voice:

"Clyde Jones?"

I thought I was going to bust open. C.W. never uses the name Clyde; I hear he hates it. That's why he uses C.W.

C.W. turned red in the face and then stood up. The man said he had passed the test.

On the way back to school, he said, "No need to broadcast this."

Sure.

MAY 28

AT breakfast this morning Dad said I had to get a haircut after school. Just when I was really starting to feel like I looked good.

Mr. Schacht had a cupcake on his desk in Algebra today. When he wasn't looking Jack put chalk from a blackboard eraser on it.

Dave Frasch and I were passing notes back and forth in History class seventh period, and Mr. Millard said, "Are you two going steady, or what?"

The *Bexleos*—our yearbook—came out. I counted up seven pictures of myself in it. I wonder if Lindy's looking at them right now?

Hannah Frankel saw me walking to the barber shop and gave me a ride. I got a college-type haircut, which Dad should like but which I hate.

Tomorrow's our Epsilons meeting at Chuck's. I'm real nervous.

MAY 29

EPSILONS is okay. Right after school Chuck and I went to his house to make plans for the meeting. His older brother Bill and Bill's friend Mark LaPine were there; they said that their fraternity at Ohio State had had the same problem, with some of the members wanting to get rid of the officers.

"The thing you've got to remember," Bill Shenk said, "is not to let it come to a vote. As soon as you let them take a new vote, they've won. You guys are the officers, and you can't let them get the idea that there's any chance for a new election."

"But what if they say we have to do it?" I said.

"Then tell them you'll quit," Bill said. "It's better to quit and hold your head high than to give them a chance to vote you out."

About seven o'clock the members started showing up. We all went down to Chuck's basement. Chuck and I stood at the front of the room, and I called the meeting to order.

"I know that a lot of you aren't happy about missing the election the other night," I said. "We just wanted to call this meeting so everyone can talk about it."

There was some grumbling, and a couple of guys said we should have the elections over, but Chuck and I kept saying no.

"We really want to make Epsilons great next year," Chuck said. "We're willing to work as hard as we can. But if you say you have to have a new election, then Bob and I quit. We won't run in a new election."

We talked for about an hour, and every time the idea of a new election came up Chuck and I went into our Bill Shenk-Mark LaPine stance: If there's a new election, we're out.

Finally Gary Herwald, who was one of the guys at the spring sports banquet who missed the election, said, "Why don't we quit bitching at each other and just go forward? Greene and Shenk sound like they want to do their best for the fraternity, so let's get behind them." That seemed to turn the tide—everyone respects Gary—and within five minutes we had agreed to have an open-house dance next week after school lets out for the year, in Eddie Weston's driveway.

It was a close one, but now I feel I can breathe a little easier.

MAY 30

IT's Saturday morning; when I woke up it was really warm, so I didn't wear socks for the first time of the year. The feeling of my bare feet against my shoes reminded me of summer.

Went to Dan's, and then we picked Jack up. Some seniors

were playing wiffle ball, and we got in the game. After the game I was driving Mom's station wagon, and I saw Lindy riding in Bruce Byrnes' car. She motioned for me to follow.

Byrnes drove to the parking lot of the Excelsior Club, and I pulled up next to him, but it was awkward; I didn't know if Lindy wanted to ride with me or not, so I just left. Jack and Dan and I went back to my house and we were in my room playing records—and I just went into a daze. I don't know how else to explain it—I knew for sure that Lindy was out there.

So I left Jack and Dan in my room and got back in Mom's car and drove down the street, and there was Lindy, standing on the corner. She got in the car and we cruised for an hour.

She said she had called Red Thomas. Red is the tennis pro at Winding Hollow Country Club; before I met Lindy I would spend all my time at the courts, but after I met her last summer I'd spend most of my days with her. We'd go out to talk to Red sometimes, though, and he thought it was funny that a girl could take me away from my great love of tennis.

Anyway, Lindy said she had called Red, just to see how he was. I said that maybe the two of us could go out to Winding Hollow and see him tomorrow, and she said maybe that would be all right. I dropped her off a block from her house.

Am I hoping for too much? When I got back to my room, Jack and Dan were still there.

"Don't even tell us," Dan said. "Lindy, right?"

MAY 31

THIS day leaves me frantic with wonderings. Jack slept over last night; I couldn't get to sleep—all I could think about was going out to Winding Hollow to see Red with Lindy. Somehow it symbolized this whole last year for me—if Lindy and I could get out there together, it would be just like last year. And with summer starting again, it could be a new beginning for us.

I finally fell asleep; Jack and I woke up at eleven, and I

drove him to his house. Then I came back home, brushed my teeth, ate lunch, closed myself in my room with the phone, and called Lindy.

She sounded completely cold—like yesterday never happened. When I mentioned going to see Red, it was almost as if she was surprised by the whole idea.

"I'm not going," she said.

"Why not?" I said.

"It's not a nice day, and I don't look good," she said.

Just like that. I hung up. Half and hour later, she called me back.

"Bobby, I'm at Wendy's," she said. "Are you mad?"

I was sick of being made a fool of. "What do you think?" I said.

"If you really want to go to Winding Hollow that bad . . ." she said.

"I gotta get off," I said.

"What's the matter?" she said.

"I have to study," I said, and hung up again.

I drove over to Jack's and told him how I was feeling. I base all my hopes on something like this, and then it just goes away. We had a good talk, and when I was driving home I saw Lindy and Wendy walking down Roosevelt.

I drove past them without looking, but I heard one of them yell, "Snob."

The Dave Clark Five were on TV tonight. I watched them and studied Chemo. Finals are tomorrow, Tuesday, and Wednesday. Then summer.

JUNE 1

CHEMO final was a bitch. After school I went to Chuck's, and cruised with him and Jack and Dan. I was wearing this light blue shirt that Lindy gave me last summer.

Chuck stopped the car.

"You've got to get over this Lindy thing," he said. He and Jack and Dan got out of the car, so I got out too.

They all jumped on me and started ripping the shirt off me. We were in somebody's front yard.

I started yelling, but they were tearing the shirt to shreds.

"Maybe this will end the daze for you," Dan said. We were all laughing, but the shirt meant a lot to me. When they got done it was hanging off me in tatters.

Jay Maupin and Jeff Schmidt came by and hit us with bean-shooters. Then we drove back to Chuck's house; I had Mom's car there, and I headed home. Lindy was walking down the street and I heard her yell, "Why don't you stop, Bobby?"

So I circled around the block and pulled up to where she was standing on the sidewalk. She looked inside the car and said, "Your shirt."

I started to explain what had happened, but it wasn't worth it. Instead I asked her if she wanted to get in.

"I can't," she said. "I have to go home to dinner."

So I went home to dinner, too.

Chuck says there's a girl in his Spanish class who wants him to screw her. He think's it's really true.

Her name is Carla Crowe, and she's a sophomore, and she's moving out of town next week. Chuck has this mark on his arm where the doctor stuck a tube in when they thought something might be wrong with his heart. He says that Carla makes a point of touching it and rubbing her hand over it every day during Spanish.

She's been saying suggestive things to him all week. He says he's going to try before she leaves town.

JUNE 2

ALGEBRA final was horrible; History and French were okay. When school was over, Allen was waiting outside on Cassingham in his car. He had just gotten back from military school.

It was great to see him. Now it really feels like summer is ready to start—ABCDJ are together again.

We rode all over Bexley in his car. There's a terrific new song out by the Beach Boys—it's called "I Get Around," and it's a summer song if I ever heard one. WCOL played it twice while we were cruising. One more final tomorrow, and that's it for this school year.

JUNE 3

HAD my last final—English. It wasn't that hard. It felt so good when the bell rang to end the school year. We drove by the junior high school building yelling and honking our horns.

It feels just like breaking out of prison. Tomorrow is a free day, and Friday we have to go back and pick up our report cards—but this is it. School is out.

Our Epsilons open house was tonight in Eddie Weston's driveway. It was packed—it seemed like the whole school was there. We had a band, and Kenny Stone playing records, and an off-duty Bexley cop to keep control. Eddie Weston's parents had strung colored lights up in the trees and bushes, and the weather was warm—it felt like summer for sure.

I was talking to Mark Smilack, and Lindy walked up and said to him, "Bobby and I are good friends—aren't we?" I didn't say anything.

Chet Crosby was there. Rumors are that he doesn't like Lindy anymore, and that he wants to go out with Mark Smilack's little sister Marcia. Chuck and Jack and I were standing around, and Chuck saw Chet Crosby talking to Marcia—so Chuck walked right up to her, right in front of Crosby, and asked her to dance. She said yes. It was great.

ABCDJ went to the Toddle House for cheeseburgers and banana cream pie after the open house ended. We were all sitting there at the counter, on five stools right in a row, and I thought about how nice it is not to have to worry about getting up for school in the morning.

JUNE 4

WE were hanging around Dan's house this afternoon and Pongi started acting tough and slugged me in the arm three times. Really pissed me off.

Tonight Dan and I were cruising past the school in his T-Bird and someone threw pebbles at us. Based on the direction they were coming from, whoever threw them had to be up on the roof of the junior high school building. Dan slammed on the brakes and we got out of the car, but we couldn't find anybody.

Chuck called Carla Crowe and asked her out for night after tomorrow. He really think's he's going to get her.

JUNE 5

UP at eight o'clock; Dan, Chuck, Jack, and I went to breakfast at the Eastmoor Drive-In, and then went to school to get our grade cards. Mine were pretty awful. Pongi had his convertible at school and we cruised through Bexley in it with the top down. "I Get Around" kept playing on WCOL. It was really hot out.

Some guys threw water balloons at Pongi's car, so we went to Rogers' Drugstore and bought our own balloons and filled them up. We drove around throwing them at people.

It's hard to believe—we're the seniors now. School doesn't start again until September, but we are definitely the seniors.

At night there was an open house at the Jeffrey Mansion. A lot of girls from other schools were there—Judy Newpoff, Anita Paul, Tiffany Coleman. Boy, they are great-looking.

Only a few people from this year's graduating class were at the open house. They seemed out of place. It's funny—they've only been out of school for one day, but already it seems like they shouldn't be at Bexley functions. It's our turn to be the oldest guys in the school.

JUNE 6

WHAT a historic day. Chuck screwed Carla Crowe. A first for ABCDJ.

It all started in the afternoon. Allen, Chuck, Dan, Jack, and I were driving around Bexley, and we decided to go the the Excelsior Club. When we got there, Lindy was in the parking lot talking to some people. She started to walk over to Chuck's car to talk with me—and Chuck laid rubber and squealed out of there.

We were driving down Cassady, and I said to Chuck, "Why did you do that?"

"You think about Lindy too much," he said.

"I'm going to get you back for this," I said.

"Yeah, you're going to get me back," he said.

"In spades," I said. "In spades."

We cruised around most of the day. Chuck said that he was supposed to pick Carla up at about seven o'clock for their date. Allen had said that his parents were going to be out for the night; Chuck asked if he could use the apartment, and Allen said that would be okay. He gave Chuck a key to the apartment.

We all kept debating about how much of a chance Chuck really had to screw her. He had already gone out and bought rubbers.

"You'd better use two of them," Jack said.

"What do you mean?" Chuck said.

"Just to be safe," Jack said. "In case one breaks."

We discussed that idea, and we decided it probably was a good one.

"I don't know," Chuck said. "I never heard of using two rubbers before."

Right before dinnertime he dropped us off so that he could get ready for the date. Allen and Dan and Jack and I had switched over to Allen's car when I came up with the idea.

"You know that bathroom that connects to your bedroom?" I said.

"Yeah?" Allen said.

"I think we should be in it when Chuck comes to your apartment," I said.

All of a sudden everyone in the car stopped talking.

"What if Chuck tries to get in the bathroom?" Jack said.

"It locks," I said. "We'll just lock ourselves in."

We started talking about it. The beauty of the plan was that there could be no way for Chuck to put one over on us—if Carla wouldn't go to bed with him, or if Chuck chickened out, we'd be right there to hear it. We had made plans to meet Chuck back at Dan's house after the date. Now we could compare what he told us with the real truth.

We drove to Allen's apartment building. His parents were already gone. We put signs up in the living room and the den; we wrote on pieces of paper: "ALLEN'S PARENTS SAID NOT TO GO INTO THIS ROOM. PLEASE USE ALLEN'S BEDROOM."

Then we sat in the den and waited. We took turns looking

out the window to the street below; finally Jack said, "Here he comes."

We all looked out the window. Chuck was in his brother's white convertible, and there was a girl next to him on the front seat. We looked down seventeen floors and saw him turn into the apartment building's parking garage.

We hurried into Allen's bedroom, and then into the bathroom. We locked the door. The four of us sat on the floor.

Within a few minutes we could hear them coming. Then we heard Chuck's voice:

"This is the room of the guy who lives here."

Apparently Chuck was flipping through Allen's yearbook from military school, because Carla's voice said, "Why is he wearing that funny uniform?"

"They all have to wear them there," Chuck said.

We were all biting the insides of our mouths and trying not to laugh out loud.

Chuck and Carla talked about school, and about her moving out of town in a few days. This went on for several minutes. Then, for about twenty minutes we didn't hear anything.

We thought they might have left the room, but then Chuck's voice said, "I can't get this damn package open."

"The rubbers," Jack whispered.

Then Chuck's voice said: "Oh, yes I can."

There were another few seconds of silence, and Chuck's voice said, "Now I can't get the *other* package open."

Allen held up two fingers—Chuck was really going to use two rubbers at once.

Then all of a sudden there was the sound of Carla breathing real hard and moaning out loud. The sound grew even louder; she was going crazy.

"He's doing it," Jack said.

The four of us were scrunched up on the floor, and we didn't know what to do. We kept hearing what was going on in the other room. Dan stood up in the bathroom and said in his normal voice, "This is perverted. I've got to get out of here."

We grabbed his shirt and pulled him back down. "Shhhh!" Jack said.

Fortunately Chuck must have been too involved with Carla to hear Dan's voice, because he didn't say anything about it.

Things got quiet out in the bedroom, and then we heard Carla's voice say that she wanted to use the bathroom.

We could hear them walking over to where we were. Chuck tried the door. It wouldn't budge; the lock worked.

He tried tugging on it, and then said, "I guess it's stuck."

They must have been putting their clothes on, because Carla's voice said, "It's pretty early for me to be getting home from a date. What am I going to tell my parents?"

Chuck's voice said, "Tell them we went to Putt-Putt and it's all over."

We heard them leave the apartment. We ran to the window and made sure we saw them drive away. Then we raced down to Allen's car and headed for Dan's house. We had to get there in the time it took Chuck to drop Carla off and get there himself.

We made it by five minutes. By the time Chuck pulled up, we were leaning against Allen's car underneath a streetlight, as if we had been there all evening.

Chuck pulled the convertible up to the curb and hopped out. He was wearing Bermuda shorts, a white T-shirt, a regular shirt unbuttoned over the T-shirt, and sunglasses.

He sauntered up to us very casually.

"Well?" Allen said.

"Well what?" Chuck said.

"What happened?" Allen said.

Chuck shrugged.

"Did you screw her?" Jack said.

"Yeah," Chuck said.

"You bullshitter," I said.

Chuck shrugged again. "Call me a bullshitter if you want," he said. "I know what happened."

Dan said, "Aw, you're lying."

"Look," Chuck said, as if he was talking to a group of children. "I really don't care if you guys believe me or not. When it happens to you, you don't need to talk about it."

This went on for a few minutes, and then we asked Chuck to tell us how it happened. He went through the whole evening, from the time he picked Carla up. We listened intently.

When he had finished with the story, I knew it was time. I said:

"But how was Carla going to explain getting home so early to her parents?"

"I told her to tell her parents that we had gone to the movies, but that it was all over," Chuck said.

"You mean Putt-Putt," I said.

"Yeah," Chuck said. "Putt-Putt."

It took him only half a second to realize what had happened. Allen and Dan and Jack were already cracked up and rolling on the grass. Chuck started chasing me around Allen's car.

"In spades," I kept yelling when I could stop laughing. "In spades!"

Finally Chuck started laughing, too, and we all sat down on Dan's front lawn. We explained what we had done. Chuck wasn't mad; he thought we were crazy for doing it, but I could tell that in a weird way, he was glad that we had. It was such a milestone for all of us; somehow it was fitting that we had all been there.

We ended the evening over at Chuck's house, sitting around the kitchen and eating and talking.

What a night. Boy, I have to get a screw. It sounded like hell, but it's just something I have to do. That's my goal for this summer.

JUNE 7

NEVER a dull moment. Chuck and Jack came over to our house in the morning and woke me up. We went to the Excelsior Club and played basketball on the court next to the swimming pool. Lindy was there in a two-piece bathing suit. She looked great. She was standing by the snack bar and winked at me real sexy.

It started to rain, which broke up the basketball game. I had Mom's station wagon, and I ran to it to get out of the rain—and there were Lindy and Debby Harbold and Janie McKenney in the back seat. I drove them to Janie's, and then cruised through the rain. "I Get Around" came on the radio twice.

When the rain stopped I went back to the Excelsior Club. Just as I was walking through the entrance to the pool area, Judy Morse saw me. I hadn't really talked much to her since last winter, and those times I made out with her over at her house. She told the manager of the Excelsior Club that my family didn't have a membership—which is true—and that he should kick me out. But some guys who are members let me stay as their guest. Then Judy told Gregg Robins that I had called to ask her out and that she had said no—a complete lie—and that Lindy was just leading me on.

Dan and Chuck and I went to Javan's and got ribs for dinner. Then we went back to my house. Dan said that I should stop being in such a daze over Lindy and just ask her out.

"This is ridiculous," he said, "Quit playing these cake-dialer games. Just pick up the phone and ask her for a date tonight."

I thought he might have a point; maybe the trick was just to ask her out straightforward, like any other guy asking for a date.

I called her number. She answered.

"Hi, Lindy," I said.

"Oh, hi," she said.

"Listen," I said. "I was thinking about going to a movie tonight, and I wondered if you'd like to go with me."

"Oh, gee," she said. "I'm doing something with Debby Harbold tonight. I wish you would have called five minutes earlier."

My heart sank. "Are you sure you couldn't change your plans and go out with me?" I said.

"I really can't," she said. "And anyway, if I said yes on such short notice, I wouldn't be playing very hard-to-get, would I?"

Dan had his head up next to mine, with his ear on the back of the phone receiver, listening to the conversation as I talked. He grabbed the receiver from me and said to Lindy:

"You no-good!"

Then I took the phone and hung it up.

There was an open house later on at Cynthia Blatt's house. By the time we got there, everybody already knew that Lindy had shot me down. Joel Seiferas said he'd seen her and she'd told him I had asked her out. Everyone was laughing about it. Except Dan. He's a good guy.

At the open house I saw Susie Young. She's really pretty. I was trying to get up the nerve to dance slow with her. I told Allen and Chuck and Dan and Jack that I was going to do it, and as soon as the words were out of my mouth, Chuck walked up and asked her to dance himself. After last night, I guess he thinks he can get any girl.

As they were dancing he looked over at me and said, "Ace of spades."

JUNE 8

DAD woke me up today and said that I had to cut the lawn and get a haircut.

I put the earplug in my transistor radio, stuck the radio in the pocket of my pants, and went out to cut the lawn with no shirt on. It was hot, and I could feel the rays on my back.

I bitch every time dad asks me to cut the lawn, but in a way it feels good. Especially when the grass has been growing a little too long—I like the way that the lawnmower makes stripes as I push it back and forth and move down toward the sidewalk. I always do it the same way—first the front yard, then the narrow strip that goes along the east side of the house, then the backyard, then the strip of grass that separated our driveway from the Dormans' driveway on the other side of the house, and finally that little bit of grass between the sidewalk and the street.

I always work up a sweat when I'm mowing the lawn—not a real extreme sweat like when I've been playing basketball or something, but a good sweat. The first time I really felt grown-up was when Dad asked me to mow the lawn for the first time. Before that, I was always too little—he did it himself. Now he almost never does it. My brother Timmy would love to try it, but Dad says that ten is way too young.

I went to the icebox and drank a Coke out of the bottle after I had finished. Then I went to the barber shop and got my hair cut, which I didn't want to do.

When Dad got home from work he said that I had missed a patch of grass in the backyard, and that my hair was still too long on the sides.

JUNE 9

EPSILONS meeting tonight. It felt real natural running it; all those troubles seem to be over. We all got along great, and everyone was happy about the way the open house at the Westons' had gone.

After the meting ABCDJ went to Allen's apartment. His parents were out again, so we drank some beer we had gotten hold of. I had three, and was really drunk. Dan said that was because I was drinking on an empty stomach. He said you should always coat your stomach with milk.

JUNE 10

WE played basketball at the Excelsior Club again today; all the girls got out of the pool and watched us while the sun dried them off in their bathing suits.

Susie Young was one of them. She is so pretty. But Allen and Jack walked across the street to get ice cream with her and Judy Engelman, and as I joined them to walk, Jack said, "You stay here, Bob." What a shitty thing to say—especially for the person who's supposed to have been my friend for the longest time of anybody. Boy, I felt low. Later Jack told me that Susie Young doesn't like me—he says he knows that she has a crush on Allen. Par for the course.

Tonight Chuck and I cruised in his car. He said that Carla Crowe and her family had left town today. We talked a lot about him going to bed with her. He seemed so calm about it—like it was no big deal. I can hardly imagine what it would be like.

"I know it seems like it's impossible," he said. "But when

it's happening, you don't even think about it. It just happens.''

"That's easy for you to say," I said. "You've done it."

"It'll happen to you," he said. "Don't think so much about
it. Just cool it, and it'll happen."

For the first time in my life, I felt like I was much younger
than Chuck.

JUNE 11

DAD told me that I can have a summer job in the factory of
his plant. He said the Bron-Shoe Company is behind in its
orders; the baby shoes and stuff are coming in faster than
they can plate it, and he wants me to work in the receiving
department, opening up packages and getting the shoes ready
for the plating process.

I'm supposed to start in four days. I'm kind of happy about
it; I had planned to bum around all summer, but Jack and
Dan and Chuck are all working, and Allen is looking for a
job, so there wouldn't be all that much to do during the day,
anyway. I won't be able to catch as many rays as last summer,
though.

JUNE 12

I was at Dan's house this afternoon, and we heard some people call our names.

We looked over at the house next door, and there were
three painters on the roof. We walked to the house—and we
saw that it was three teachers: Mr. Eliopulos, the Speech
teacher; Mr. Millard, the History teacher; and Mr. Smith,
the Spanish teacher.

They were wearing white painters' uniforms and caps. We
yelled up and talked to them for a while. I guess that they
paint houses during the summer to make money. It was funny

seeing them that way; I never thought of them outside the halls of the high school.

Tonight I got so drunk and sick.

Chuck and Allen and I went to Allen's apartment; his parents were out again. We had managed to get three six-packs, and we each drank a whole six-pack.

There was a big thunderstorm outside. We were laughing and feeling great, and we thought it would be fun to walk to Chuck's house. Chuck lives about three miles away from Allen's apartment.

So we went out in the middle of all the thunder and lightning and rain. We were running down Broad Street; our clothes were completely soaked. When we got to Chuck's we realized we couldn't go inside—his parents would know right away that we had been drinking.

I went out onto Chuck's front lawn and lay on my back with my arms and legs spread out, just like little kids do in the snow. The rain was just beating down on me. Chuck and Allen pulled me up and said that we should walk back to Allen's apartment. After we got about a block from Chuck's house, I started to throw up. I stopped about three times to throw up before we even got back to Broad Street.

We were the only people walking. People who were driving their cars looked at us like we were nuts. Finally a bus came along, and Allen jumped in front of it and made it stop, even though we weren't at a bus stop. The bus took us down to Allen's.

We went up to his apartment. I called home and told Mom that I was going to sleep over. I tried to talk real slow and clear so that she couldn't tell what I had been doing. We all took our clothes off and went to sleep in Allen's room. I heard Chuck get up in the middle of the night and throw up in the bathroom.

JUNE 13

WE all got up late; we were feeling pretty sick. We had soup for breakfast.

Had to take Mom's station wagon into Gager-Keim Ford to get fixed. Pongi followed me, and after I had dropped the car off we went out to Winding Hollow Country Club and caught some rays by the pool.

Chuck came over to my house around six o'clock and asked if I wanted to go to dinner. I said okay, and we drove out Broad Street to the Ranch, but it was too crowded. So we went to Eastmoor Drive-In.

While we were eating, Lindy came in. She walked over to our booth. We talked and compared tans, and then she left, taking my heart.

JUNE 14

THIS morning Robyne Finke came over to see Debby, and Chuck and Jack and Allen came over to see me. We all went to the Pancake House together for lunch.

It always feels weird to be with a bunch of guys and girls when Debby's there. Because she's my sister, it feels funny—she's seen me around our house for our whole lives, and she knows me too well. I catch myself acting differently when she's there—not saying certain things that might sound cool at any other time, but that she might laugh at and make fun of.

We all went back to our house and had a lethargic afternoon watching TV and listening to records. Jack asked me if I wanted to go out to dinner, and Dad said that I had been eating out for every meal.

"But it's summer," I said.

He made me have dinner at home. Jack waited for me, and

after dessert I went out to his car and we went to Burger Boy Food-O-Rama. I went to bed early, because my first day of work is tomorrow.

JUNE 15

UP at 6:30 A.M., and got to the Bron-Shoe plant by 7:20. There was a card for me by the time clock, and I got in line with all of the other workers and punched in.

I was assigned to the receiving room. I was supposed to work with an older guy named Ronnie Rummel; we stood in front of a big table, used knives to open up all the packages, and then tagged the baby shoes and the other stuff that people wanted to get plated.

I got the hang of it pretty well. Ronnie seems to be a nice guy; he's been working there for a long time, and he said he was glad to have someone to help him open the stuff. The baby shoes come in from all over the country; I kept looking at the return addresses on the packages, and it seemed that each one of them was from a different state.

There was an open house tonight, and we all agreed to wear jackets to it, just to be different. I wore my Epsilons blazer with white Levi's and Weejuns and no socks.

There was this girl from Eastmoor named Nancy; I made a small play for her and twice danced slow with her.

After I walked back to my friends, Dan said to me, "Have you noticed that you're always attracted to girls with smashed-in faces?"

"What do you mean?" I said.

"Every time you ask a girl to dance, she has a smashed-in face," he said, and laughed.

I looked over by the bushes, where this Nancy girl was standing. I didn't think she had a smashed-in face.

JUNE 16

I was exhausted this morning. We didn't get in from the open house until 2 A.M., and I had to get up at ten minutes before seven to get to work. Ronnie Rummel and I opened packages all day again. He's a good guy to talk to, but it didn't seem as interesting as it did yesterday.

I stayed in at night, and fell asleep in my clothes.

JUNE 17

I punched in at 7:23 this morning, and I got a message that I was supposed to go up to the second floor to fill out some paperwork so that I would get my paychecks.

When I got up there I was looking for the right office to go to, and I ran into Dad. This is the first I've seen him at work.

He was with some other men from the company. He was real friendly to me—asking me how things were going, if I was having any problems, etc. It was really strange—he was treating me differently than he does at home. I like Dad fine, but we never have real long conversations. It's like we both agree that he lives in his grown-up world, and I live in my world, and we just go along keeping that in mind. We don't discuss stuff much. Today, though . . . the conversation was almost like a movie dad and son.

I guess that's because we were at the office, and his co-workers were around. I got the forms filled out, and then went downstairs to open boxes with Ronnie Rummel all day.

After work I went home and took a shower, then borrowed Mom's car and cruised around Bexley. "I Get Around" is number one on the new WCOL survey.

Lindy and Janie McKenney and Wendy Clowson were walking down Drexel. They waved, and I stopped. They got in the car. Lindy was in the front seat with me, and the other two were in the back seat.

I drove to Chuck's house, and pulled into the part of his driveway that winds around behind the house. That's where Lindy and I always used to go last summer when we just wanted to talk and not be bothered by anybody.

So the four of us were sitting there. We'd only been there a few minutes when Chuck's older brother Bill pulled into the driveway. He always used to come home from Ohio State last summer when Lindy and I were there, but this was the first time in a long time that he'd seen us there.

He walked up to the car. "So, Lindy," he said. "Greene's waited more than a year now. Are you finally going to wear his ring?"

The girls all laughed and Lindy said something about Chet Crosby, which didn't make me feel too good.

Bill went into the house, and Lindy and Janie and Wendy and I kept talking . . . and it was just so different than last year. Last year Lindy and I were in the driveway alone, and all we wanted to do was to be with each other. No matter how much time we had, it never seemed like enough time. Now here the four of us were, and it felt awkward. I was trying to talk to Lindy, and she kept saying things to Janie and Wendy. She was making references to people I didn't know and stuff I didn't understand.

I didn't like it. So I started directing my conversation at Janie and Wendy, and a couple of times Lindy would say something and I would make fun of it.

The third time I did this Lindy said, "Bobby, I hate you. You treat all my friends nice and me mean."

A few minutes later they asked me to drive them to the Bexley Pool, which I did. I drove home for dinner. I am so screwed up.

JUNE 18

I was completely tired and hungry at work today. Ronnie Rummel said that the word had come down that we were supposed to keep track of how many packages we opened up and tagged. By the end of the day I had opened 206 packages.

After work I cruised. I saw Lindy walking down Roosevelt with Janie. Lindy looked like the most beautiful girl in the world. I circled the block and looked for her, but she was gone when I got back.

After dinner Dan and I went to look for moccasins to buy. When I got back home Mom said that someone had called and hung up.

So I dialed for cake at Lindy's, but got no response. Later on I called and stayed on the phone until she said hello and then I hung up. Boy, just hearing her voice puts me in the damn daze.

God, why can't I have her back? In two days it's June 20— exactly a year since I met her. I've lived a whole year for nothing but her. If Chet Crosby loves her as much as I do, he deserves her. But no one's love is that great.

JUNE 19

OPENED 259 packages at work. But they keep coming in, every day; it seems like as many packages as Ronnie Rummel and I open up, we don't make a dent in the pile.

After work I went to Dan's, and we got in his family's Thunderbird and went up to the Ohio State campus to buy moccasins. When we looked for them the other night, we couldn't find any good ones.

At Ohio State I found a pair I liked at Moe Glassman's Men's Shop, and Dan found a pair he liked at Flagg Brothers. We took off our socks and our other shoes and wore the moccasins right out of the stores.

There was an open house later on, but it turned out to be crummy. I left and went over to Pongi's house, where a bunch of guys were watching *King Creole* on TV. After the movie was over we went to get hamburgers at the White Castle that's next door to the Bexley police station.

JUNE 20

You know, you wait so long for something to happen. You convince yourself that it won't, but in the back of your mind you still have that hope that won't die, no matter how much discouragement you receive.

I woke up around 8 A.M.; it's Saturday. June 20; one year ago today I met Lindy.

I guess I always thought that maybe on June 20 things would get good again. There was no sign that they would, but I just thought that maybe on June 20 something would happen that would start Lindy and me going together again.

So I woke up, and Mom reminded me that we were all going to Hideaway Hills for the weekend. She said she had some errands she wanted me to run first.

I took her car and went to Kroger's to get her some groceries, and then made some other stops for her. I kept half expecting to run into Lindy, but there was no sign of her. When I got home Dad and Mom and Debby and Timmy were waiting for me. We loaded the car and drove down to Hideaway.

I guess Mom and Dad could tell that I was a little down, but they didn't know why. I was just hanging around the cottage. Mom told me that there was a one-day tennis tournament up at the dirt court, and said that I ought to go up there. At first I didn't want to, but finally I did, just to get out of the cottage. The tournament lasted all afternoon, and I won, which was no big deal; there are no good players at Hideaway Hills. In the finals I beat this old man 6–1, 6–3.

There was a style show in the lodge, and then later in the evening there was a hayride. Debby and Timmy and I went on it. It was real corny. The haywagon just kept driving around the hills. After it was over I went to bed thinking about this past year. I wonder if Lindy even knows what day today is?

JUNE 21

I was lethargic all day. Dad wanted to stay at Hideaway as long as possible, so we spent the whole day there. We ate breakfast at the lodge, and then hung around the cottage for the rest of the time. It was hot and muggy. We drove home in the evening; by the time I got back to Bexley everyone I called was already out. So I'll just turn in and get rested for work tomorrow.

JUNE 22

I really got embarrassed at work this morning. I was opening up packages, and one of the supervisors called me over.

"There's a truck parked out in back," he said. "Here's the keys. Will you go out and pull it up to the loading dock?"

I took the keys and went out there and got into the truck. I put the key in the ignition—and I realized that the truck was stick shift. I've never driven a stick shift before—every car I've driven has had automatic transmission.

I didn't know what to do. I didn't want to go back in and say that I didn't know how to drive the truck. It wasn't that I was afraid that they'd get mad. It was almost the opposite— because my dad is vice-president of the company, I'm always worried that they're going easy on me. If I told them that I couldn't drive a stick, they'd just have someone else do it. But they'd think that I was hopeless.

So I tried to figure out how to drive the truck. There wasn't even a gearshift pattern on the knob; it was a plain black knob. For about ten minutes I tried to do it. The truck kept lurching back and forth, but I couldn't get the hang of it.

Finally I went in and called Ronnie Rummel aside. I told him what the problem was, and that I didn't want anyone to know about it. He said not to worry; he said he'd do it for me. He slipped out and backed the truck up to the loading dock while no one was looking. He's really a good guy.

JUNE 23

IT was really hot at work today; I sweated through my T-shirt the whole day as I opened up the packages. I was in a bad mood to start with because Dad told me I had to get another haircut, which I did after work was over.

Tonight Allen picked me up and ABCDJ all went to an open house on Cassingham. Kenny Stone was playing records for the party.

It's funny what the difference is in dancing fast and dancing slow. When you dance fast, it doesn't much matter who you're dancing with. The record comes on and you ask a girl and you go out there and you dance and that's it.

But when you dance slow . . . the whole thing has a different feeling. When a slow song starts, you're a little more careful in who you ask. On a slow song you're going to be holding each other close and dancing cheek-to-cheek. The other people at the open house notice who you're dancing with when it's a slow dance. And it's easier to get shut down by a girl when you ask her for a slow dance. The same girl who might say yes to you on a fast dance might say no to you on a slow dance, just because it means so much more.

I danced fast a couple of times tonight, but I didn't dance slow. There was no one there who I liked enough or felt confident enough to ask. Mostly ABCDJ stood around watching everybody else and talking among ourselves. That's what we usually do at open houses. We ended the evening at the Pancake House. I had the little ones (they're called silver dollar pancakes) with blueberries.

JUNE 24

SOMETIMES at work I think about the people who have sent in all the baby shoes. Ronnie Rummel and I will stand there hour after hour, opening up the packages, taking out the baby shoes, putting tags on them. Almost all of the shoes are white;

they're scuffed and worn, and they come from all over the country, and here they are on our table.

I wonder why it's so important for parents to get their babies' shoes bronzed? On my first day at work one of the supervisors told me that it was very essential not to screw up the identification of the shoes. He said that if a mother and father got the wrong shoe back, they'd know it right away.

I said, "Even after the shoes have been bronzed?" And the supervisor said yes, the parents always know what their children's shoes look like.

I open the packages and tag the shoes, and I think about all of those families, and all of those babies, and here the shoes end up, in front of me on a table in a factory in Columbus, Ohio. It makes me feel strange.

There was another open house tonight. On our way there we ran into some of the seniors who just graduated—Jay Maupin and some of the other guys from last year's football team. They were riding Hondas.

We were in Chuck's car and he honked for them to get out of the way. Last year he would never have done that—Maupin and those guys owned the high school. But I guess that now that we're going to be the seniors, Chuck felt he could honk his horn at them.

They stopped their cycles right in front of Chuck's car and came up to the car and opened the doors and pulled us out.

"You guys have been calling us and threatening to slit our tires," Maupin said.

"Look, we didn't do it," I said. He was holding me by my shirt.

"We know you did it," Maupin said. He let go of me and said to his friends, "Come on—we'll get 'em later."

We got back in the car and they drove off on their cycles. Everybody knew that everybody else was just screwing around. Still, it put a little action into the evening.

JUNE 25

AFTER work today Jack and I went to look at used cars. His dad says that maybe he can get one. We saw some cool foreign cars—Triumphs, Austin-Healeys, MGs. Jack's dad drives a big Pontiac, though, and Jack thinks that his dad won't let him get a little foreign car because they aren't "safe."

Jack said that his dad said, "If you roll over in one of those things you're dead." But it was great looking at them.

We had an Epsilons meeting tonight. I'm getting pretty good at running the meetings. Afterwards there was another open house. Allen invented a dance called the "Jungle Rot." It's great—he bends over like a monkey and lets his hands hang down to the ground, and then he moves from side to side. The girls don't know if he's serious and they're supposed to dance with him, or whether it's a joke and they're supposed to laugh. When they ask him he just says, "Hey, it's the latest dance—the Jungle Rot!" By the end of the open house, we were all doing it.

JUNE 26

OH, have I got troubles. At the end of work today I got my first paycheck. After taxes and Social Security were taken out, it came to $24.09.

I folded the check up and put it in my back pocket. Dan and I went to the Excelsior Club and sat by the pool catching rays. Then I went home for dinner; after dinner Allen picked me up, and we went back to Dan's. Allen and Chuck and Dan and Jack all had dates tonight; they were going to have a party at Allen's house. They got some older guys to buy them beer. I didn't have a date.

So I went over to Pongi's and watched TV. While I was there I reached into my back pocket—and the check was gone.

I retraced my steps and looked everywhere. No check. I tried to think of where I could have lost it, but I have no idea. I'm just sick about it.

It would be bad enough no matter where I worked. But working for Dad's company—if I go in next week and tell them that I lost the check, it will get back to him right away. My very first paycheck—I know what he'd say about my sense of responsibility, etc.

I'm at home now, getting ready to go to bed. I don't know what I'm going to do about this. I just have to find it. How could I lose my first paycheck?

JUNE 27

DAD woke me up yelling at 7:30 A.M. He was holding my paycheck in his hand.

He said that Debby had found it on our driveway; it was folded up and just lying there. I guess it must have fallen out of my pocket when I got home from work yesterday.

He threatened to ground me for the weekend; today's Saturday, and he said he just might make me stay inside until work Monday morning.

"Do you know how hard people have to work for their paychecks?" he said. "Doesn't the value of money mean anything to you?"

"I didn't mean to lose it," I said.

"You didn't mean to lose it," he said. "You didn't mean to lose it."

He cooled off by the end of breakfast, and let me go out. Dan and Chuck and I went to the Excelsior Club and to the Columbus Country Club. They had dates tonight, but I didn't, so I went to Mark and Judy Engelman's house, where there were a lot of people over. Everyone was watching TV in the den; Susie Young was sitting on the couch, and she let me sit on the floor and lean back against her legs while I looked at TV.

JUNE 28

EPSILONS had a fraternity league softball game today. I borrowed Mom's car to drive to the field, but it was almost out of gas, so I stopped at Luke's Shell Station and put in fifty cents worth of regular.

We played a good game. We won 12–7; I played the whole game at second base, and went two for four at the plate. I felt great out in the field; I smacked one guy with the ball when he tried to run into me to break up a double play—and later, when I was running to second, the same guy was trying to make a double play work and I ran into him so he couldn't get the throw off.

Tonight there was an open house in Berwick. Allen and Chuck and Jack and I went; we all found girls to hang around with, except Jack. Harvey Handler asked me if I liked Susie Young, and said that he heard she kind of liked me. So when I saw her I put my arm around her and held her hand. I don't know if there's anything there or not.

JUNE 29

AFTER work today I drove to the Excelsior Club, where a lot of people were still sitting around the pool. Susie Young was one of them, but she acted kind of distant. I don't know how she feels about me.

The cake dialers hit our house at dinnertime. It seems like a long time since I've seen Lindy around, and when I dialed her house and let it ring, there was no response.

At night ABCDJ cruised, and then we had a late snack at the Toddle House. It made me feel sick, which I am right now.

JUNE 30

I punched in at 7:25 at work today, and they told me that I only had to work a half day. So when I got off I went down to the Lazarus department store to do some errands.

Mom had let me drive her car to work in exchange for me getting her tires changed. I went to the Lazarus parking garage on Front Street and asked the people in their service department to do it while I was in the store.

I bought a pair of white Levi's, and then went to the record department. They had a brand-new Beatles album—it's called *A Hard Day's Night*, and the songs are from the movie that they're going to be in later this summer.

I took it home and played it. It's really great—especially the title song. At night we all went to the TAT and bought poor boys. We took them over to Pongi's to eat them. His parents weren't home, so we all made ourselves Bloody Marys. It really set me off—my first hard stuff.

We cruised. WCOL was playing a lot of songs from *A Hard Day's Night*, and I felt good because I bought it first, before people were hearing it on the radio. We stopped at Rogers' Drugstore before we went home for the night, and bought gum so our parents wouldn't smell the booze on our breath. Dan said that vodka doesn't have a smell, but we chewed the gum anyway, just to be safe.

July 1

Mom let me drive her car to work this morning, and I pulled too close to the curb in front of the Bron-Shoe Company and scraped the tires real bad. I thought I might have busted them, but when I came out of work at the end of the day they were still all right.

After work I went home and played the *Hard Day's Night* album for a few hours. Then Allen picked me up, and ABCDJ went to an open house. I danced slow twice with Susie Young; she kind of squeezed my hand.

"Rag Doll" by the Four Seasons is number one on the new WCOL survey.

July 2

Things are happening. I got my paycheck at work; it was up to thirty-three dollars this week because I worked some longer days. I made sure I didn't lose it.

When I got home there was a message that I was supposed to call the *Citizen-Journal*. Bill Moore, the city editor, had called my house.

I called him. The paper had been on strike for a few weeks, but now the strike is over and they're back at work. Their copy-boys and copygirls had all been Ohio State students—but the students went home for the summer when the strike started. So now the paper needs copyboys, and they still had my name on file.

Bill Moore asked me if I could come down right away and talk to him. I said sure; I walked over to Main Street and caught the downtown bus.

At the newspaper building I rode the elevator up to the mezzanine. When I walked into the city room it was like everything was going on at once. Telephones were ringing and people were typing and everyone was walking around from desk to desk. I stood there for a minute and no one said anything to me. So finally I asked someone who Mr. Moore was, and they pointed me toward a desk in the middle of the room.

He had a crew cut and was smoking cigarettes. I introduced myself to him. He seemed to be in a big hurry; he said he needed someone who could start right away. He told me that because the *Citizen-Journal* is a morning paper, I'd have to work from 2 P.M. until 11 P.M. I didn't know what to say; that will limit my nighttime activities with ABCDJ.

But I looked around the room, and I really wanted to work there. So I told Mr. Moore okay. He said that my pay would be sixty-five dollars a week; the paper is unionized, and that's their minimum wage. It's a lot more than I'm getting at the Bron-Shoe Company, and I said that would be fine. He said to come back tomorrow and fill out my employment forms. As I left the city room things were still as noisy as before.

I rode the bus home and told Mom and Dad about the job offer. They seemed pleased, but Dad said that I couldn't just quit the Bron-Shoe Company without giving notice. He said that I had to follow the same rules as everyone else who works there. So next week I have to work both jobs—the Bron-Shoe job in the morning, and the *Citizen-Journal* job right after that.

Allen and I had dates tonight; his was with Marcia Smilack and mine was with Susie Young. We asked them to go to the movies—*What a Way to Go!* with Shirley MacLaine and Paul Newman was playing downtown at the RKO Palace.

It was embarrassing—we picked them up at Marcia's and they were both dressed up; high heels and everything. Allen and I were dressed like slobs—shorts and T-shirts. So the girls had to change before we even got started.

On the way downtown WCOL kept playing songs from *A Hard Day's Night*. During a newsbreak the announcer said that the civil-rights bill had passed in Washington.

The movie theater was pretty empty. I held hands with Susie for almost the whole movie. Afterward we went to Howard Johnson's. I'm pretty excited about the *Citizen-Journal* job.

JULY 3

WE had the day off at the Bron-Shoe Company, because the Fourth of July is tomorrow and it falls on a Saturday, and everyone gets the day before as a vacation day. So I rode the bus downtown to the *Citizen-Journal* to fill out my paperwork.

Bill Moore told me to talk with Jean Allison, who is the editor's secretary. She was really nice to me. She said that when I'd been in yesterday, she had noticed that I had worn the backs of my loafers down and that my heels were sticking out of the backs of my shoes. She said that was bad for my feet. I hadn't even realized that she had known I was there.

Miss Allison said that even though they had told me I had to work from two till eleven, they'd checked the rules and I can't work that late. There's some Ohio law or something that says if you're under eighteen you can work only until nine o'clock. So now my hours are noon to nine—which is a lot better. Now I can go out with my friends after work.

There's a vacant one-room apartment next to Allen's parents' apartment in the Park Towers. His parents rent the little apartment and use it as a storeroom.

Tonight we all decided to sleep there. Allen had another date with Marcia Smilack, and he took her home around midnight. Chuck and Dan and Jack and I stayed in the little apartment; there's a stove in there, and we made ourselves some soup at about 1:30 A.M. It really tasted great.

Apparently, we were making a lot of noise, because at two-thirty Allen's father came into the apartment. First he asked us what we were doing there. Then he looked around and said, "Where's Allen?"

We said that Allen had taken his date home. His father said, "You boys aren't supposed to be in this apartment. As soon as Allen gets back, you tell him that I want to talk to him."

We didn't know what to do. It kept getting later, and at three-thirty Allen's dad came in again. Now he was really steaming. "Where is *Allen*?" he said, and we said we hadn't heard from him.

It was too late for us to go back to our own homes, but we were dreading the next time Allen's father came in. Finally, at about four-fifteen, Allen walked in the door. At four-thirty his father came in and totally blew up at us. He said that we were never to go in that apartment again.

But he let us stay there, and we all slept on the floor.

JULY 4

I had two beers at night. My powers must really be building up; they didn't have any effect on me at all.

We all went over to the high school and watched the fireworks. Afterwards Chuck's parents weren't home, so we went to his house and fixed ourselves hard drinks. I had an almost fifty-fifty screwdriver—it put me on my ass. We went to an open house at the Bexley Pool. Everyone knew we had been drinking. Susie Young was there, and I got mad at her because she wouldn't leave the party with me. She said, "I know what you guys have been doing." So we all went to the Toddle House with no girls.

JULY 5

JACK came over at noon and we made little frozen pizzas in the stove. We thought the pilot light went out, and I ran out the front door like the house was going to blow up or something. But Jack fixed it.

We had another Epsilons softball game. We won 18–10. I was real sharp in the field, but only got two hits. I could have done better.

That's the one thing that bothers me about the job at the *Citizen-Journal*. If I have to work weekends, I won't be able to play on the softball team. Dad says that's the choice I have to make. I guess he's right; getting the experience on the newspaper is better than playing for Epsilons. But I sure love to play.

JULY 6

BRON-SHOE was a bitch this morning. I started opening packages at seven-thirty and didn't get a break until just before noon. Then I gulped down my lunch out a paper sack, put on a shirt and tie, and ran to the *Citizen-Journal*.

It was great. I got to talk to all these people—Jack Keller, the managing editor; Al Getchell, the editorial cartoonist; Ben Hayes, the columnist . . . they all treated me nice and welcomed me to the paper.

What I did most of the day was run copy to the pneumatic tubes. What happens is that when a reporter finishes a story, he yells "Copy!" or "Boy!" Then I hurry over to his desk and take the story to the city editor. It goes to the copy desk then—and when the copy desk is done with it, I take it, roll it up into a cylinder, stick it in a container, and then shove the container into the big pneumatic tubes. Air pressure takes it down to the composing room to be set in type.

There's a copygirl there named Doris. I can't figure her out yet—she could be the world's nicest, purest human, or she could be a whore. Probably the former.

I went to Woolworth's and had dinner at the counter by myself. At nine o'clock, after work, I rode the Broad Street bus back to Bexley. There was an open house at Doug Felger's. Al and Chuck and Dan and Jack were already there; they said they had seen Lindy, but she had left. I talked with Susie Young, but she acted quite cold.

I dread getting up for Bron-Shoe tomorrow. A week of working both jobs is going to kill me. Bill Moore looked up from the

city desk on my way out tonight and said, "You'll be one tired
boy by Friday."

JULY 7

I just sleepwalked through Bron-Shoe this morning. It was pouring rain at noon, so I ran to the *Citizen-Journal* through the
downpour. I was soaked when I got there.

I was on the move all day. Al Getchell let me watch him draw
his editorial cartoon for tomorrow's paper. He's a real old guy—
in addition to doing his cartoons, he has to retouch every photo
that goes into the paper. I ran about a dozen of the photos down
to the engraving department for him. He said he appreciated it,
and said that he'd draw a picture of me someday.

I saw Ron Pataky sitting in his office. He's the *Citizen-Journal*'s movie critic—I always read his stuff. I got up the nerve to
knock on his door. I said, "Mr. Pataky, my name is Bob Greene,
and I'm the new copyboy here, and I just wanted to introduce
myself."

He said, "I want to tell you two things, Bob. First—you
have to learn to project your voice. Enunciate! Make sure that
people hear you! And second—don't call me Mr. Pataky. Call
me Ron."

I went on two coffee runs for the staff. You have to go around
to every person in every department—city room, sports, wom-
en's department, photo lab, everything—and ask every person
if they want something to drink or eat. Then you have to leave
the building and go to Paoletti's Restaurant next door, and bring
all the drinks and sandwiches back to the people.

I went to Mills Cafeteria on High Street for dinner. I think I
saw Gail Lucas eating there, too. She's real pretty—she writes
for the women's section. I thought about going up to her, but I
didn't have the nerve.

Mom and Dad picked me up outside the paper at nine o'clock.
I picked up a *Citizen-Journal* blotter from the public service
desk in the lobby. When I got into the car, Dad said, "Hi,
Scoop."

I think this is really going to be fun.

JULY 8

AT Bron-Shoe, Ronnie Rummel and I finally opened everything that was there. For the first time since I started working there, there is no backlog of packages.

At the *Citizen-Journal*, I got to meet the editor, Don Weaver. His secretary, Miss Allison, said that he wanted to read some page proofs, so I went downstairs, got them, and took them to him. He told me he was glad that I was getting the chance to work there.

I had dinner alone at Mills Cafeteria again. Salisbury steak—pretty good. On the way back to the paper, I saw Ben Hayes on Third Street. He stopped and waited for me to cross with the light. He shook my hand and asked how things were going, and then walked back to the paper with me. It made me feel great. He's just about the biggest celebrity in Columbus—everyone reads his column in the morning.

I took the bus home and met up with Allen and Chuck and Dan and Jack. Kenny Stone and some guys threw water balloons at us. We retaliated with eggs.

JULY 9

BRON-SHOE was a snap this morning. With all the packages opened up, there's not much for me to do. But I'm really getting tired, working both jobs. Tomorrow will be the last day at Bron-Shoe.

They ran me like crazy at the *Citizen-Journal*. I had to go out on six coffee runs to Paoletti's, and then I had to go over to United Press International and to the post office. I felt like a real goon—Dick Tracey, the director of promotions, gave me some packages to deliver, and by mistake I knocked over his secretary's stamping machine and water got all over everything. I was just standing there; I didn't know what to say. But she was nice about it.

I got real friendly with Getchell and Pataky. Also with Dick

Garrett, who's a photographer, and George Strode, who's a young sportswriter. Bill Moore was off today, so Bill Keesee and Wink Hess were acting as city editors. It's a funny feeling—a week ago I didn't know any of these people, and now we're part of each others' lives. Not that they think about me—but now they're people who I work with and talk with.

I had dinner at Mills for the third night in a row. I'm going to have to cut that out. When I go through the cafeteria line, everything looks so good that I put it on my tray. It ends up costing me too much—tonight my dinner bill was $2.11.

There was another open house tonight. Just as I got there, I saw Lindy walking out with Chet Crosby. After all this time, it doesn't hurt any less.

JULY 10

I was so tired when I got up this morning. I just had a Coke for breakfast and went down to Bron-Shoe for my last day.

The *Citizen-Journal* was great, as usual. There's this new thing called the topless bathing suit, and the wirephoto machine ran a picture of Mamie Van Doren wearing one of them. She was holding two martini glasses up so that her breasts didn't show in the picture. We were all passing the picture around and looking at it, and then Charlie Stine, one of the copy editors, said, "Look, here's another picture on the machine—and the martini glasses broke!" We all ran over to look, but he was only kidding.

That's the kind of atmosphere that goes on at the paper all day. It's not even like working; everybody seems to be having a good time. When they handed me the picture of Mamie Van Doren, it really made me feel good—like they were including me.

After work I went to Pongi's, where everybody was hanging out. On my tie I had been wearing a tie pin that Lindy had given me last summer. It was one of those laughing-faces/crying-faces pins—the kind of design they use to symbolize drama: comedy and tragedy. When she gave it to me last summer she said, "This is because I'm happy when I'm with you, and I'm said when we're apart.''

At Pongi's I looked down at my tie—and the pin was gone. I looked everywhere for it, with no luck. Lord, can't I even have my memories?

JULY 11

SATURDAY; at last a day off. Allen and Chuck and Jack and I decided to drive to Cleveland and mess around. We took Allen's dad's car; about halfway there the convertible top broke. We had to take the car into a gas station in this little town. We had brought an eight-pack of beer to drink in Cleveland, but we ended up giving all the beer to this young mechanic at the gas station in exchange for him fixing the top.

Cleveland was kind of boring. We just drove around waiting for something to happen, but nothing did.

JULY 12

I had to work at the *Citizen-Journal* even though it's Sunday, so I missed an Epsilons softball game. When I got to work Bill Moore was on the city desk; someone called, and he picked up the phone and said "City desk." Then he said, "Dammit," and hung the phone up.

"What happened?" I said.

"They hung up," he said.

"The cake dialers," I said.

"Huh?" he said.

I tried to explain it to him, but he didn't seem to understand.

It was a quiet day in the city room. Paoletti's is closed on Sundays, so they gave me the keys to a press car and had me go to the Big Bev to get hamburgers and milkshakes for everybody.

Then, when I got back, Bill Moore told me how to do the emergency runs. What you do is, you call the police department and the fire department and they tell you every time an ambulance or a fire truck has gone out during the day. You get the details and write up a list of the stuff, and the paper runs it in real small type.

It was my first printed work in the paper! I know it's simple, but I wrote it, and it got in. It made me feel more like part of the staff.

Things were slow after that, so I went over to the sports department. Kaye Kessler and Tom Pastorius and Clarence Young were sitting around talking. I knew Kessler and Pastorius from their bylines; Clarence Young is a desk man, who just works on putting the sports section together. He's been calling me "Brownie" all week, but today he figured out my name is Greene and started calling me "Greenie."

After work I met up with everybody. Pongi said he'd seen Lindy, and had told her that I had lost the tie pin. According to him, she said, "He still had that? I thought he wasn't even my friend."

JULY 13

DAD made me get a haircut before I went to work. You'd think he'd leave me alone about that during the summer.

I kept paying attention to Bill Moore at work all day. He's my idea of what a journalist should be. He runs the city desk like it's the Army or something. He's always got a cigarette in his mouth, and he gets his phone calls done in the briefest possible amount of time. "City desk. Yeah? Yeah? What time? Okay, we'll have someone there." And then he hangs up. And all day long he's reading the copy from every one of the reporters. It's like he never stops doing things.

The Republican National Convention starts tonight. Late in the afternoon the UPI wire ran an advance copy of the entire text of the keynote address. The wire editor let me keep it as a souvenir.

That's one of the things I like about newspapers—I was reading the keynote address hours before the rest of the nation would be seeing and hearing it on TV. It's a neat feeling.

JULY 14

THAT copygirl Doris—boy, I'd like to smack her. She talks in this sweet voice all the time, but today she said, "Bob, coffee runs and pastepots are handed down from the senior copykid to the junior." Meaning that I have to do all of the coffee runs and all of the pastepots.

The coffee runs I don't mind so much—it's a pain going out of the building and lugging all those sandwiches and cups of coffee back, but it gives me a chance to talk to everyone on the staff. When you go around to get orders people get mad if you skip them, so you have to make sure you talk to 100 percent of the people. It's a good way to get to know them.

But the pastepots—the pastepots are awful. There is a paste-pot on every reporter's and editor's desk. What they are are white enamel coffee mugs, filled with gooey white paste so that the reporters can paste the pages of their stories together. Every day I have to take them all into the men's room, wash them out, then fill them up again with new paste. Then I have to clean the brushes that are stuck into every pastepot. By the time I'm done there's paste all up and down my arms, and I smell like the stuff.

Ron Pataky gets publicity photographs for all of the movies that come to town; today he gave me a stack of them to take home to Debby. I thought that was a nice thing for him to do.

After work I got together with ABCDJ. It feels funny, not meeting up with them until after nine o'clock every night. They're already talking about stuff that happened earlier in the evening, stuff that I wasn't a part of. But I think the newspaper job is worth it.

When I met them tonight they had a case of beer. I drank a whole six-pack. I was drunk as hell, but I can really hold it now.

JULY 15

Took the Main Street bus down to work and got my first *Citizen-Journal* paycheck. It was $58.50, after taxes were taken out. The first thing that happened was that Bill Moore called me over to the city desk, gave me thirty-five cents, and told me to go out and get him a pack of Larks.

I didn't know what to say to him; I've never bought a pack of cigarettes in my life, and I didn't know if I had to have an ID or what. But I walked over to the Sheraton-Columbus, went into their cigar shop, and said, "One pack of Larks." The woman behind the counter hardly even looked at me; she just took the money from me and gave me the cigarettes.

When I got back to the office with the cigarettes, a big story was breaking. Dr. Sam Sheppard, who has been in the Ohio Penitentiary for murdering his wife in Cleveland, was set free. The newsroom went crazy. Every reporter was assigned to some part of the story. There was a rumor that Sheppard was already having a drink at Benny Klein's Restaurant near Broad and High, so Bill Moore sent me over there to look for him. I wouldn't know Sam Sheppard if I walked right into him, but there was nobody in the restaurant anyway.

After I had returned to the office Bill Moore had me go back into the newspaper's library and start going through old clippings and photographs of Sheppard, so that the reporters could work from them. It was a great day—by the time the first edition was ready to come out I felt that I had really played a part in putting it together.

When I got home tonight the phone rang. I answered it and some guy said, "Wanna fight?" Then he hung up. I have no idea who it was.

JULY 16

IT's my day off, and the PGA Golf Tournament is being held at
Columbus Country Club, so Allen and Dan and I went to watch
it. It was really cool—we followed Arnold Palmer around for
most of the time. Then the crowd started to switch to a young
golfer named Bobby Nichols who was having a great round. We
watched him finish—he got a 64 to lead the tournament.

The sports staff and photographers from the *Citizen-Journal*
were all out there covering it. When Allen and Dan and I were
walking near the clubhouse, I ran into Tom Pastorius and George
Strode and Dick Garrett from the paper. They were all wearing
press tags around their necks.

I started talking real familiarly with them—like we were the
oldest friends in the world. I guess I was trying to impress Allen
and Dan. Pastorius and Strode and Garrett kind of smiled, but
they treated me real nice. I hope I didn't make an ass out of
myself, and that they still like me.

I got home from the PGA about six-thirty. Pongi and Dennis
MacNeil came over on their motorbikes—Pongi had his Honda
and Dennis had his Vespa. Dennis rode me around on the back
of his. It was great—I would love to have one of those.

Dad came out the front door and asked Pongi and Dennis if
he could ride their bikes. They said yes. So he got on Pongi's
Honda first and rode it down Bryden Road and back; then he
got on Dennis' Vespa and rode it for a while. He said that he
loved it.

It was weird, seeing Dad on the motorcycles. Usually I think
that if something's fun for me, then it wouldn't be fun for him.
But he seemed to have as good a time on them as I did. When
Pongi and Dennis left, he seemed really sad to see them go.

JULY 17

USUAL good day at work. Doris the copygirl was hard to take as always, but the sports guys couldn't have been nicer. Mostly I did stuff around the city room, with one run over to UPI.

When I got off work I went straight to the Bexley Pool, where there was an open house. I don't know what it was—there was a real strange atmosphere in the air. About twenty guys wanted to start fights with us—including Van Snider, one of last year's seniors, who was always one of the nicest guys in the school. I was glad to get out of there and get home.

JULY 18

WENT to the PGA again, because it's Saturday and everybody gets Saturday off because the *Citizen-Journal* doesn't print a Sunday paper.

Dan and I walked around the course, and he said that no matter what, he was going to get one of the golfers' gloves as a souvenir. When we were kids we used to run onto the football field after a Bexley game and ask the players for their chin straps; at Ohio State games we'd do it too, but those guys were more reluctant to give us the chin straps.

So we hung around the eighteenth green all day. Every time some golfers would come off the course, Dan would say, "Can I have your glove?" But they all said no.

Finally, Mike Souchak made his final putt of the day and walked toward the clubhouse. He had stuffed his golf gloves into the waistband of his pants. Dan got off to a running start, ran in front of Souchak, grabbed one of the gloves, and took off into the crowd. Souchak looked startled for about half a second; he took a step forward like he was going to run after Dan, but then he just walked into the clubhouse.

I caught up with Dan in the parking lot. He was laughing. "How's that for balls?" he said. We rode back to Bexley.

* * *

Pongi let me ride his cycle tonight. It was really fun, but I have a little trouble doing it right.

Later on some younger guys from Bexley tried to start something with us. Joe Thiebert, Steve Stout, Mike Peters, and Dallas Sturgill were hanging around outside Pongi's house talking real hard to us. Chuck and Pongi really backed them down. Especially Pongi. He walked up to Thiebert and said, "Let's go. Right now." Thiebert said to him, "Look, I don't have any fight with you. I don't have anything against you." So Pongi spit right in his face and said, "Now you do." They all just turned around and left. It was pretty cool.

JULY 19

I saw another side of Doris the copygirl at work today. We were supposed to go down to the composing room to pick up some galley proofs. I've always gone down there on my own before, but today Doris walked with me.

As soon as we got into the room, all of the printers and linotype operators started screaming and howling. At first I didn't understand what was going on, but then I figured it out: They were doing it to Doris.

We were only down there for about three minutes, but it never stopped. Guys were yelling "Woof-woof-woof"; they were shrieking and whistling; they were barking like dogs.

Doris is a pretty attractive girl, but it's not like she's Marilyn Monroe or anything. When we were on our way back to the city room, I asked her what that had been all about.

"They do it to any woman who walks into the composing room," she said. "It's just how they act around women. I just stare straight ahead and don't say anything. Some women from the city room refuse to go down there because of it. I was warned about it when I started here, and it never lets up."

I had to go get food for the staff at the Big Bev again. While I was waiting for the order to get filled, I looked at the jukebox. "I Can't Stay Mad at You," the Skeeter Davis song, was on it. That used to be one of Lindy and my songs; once she took the

"I Can't Stay Mad at You" tag off one of the record bins at
Lazarus and gave it to me.

It seems like I never even see her around anymore.

JULY 20

I did the cop and fire emergency runs at work again today;
they're letting me do them more and more often. Even though
you just take down the bare information that the cops and fire-
men tell you, and it just runs in agate type, I get a kick out of
seeing something I wrote end up in the newspaper. What would
really be great would be to have a story in the paper—something
I really wrote, with a headline and everything.

Allen and Jack and Jack's cousin came down at dinnertime,
and we went to Mills Cafeteria. Then we went over to Lazarus
and I bought the Peter, Paul, and Mary *In the Wind* album and
the Bruce and Terry "Summer Means Fun" single.

There was an open house later tonight, and I went to it when
I got done with work. I danced some with Susie Young. Lindy
was there; she was walking around with a guy named Jerry
Carter. She said, "You aren't very friendly to me." I didn't
know how to answer, so I just said, "You're real cute," real
sarcastically.

JULY 21

TODAY at work Brian MacNamara, the women's page editor, was
explaining some stuff to me that he wanted me to do. I had never
done it before, and in the middle of his explanation he said,
"Damn, I wish Doris was here today." Even though it wasn't a
personal cut at me—he just meant that Doris already knew the
procedure—I got pissed.

I had to do all the coffee runs at Paoletti's, as usual. I was
getting tired of just getting stuff for everybody else, so I decided
to buy myself some food, too. On the two o'clock run I got

myself a bacon-and-egg combination sandwich. On the five o'clock run I got myself a cheeseburger deluxe. Then at dinner-time Dennis MacNeil came by, and we went to Mills Cafeteria. I was pretty stuffed.

The bus I take home every night picks me up on Broad Street just east of High. There aren't many riders on the bus at nine o'clock, but most nights there's this really pretty girl who gets off at Ohio Avenue, and then walks north up the street. I know she has to know who I am; sometimes we're the only passengers on the bus. But we never talk. I wonder how you get to meet a girl like that? Do you just introduce yourself? Do you just start talking? Or do you just keep watching her get off the bus at Ohio Avenue every night and never say a word?

Another open house tonight. Lindy was there; she came up and said something about Wendy Clowson being in love with someone. I said, "She's another one who doesn't know the meaning of the word 'love.'" Lindy got real mad, and I apologized. The thing is, it's easier for me to say things like that to her than to try to tell her how I really feel.

JULY 22

IT was just as if it had been planned. I kept telling myself that if I cooled it, a girl would come along. Tonight she did.

Work went okay, and afterwards I took the bus back to Bexley, where there was an open house at Steve Gutter's house. As I walked in, this really pretty girl looked at me. I had never seen her before. I thought about walking back through the crowd and looking for her, but then I saw Susie Young and stood by Susie.

Harvey Handler called me over. He said that Susie Young had been going around telling everybody that I loved her. So I thought, forget her. I walked around looking for the other girl.

I saw her standing on the edge of the driveway. She said, "Hi." Then she looked at me like she wanted to dance.

But I said to her, "Let's get out of here." We did. She just clung to me as we walked down the driveway to the sidewalk.

As we walked down the street we kissed about seven times. Once she let me put my hand over her blouse.

Her name is Tina Flaker and she goes to Bishop Hartley High School. We went back to the open house, and she gave me her phone number. As we were standing around, she purposely bumped her front against me once. The open house was ending, and as my friends and I were leaving, she said, "Bye, honey."

I'm going to call her right away. This could be the answer to my prayers.

JULY 23

I think I understand all girls, and now this.

Today was my day off, so I got up and went out with Dan. We walked all around Bexley—the Excelsior Club and the Bexley Pool. I went to a pay phone and called Tina. She said she couldn't talk at home, but I should call her later where she works. She gave me the number.

At the Bexley Pool Lindy was there. She looked okay, but I kept thinking about calling Tina back. Early in the evening we had an Epsilons meeting, which went fine. Harry Post, our adult adviser, might have called me a show-off.

After the meeting was over I went to another pay phone and called Tina. She said that she was too tired to go out tonight, but didn't have to work day after tomorrow—Saturday—and that if I still wanted to go, she could go out then.

I said, "Do you want to go?"

She said, "I don't care."

That made me mad. She said I could come over to her house tonight and talk, and I said I'd think about it. I rode around with Allen and Jack, but they were acting shitty and they pissed me off.

So I picked up Dan and we went over to Tina's house. Her parents were home; Tina and Dan and I went down to their basement.

I said, "Saturday?"

She said, "Maybe."

I said, "Don't do me no favors."

She said, "I won't."

That really made me feel down, but on the way up the stairs from her basement she kissed me so good.

I have no idea what is going on here.

JULY 24

I'M nervous.

I missed my bus downtown, so I had to ask Mom to ride with me in her car to work. I drove down there, and then she drove the car back home. Hectic day—I had to type up *thirty-five* fire runs That really wears me out.

Jack picked me up after work. We planned tomorrow night. Mom and Dad and Debby and Timmy are going to Hideaway Hills in the morning, so I'll have the house at night.

Jack has a date with a girl named Cindy McCarthy. She's a car hop at the Ranch Drive-In; she flirted with him a couple of times when he was ordering there, and this week he asked her out and she said yes.

The way we figure it, we'll bring the girls to my house. If we can get the girls to go upstairs, I'll use my room, and I told Jack that he can use Debby's room.

We planned all the details so carefully. But I know it won't work out. I'm so used to getting screwed over that it will probably happen again. Tina either won't go out with me or she won't come to my house or something unexpected will come up or *something*.

I cruised with Jack all evening talking about it. He dropped me off at eleven. I just keep thinking of walking into my room with Tina. It's just too good to be true.

JULY 25

AMAZING.

I got up early. My parents left for Hideaway with Debby and Timmy; they took the Thunderbird and left me the station wagon.

I put off calling Tina. Dan and Chuck and I went to the

Excelsior Club and caught some rays. Then I picked Jack up and we went to my house and fixed it up.

I called Tina's. Her grandmother answered. She said to call Tina at work. She said, "Have a good time tonight."

That was a good sign. I called Tina at work, and she said tonight was okay. She said, "We have to tell my parents that we're going somewhere, but we don't really have to go there." I was ecstatic.

I borrowed five dollars from Chuck, and then Jack and I went to the Eastmoor for dinner. He had fried chicken and I had a cheeseburger. He doesn't have a car tonight, so the plan was for him to use my Mom's station wagon to pick up Cindy at the Ranch, then to come back to the house, then for me to take the car and pick up Tina.

He got in the car and backed out of the driveway. When he came back with Cindy, I was pretty surprised at what she was like. She's got a good body, but she's really pretty much a hillbilly. She was wearing all these plastic bracelets on her wrists.

I sat around the living room with Jack and her for a few minutes, and then I said I had to go to pick up Tina. When I got to her house, her parents wouldn't quit bitching at me. They kept asking me where we were going, and how long we would be out, and saying what time Tina had to be home. They said that if I planned on taking Tina to a movie, it couldn't be a drive-in movie. They were doing this right in front of Tina. I felt embarrassed for her. Finally I just told her parents that we were going to play Putt-Putt.

As soon as we got into the car I asked her if it would be okay to go to my house. She said that would be fine with her. I drove there, and we walked in and Jack and Cindy were still in the living room.

Our plan was to offer to show the girls around the house, and, as soon as we got them upstairs to go to the separate bedrooms. It worked like a charm. Jack said, "Would you like to see the house?" and they both said yes right away.

The four of us walked up the stairs. I took Tina right into my bedroom, and Jack headed down the hallway to Debby's room. Tina and I lay on the bed in the darkness and started making out. She was so completely willing. I put my hand under her blouse and tried to unsnap her bra. I couldn't do it with one hand, so I put the other hand under there, too. I still couldn't unhook it. So she helped me out; she reached under the back of her blouse and unsnapped the bra.

She felt so great. She let me take her blouse off. This was the first time in my life I had ever been with a girl who had her shirt off. It was just so wonderful. We weren't saying much to each other. We just kept making out.

Finally she said that she had to get home soon, or her parents would start getting suspicious. We heard Jack and Cindy downstairs in the kitchen. Instead of putting her blouse back on, Tina asked me if she could wear my shirt. I said sure.

So we went down to the kitchen. All four of us were there. No one discussed what we had been doing—but after all, there Tina was, wearing my shirt.

In a few minutes she went back upstairs and put her own blouse back on. We all got into the car; I drove, and dropped Cindy off first and then Tina. Her parents were waiting up in the living room. It's obvious they don't like me.

On the way back to my house, Jack said he had done the same thing—Cindy had let him take her blouse off. Jack slept over. In the middle of the night he got up and threw up into my waste-basket. He said he thought it was the chicken from the East-moor.

JULY 26

JACK and I woke up at ten. We cleaned up the house, made the beds, etc.

I took Mom's car to work. It was really hard—lots of typing up fire runs, plus I had to go to the Big Bev twice to get food for everybody.

Around dinnertime I went back to the women's department; there's nobody there on Sundays. I phoned Tina; called her "honey." It was hard to judge her reaction.

When I got home from work, Mom and Dad and Debby and Timmy had gotten back from Hideaway Hills. Debby came into my room and closed the door. She said, ''Were you in my room while I was gone?''

''I don't know,'' I said. ''I might have played some records on your record player or something.''

''You wouldn't have been in my bed?'' she said.

''No,'' I said. ''Why do you ask?''

She stuck out her hand. She was holding an orange plastic bracelet. ''Because this was in my bed,'' she said.

Damn. It was one of the bracelets that Cindy, Jack's date, had been wearing. We thought we had been so thorough in cleaning up the house.

I made Debby promise not to say anything to Mom and Dad. She just shook her head like I was a jerk.

I called Lindy tonight. I just wanted to talk to her. Isn't that something? Here's Tina coming into my life, and things are looking great—and I still need to make contact with Lindy. I wonder if it will ever stop?

JULY 27

AFTER work tonight I took the Broad Street bus to Bexley; Jack and Chuck were waiting at the bus stop to pick me up. We went to an open house in Eastmoor. Lindy was there. She came over and pointed up at the sky and said, ''Remember? Our star.''

As if I could forget. Also, WCOL is playing Allan Sherman's new record, ''Hello Mudduh, Hello Fadduh 1964.'' It makes me think of last summer, when the original record was out and I was with Lindy.

Tomorrow I have to go to Parker Studios up by the Ohio State campus to have my senior picture taken. I'm worried that it won't turn out good—my nose will screw me or something. Your senior picture is the most important picture of you that's taken in high school—it's the one that runs in the *Bexleo* yearbook, and it's the one that you trade with all your friends. Dad tried to make me get another haircut before going to have the picture taken, but I refused.

JULY 28

I was up before eight. I took the bus to Broad and High, and then transferred to the High Street bus that would take me to Parker Studios.

As soon as I walked in, Mr. Parker said, "What have you been doing, washing boats?" I didn't know what he was talking about. He pointed to the collar of my white dress shirt; it was all frayed.

"Never mind," he said. "We can retouch it."

He took me into the studio and sat me down on a stool and had me look off in all these different directions while he snapped the pictures. I felt completely awkward. I know I'm going to have to have retakes. I mean, I could feel the gooniness all over my face.

I was late getting to the *Citizen-Journal*, because the bus from the bus stop near Parker Studios was late getting there. Hard day at work. On the bus home at night I saw the Ohio Avenue girl again, but as usual we didn't speak.

Chuck and Allen picked me up at the bus stop in Bexley. They say they're going to take a trip up to Cedar Point, on Lake Erie. That really makes me jealous, but there's no way that I can go because of work. Chuck and I got into sort of an argument; at one point he called me a "farce." I sense that we're sort of drifting apart. He used to be such a great friend.

What a rotten day. The pictures at Parker's, the fight with Chuck . . . I felt real bad when I got home.

JULY 29

AT work today Don Weaver, the editor, was real nice to me—called me "Bob" twice. I sure would like to get a real story in print.

Pongi and Jack both got their proofs for their senior pictures in the mail. They both look good, especially Jack. If only mine turned out to look that good.

* * *

When I got off the Broad Street bus at the Bexley bus stop tonight, Chuck and Jack and Allen were waiting to pick me up again. That made me feel good. We cruised around for a while. Chuck was going out of his way to be a good guy.

Those guys leave for Cedar Point tomorrow morning at ten. I'd better find some action while they're gone; it's going to be a long week.

As they dropped me off at home, Chuck put his hand on my shoulder and said, ''See you, Greenie.'' I think things are okay with us now.

JULY 30

WOKE up early this morning after a million dreams. Really crazy ones.

At work I had a long talk with Bob Moeckel. He's a good guy—he's an editorial clerk, which is one step up from copyboy, and his job is to take the ticker tapes of the stock market reports and paste them on the page to be sent down to the printer. He uses this metal machine to do it—the ticker tape feeds into the machine, and he snips each stock's numbers off at the proper place on the page. It's really hard work—all the stocks come in at once as soon as the stock market closes in New York, and if he's late or he gets behind, he's in trouble.

I'd say he's in his early-to-mid twenties. It wasn't a very fast-paced day at work, so he and I spent a lot of time just shooting the shit.

Pongi and Dennis MacNeil picked me up after work. All I could think about is how the boys are doing up at Cedar Point—whether they're meeting any girls.

I called Tina at night. She said that maybe we can get together again Saturday night.

JULY 31

I woke up late because it's my day off. Mom bitched at me to get my hair cut. Usually it's Dad; now she's doing it. I wish they'd leave me alone.

I went out into our backyard and lay down on the grass to catch some rays.

I had my transistor radio next to me, and this great new song came on WCOL. It's called "The House of the Rising Sun," by a group called the Animals. Now there is a winner.

My proofs for my senior pictures didn't come in the mail again today. I'm getting so nervous about that.

Mike Melton got a new motorcycle, and he came by the house and gave me a ride on it. It was good being with him again; it seems like so long ago that we were doubles partners and getting our letters sophomore year. We rode his cycle all around Bexley.

Tomorrow night is the night I was supposed to see Tina, but I called her today and she said that I could come to the house where she was baby-sitting tonight. It was over in Berwick—I borrowed Mom's station wagon and went there.

It was weird—there we were in this nice house, with portraits of all the children on the wall, and the children were upstairs asleep. And Tina and I sat on the couch in the living room and made out. She let me put my hand under her blouse and undo her bra again. But I want to do more than that. Boy, my values have changed.

After leaving the place where Tina was baby-sitting I drove over to Pongi's, where a lot of guys were gathered. I sat on the curb and smoked a Tiparillo.

August 1

My proofs came. I don't know what to think. They're not great, but they're not terrible. I won't have to have them reshot. Now I just have to pick out which one to use in the yearbook.

I mowed the lawn with no shirt on today. Combined with yesterday's lying out in the sun, I'm getting pretty tan. I had the earplug from my transistor radio in the whole time. It makes the mowing go faster.

August 2

It was so hot last night, and Mom and Dad and Debby and Timmy were at Hideaway Hills again, so I slept in Mom and Dad's room with the air conditioner on.

Sundays at work are usually low-key, so I had a pretty good day. For once when I went to the Big Bev, they didn't screw our order up and I didn't have to go back again.

When I got home after work, the family was back from Hideaway. Mom and Dad had already looked at my senior picture proofs, and said they were disappointed. They said my hair was too long. I don't know what to do about it—I think I'll ask Jack. He usually has the right answer.

Damn. It's pouring rain, and I'm in bed, and I just remembered that when I drove the press car back from the Big Bev

to the outdoor parking lot at the paper, I forgot to roll the
windows up.

AUGUST 3

WHEN I got to work this morning I called Jack at his house.
He got back from Cedar Point last night, because he has to
be at work. Allen and Chuck and Dan are still up there, and
won't be coming home until the middle of the week. Jack
says they're having a great time—meeting a lot of girls and
everything.

Work was busy at first, but then it got slow. Bob Moeckel
and I walked over to Al Getchell's desk, where he draws his
cartoons. We joked around for a long time. It was funny, but
I get the feeling that Getchell is a pretty bitter old guy. He's
been the cartoonist at the paper forever, and he always seems
down about whatever is going on there.

I decided to take home some souvenirs from work. I got a
copy of the *Scripps-Howard News*, a proof of tomorrow's page
1, a *Hard Day's Night* press kit that Ron Pataky gave me,
and a promotional brochure from King Features. Jack picked
me up after work; I showed him my senior picture proofs,
and he said that there's one smiling one that looks fine, and
that I should order it.

During the day I had called Tina. She had been very luke-
warm on the phone. But Jack and I went to an open house at
Anita Paul's, and Tina was there. She was apologizing for
being in a bad mood earlier. At the end of the open house
she took my hand.

AUGUST 4

I took the Main Street bus to work, and it was late. Bill
Moore was not too pleased when I walked in past my usual
starting time. In a way I felt bad about it, but in a way I felt

good—it means he thinks that it's important that I'm there to do my work.

I finally got up the nerve to ask Ron Pataky if I could write fillers for his entertainment page. He said yes! He didn't give me any idea of when it would be, but he was a good guy about it—patted me on the back, etc.

I was at Mills Cafeteria for dinner, and a young reporter named Jim Sykes was there, too. He invited me to join him at his table. We had a real nice discussion about journalism. He gave me a lot of pointers.

After work there was an open house at the high school. Lindy was there, and said she had met Ron Pataky at some luncheon that Wendy Clowson's father gave. Pongi got a new motorcycle, and said he'd give me a ride home from the open house on it. We rode down Fair Avenue, and Pongi took the right turn onto Roosevelt . . . and he couldn't control the cycle. We went right into the opposite lane of traffic. Luckily there aren't many cars on the streets of Bexley at that time of night, so nothing happened. But for a moment we were pretty scared.

AUGUST 5

WHAT a nutty day. We got our paychecks, and Bill Moore endorsed his and asked me to cash it for him at the bank. When I got to the bank and handed the cashier Bill's check, they launched a federal investigation. I guess they thought that I stole it or something

Then when I got back to the paper, Ron Pataky really pissed me off. He wrote a whole lot of fillers for his page, and didn't ask me to do any of them. I just have to get a story of my own into the paper.

Ed Colston, one of the reporters who is also an artist, is working secretly on a color portrait of Al Getchell. Getchell's twenty-fifth anniversary at the paper is coming up in a few days, and they want to surprise him with it. Ed let me look at the portrait, but made me swear not to mention it to Getchell.

I had dinner at Paoletti's, and as I was walking back to

the paper a beggar on Third Street stopped me and said, "Could you spare a quarter?" It really made me feel funny. I've never been approached by a beggar before—I've never even seen one. So I reached into my pocket and gave him a quarter, and I found myself thinking about it until I got off work.

There was an open house. I saw Dave Frasch, who I haven't really seen all summer, and we had a long, funny talk. He's in the middle of summer football practice now. I had forgotten how much I like him.

Lindy was there, and we talked a little. I started walking home, and Mike Melton came by on his motorcycle and gave me a ride the rest of the way. After I got home Tina called. Then after we had finished talking, I dialed for cake at Lindy's, and she called back and we talked. I loved her—but *no daze*! For the first time in a long time it seemed that I could still care about her, but that I could survive without her.

I went to bed, and just as I was falling asleep I heard someone calling my name from down in the driveway beneath my window. I looked out—and it was Tina! She said she was running away from home!

I didn't want to wake Mom and Dad, so I told Tina to be quiet and that I would be right down. She was in a car with the lady she baby-sits for—she really wasn't running away from home, she was just thinking about it, and she asked the lady she baby-sits for to drive her to my house so we could talk. We did, for a while. Then she said that she was going home after all.

AUGUST 6

ALL summer long Nana has been saying that she wants to take Mom and Debby and Timmy and me to the New York World's Fair at the end of August, as a treat.

But today was my day off, and Allen and Chuck and Dan buzzed in from Cedar Point around noon. Allen met a girl up there who he's started to date, and he promised her he would come back before the end of the summer. He told me that if Jack and I want to come along, that will be fine.

I don't know how Mom and Dad will handle that. All of us went over to the Excelsior Club and played basketball with our shirts off, then went swimming and lay in the sun. It's good to have those guys back.

We had lunch at the Toddle House, and then we went to Chuck's. His senior picture proofs were there. He's having the same trouble with his dad that I had with mine—as soon as his dad saw the proofs, he said, "If I'd wanted a picture of a Beatle, I would have ordered a picture of a Beatle."

At dinner I approached Dad about Cedar Point. He said he'd think about it, which surprised me—I thought he'd give it an automatic no.

Then, right after dinner, Lindy walked up to our front door. That almost never happens. She said that she heard I got my senior picture proofs back, and she wanted to see them. I showed them to her, and she picked the same one that Jack did—a smiling one.

Cruised with the boys at night. Smoked two Tiparillos.

AUGUST 7

Boy, the born loser strikes again. At work today, at four o'clock, there was a surprise party for Al Getchell. Ed Colston presented him with the portrait, which we had all signed.

Lloyd Flowers, one of the photographers, took about twelve pictures of the staff gathering around Getchell and admiring the portrait of him. I was in every shot but two. I knew that they were going to use one of the pictures in the paper tomorrow, as sort of a tribute to Getchell.

So Jack Keller, the managing editor, makes the selection of the picture—and damned if it's not one of the two I wasn't in. That would have meant so much to me—to be shown in the paper as a part of the staff. But when the paper comes out tomorrow morning, I won't be in the picture.

* * *

A good surprise—Dad says I can go to Cedar Point instead of the World's Fair.

"Nana and your mother would have liked you to go to New York with them," he said. "But you've worked hard all summer, and if going to Cedar Point is really what you want to do with your remaining time before school starts, it's all right with me."

I can hardly believe it. I think it must have something to do with Dad remembering what he was like when he was my age.

AUGUST 8

SATURDAY, my day off. When I woke up Dad said, "I would appreciate it very much if you would go over and get a haircut. A short haircut."

It wasn't very hard to read between the lines. He was saying that because he had agreed to let me go to Cedar Point, I had to do this. So I went to Ralph and Jim's Barber Shop and got a crew cut. I look terrible. I'm so mad at Dad, but there's nothing I can do.

Dennis MacNeil came by and rode me around Bexley on the back of his Vespa for a long time. Then he let me ride it myself! I caught on pretty quick. It's the freest feeling—just zipping down the street on the cycle, controlling the speed and using the hand brakes.

Timmy asked me if he could go out to dinner with me tonight. It must be tough being ten. Jack and I took him to Howard Johnson's. As we were paying our bill I bought another pack of Tiparillos. We went back to my house, and I smoked one as Jack and I threw a football around on the front yard.

AUGUST 9

WHEN I got to work today I gave my two weeks' notice. I had mixed emotions. I'm really looking forward to going to Cedar Point, but I have loved working at the paper.

While I was typing up the fire emergency runs, the dispatcher gave me one about a man who had been taken to the hospital because a golf ball had exploded in his face. I took down the other fire runs, but when I was done I thought that maybe this golf ball thing was interesting enough to do a little story on.

I didn't want to tell the city desk about it; if they liked it, they would just assign it to a reporter. So I took the man's name and address from the fire runs, and I called his house. I told his wife that I was from the *Citizen-Journal*, and that we were interested in what had happened today.

She said that her husband had bought one of those liquid-center golf balls, and that he had wondered what it looked like inside. So he went down to his basement workshop, got out a saw, and started sawing the golf ball in half.

When he got to the liquid center, the liquid spurted out right into his eye. It really hurt him, so his wife called the fire department ambulance, and that's how I ended up finding out about it.

I wrote the story up—just a couple of paragraphs. Then I took it over to Bill Keesee, who was working the city desk in place of Bill Moore.

I said, "I found this story in the fire runs, and I thought it was pretty good. I wrote it up. I wondered if maybe you could use it in the paper."

Keesee read my copy and smiled. He said, "This is good." He made a few slight changes, and sent it over to the copy desk.

I immediately started hanging around in back of the copy desk, just to see what the copy editors would do with it, and what headline they would put on it. Charlie Stine was the copy editor who got the story, and the headline he wrote was "Golf Ball Fights Back."

A couple of hours later I went down to the composing

room and saw it on the galley proofs. It was such a thrill to see a real story I wrote in print—even a tiny one.

I'm nervous that it won't get in the paper. I told my friends about it, and that's always a bad idea—it can jinx things. Boy, I hope they print it.

AUGUST 10

I woke up at six o'clock this morning, went down the stairs, unlocked and opened the front door, and picked up the *Citizen-Journal* from the front stoop.

I rolled the rubber band off the paper and unfolded it. I went through it once in a hurry, and didn't see my story. I was so disappointed.

Then I went through it again—and the story was there. Right down at the bottom of the obit page: "Golf Ball Fights Back." I felt so proud—when Mom and Dad woke up I showed it to them.

And then, when I got to work, Ron Pataky called me into his office and said, "I have your first assignment for you." He handed me a press release for the Cincinnati Jazz Festival. "Write this up," he said.

I wrote twenty-six lines of copy, and Ron read it and said he would put it in the paper exactly as is. That made me feel great.

Later on I was having dinner at Paoletti's. There's this palsied old man who's always sitting around in there, just to kill time. No one ever really speaks to him. But tonight Ron Pataky was sitting and talking to the man. I never had so much respect and admiration for him.

Jack called me while I was doing the emergency runs and asked if I would put his name in. I thought about it, and decided what the hell.

I wrote, "2:17 P.M., 228 S. Ardmore Road, Bexley, Jack Roth, 17, cut head. Treated and released."

* * *

After dinner Bob Moeckel said he wanted to show me something. He took me on top of the building where the presses are. From there you can see into the windows of the downtown YWCA.

Moeckel said that sometimes he comes up here and he can see the women at the YMCA getting undressed. We stood there and looked for a while, but we didn't see anything.

At one point, Moeckel said, "Remember to remind me to ask you something on your last day of work."

I said, "What do you want to ask?"

He said, "Wait until your last day, and then I'll ask you." I kept bugging him about it and bugging him about it, and finally he said: "All right. A lot of the women at the paper are curious if you've ever been laid."

"They asked you that?" I said.

"Yeah," he said. "They really want to know."

"Why would they care?" I said.

"I think they just think you're interesting, and they want to know," he said.

I just stood there for a minute.

"Well?" Moeckel said.

"Well what?" I said.

"Have you?" he said.

"Aw," I said, "I don't talk about that kind of stuff."

He laughed. "Well, if you change your mind, let me know," he said.

After work tonight I went to Pongi's. Dan fought Rocky Saxbe, a Tweed. I would have liked to fight a Tweed, but Dan and Saxbe's fight lasted only a few punches, and then everyone cleared out.

AUGUST 11

I got up early to look at the paper. My story on the jazz festival was in. It looked real nice. Two stories in two days— not bad.

Yesterday I had ordered *Peter, Paul, and Mary in Concert*

from Lazarus, and this morning before I left for work the Lazarus truck delivered the album to our house. I played it right away. It's great. It really reminds me of when we saw them at Veterans Memorial.

When I got to work, Jack called. He said his aunt had called his house, all concerned, because she had seen the item about him in this morning's emergency runs. She wanted to know about his head injury.

That makes me nervous. Even though I type up the emergency runs every day, I never think in terms of anybody actually reading them. They're set in such small type, and they're not even stories. But Jack said that his aunt had found the item about him early this morning. So I guess there must be a lot of people who read that stuff.

What makes me nervous about it is that if one of the editors of the paper finds out that I had put my friend in the emergency runs as a joke, I'll be in real trouble. When I did it yesterday, there didn't seem to be any harm to it. But now my stomach is churning, just thinking about it.

Dan picked me up at the bus stop in Bexley after work. This great new song came on the car radio—"A Summer Song," by Chad and Jeremy. It just reminds me so much of last summer, and of Lindy. I turned the radio up and didn't say anything until the song was over.

We stopped at Pongi's for a while, and then I went home and got into bed. At 1 A.M. I felt "A Summer Song" coming, so I turned on the radio next to my bed, and within ten minutes WCOL was playing it.

AUGUST 12

AT work today I called the Esquire Theater to find out what times *A Hard Day's Night* was showing. The movie finally made it to Columbus.

So many people were calling the theater at the same time that there was a big jam-up—and over the busy signal you could hear other people talking. It was like a giant party line.

I motioned for Bob Moeckel to pick up another extension in the city room, and we both started talking back and forth to people on the line. We got three girls' phone numbers.

None of the editors said anything today about me putting Jack's name in the emergency runs, so I guess I got past that one okay.

I took the bus home and walked to an open house. Susie Young was there; we started talking about *A Hard Day's Night*, and we decided to leave the open house and go see the movie.

It was unbelievable. The Esquire was packed, and every time the Beatles came onto the screen, the audience would scream. It was just the same as if the Beatles were live on stage. Even though it was only a movie screen, the girls in the audience were shrieking throughout the entire picture. I held Susie's hand the whole time.

We went back to the open house after the movie ended. Dianne Kushner called me over and said, "Haven't you been seeing a girl from Bishop Hartley named Tina Flaker?"

I said that I had; I asked her why she wanted to know.

"Because she was standing by the bushes over at the end of the driveway, making out with some guy," Dianne said. "They left together."

I don't know why that should surprise me, but it made me feel awful. That's just how I met Tina—at an open house— and the first thing we did was to leave the open house and make out. But still, I hated hearing about it. It put a damper on the whole evening.

I walked Susie home. I didn't kiss her goodnight. It's funny how you think of different girls in different ways. Susie's so nice—it's good to hold hands with her during the movie, but I wouldn't think of making a move on her. And then there's Tina.

After I got home I wrote a lead for a review of *A Hard Day's Night*. Tomorrow, if I get up the nerve, I'm going to ask Ron Pataky if he would consider running it. A review of my own, with a by-line—that would be the high point of my career.

August 13

The first thing I did when I got to work was to leave a note about my Beatles review on Ron Pataky's desk. He hadn't arrived yet.

When he did come in, he read my note and called me into his office. He said that he'd like to run a review of *A Hard Day's Night*, but that there were just too many *good* movies coming out, and he only had so much space. He gave me the impression that he didn't think too highly of *A Hard Day's Night*.

I called Tina from work. I bawled her out, and told her that I had heard about her and the guy at the open house. She seemed pretty noncommittal.

Bob Moeckel and I called the Esquire again. The line was still busy with Beatles fans. We had a lot of fun talking to the voices.

The guy who gives me the fire emergency runs over the telephone was really funny today. Usually he'll give me the name of the person the emergency squad picked up, and then say something like "D.O.A." for dead on arrival, or "treated and released." He's real routine about everything.

Today he gave me an address and the name of a man, and then he said "D.F.M."

I hadn't heard that one before. "What's 'D.F.M.' stand for?" I said.

"Dead as a fuckin' mackerel," he said.

We laughed, but afterwards it made me think. Working at the paper, I hear people talk about violence and death every day. It makes up a lot of the stuff that they write about. But before I came to the paper, I had never heard that kind of talk. The "D.F.M." thing is a good example. Here I was laughing with the guy—but the truth of it is, some man had died before the emergency squad got a chance to try to save him. That's not funny.

* * *

There was another open house tonight. Lindy was there and she looked wonderful. The disc jockey played "Please Write," a local Columbus hit that had been one of our songs, and she danced with Tim Greiner. I caught her eye during the song, but apparently it didn't faze her.

AUGUST 14

DAY off. I went over to the high school to interview C.W. Jones for the first fall issue of the *Torch*. Then went to Dan's. I got on the back of his Honda, and we rode around Bexley. We ran into Dennis MacNeil and Mike Melton on their cycles, and all of us rode together for most of the day.

At night Dan and I went over to the Esquire to look at the crowds waiting to get in to see *A Hard Day's Night*. We thought we saw two girls who were giving us the eye. His parents weren't home, so we went to his house and had some beer to get our courage up. We went back to the Esquire—and the same two girls were giving us the eye. Then they went into the theater.

We waited a few minutes and snuck in. But it was too crowded; we couldn't find the girls. Damn it. We went to Pongi's and just hung out.

AUGUST 15

WHAT a confusing day.

It's Saturday, and Mom and Dad and Debby and Timmy are down at Hideaway Hills again. They left before I woke up this morning, and when I went downstairs, I saw that Dad had taken the station wagon. He left the Thunderbird for me. He's never done that before.

I called Tina and asked her if she wanted to come over tonight. She said yes. I figured that this was finally going to be the night—it was finally going to happen.

So I got the house all fixed up. Chuck and I had dinner at HoJo's. Right before I went to pick Tina up, I went back to the house, reached down into my *Sports Illustrated* drawer, and pulled out the pack of Fourex rubbers. I put them under the night table next to my bed, so I could get them as soon as I needed them.

I got into Dad's Thunderbird and started backing it down the driveway. I guess I was thinking so much about what might happen in the next few hours that I wasn't paying attention. I let the side of the car brush against some bushes that are next to the driveway—and the bushes snapped off the Thunderbird's radio aerial.

I got out of the car to see how bad it was. It's pretty bad. The aerial is snapped off clean, right at the base. Dad is absolutely going to kill me.

I went to Tina's and picked her up. We came right back to my house, and sat around the living room for a while. Then I asked her if she wanted to come upstairs, and she said yes.

It was going great. I got her shirt off, and she let me put my hand in her pants—a first for me. I was sure it was going to happen.

After a few minutes I reached under the night table. The Fourexes were in a cardboard box; I opened it and pulled one of the little blue capsules out. You're supposed to snap the capsule open and take out the rubber.

I tried to snap the capsule, and I couldn't do it. Tina was just lying there. I took both my hands and bent the capsule in the middle, as hard as I could. Nothing. So finally I put the capsule in my mouth and bit down real hard.

It snapped open, but the lubricating solution got into my mouth, and it tasted terrible. I pulled the rubber out. Now I was going to have to get it on. Which promised to be no easy task—I have never had a rubber on in my life.

Just as I was getting ready to try, Tina said, "Stop."

She said she didn't think she could do it.

I didn't know what the proper thing to do was. The first thing I did was put the rubber back on the floor. We just lay there in the darkness, and finally Tina said, "If you want everything, go ahead."

I felt so sorry for her. I thought she was saying yes just so I wouldn't drop her. This isn't how I had wanted it to be. So

I just said, "No, it's okay. If you want to get dressed, I'll take you home."

She put her shirt on and I put my shirt on, and we started walking downstairs. Just then the phone rang. It was the boys. They were over at Allen's apartment—his parents were out for the evening—and they were drunk. I told them I couldn't talk to them.

Tina and I got downstairs and were walking through the kitchen to the back door and the driveway when she said, "Okay, I'll do it." She took my hand and pulled me back toward the stairs.

So we went to my room again. We lay down—and then she said something crazy. She said I should call my friends and let her talk to them, and that if they said it was okay, she'd do it.

I had never heard of anything like this. But I went out into the hallway, and pulled the phone into my room. I dialed Allen's apartment.

Allen answered. There was loud music playing, and it was apparent that they were really bombed.

"I have someone who wants to talk to you," I said. I handed the phone to Tina.

I put my ear against the receiver so I could hear what everyone was saying. Tina said to Allen, "Bob wants me to go all the way. Do you think I should?"

Allen, drunk, said, "No! Don't do it! He's only using you!"

I heard laughter in the background. I could hear Allen telling Chuck what Tina had asked. Chuck got on the phone and said, "Do yourself a favor. Get out of there. Greene's a terrible guy. Run away!"

By now everyone at Allen's was laughing. I hung up the phone.

"I guess I should take you home," I said.

She stood there for a minute, and then said, "No, it's okay." We got back on the bed and she started taking her clothes off.

Then she started crying—really sobbing—and saying that she was too scared. I knew that I had to take her home. We were pretty silent during the ride.

As I drove back to my house I wondered if I had chickened

out or not. I suppose I did. But I just felt too sorry for her.
It just wouldn't have been right.

When I got back to my room and turned on the lights,
there was the dried-out rubber on the floor.

Maybe someday.

AUGUST 16

I woke up and took the Thunderbird to Luke's Shell Station
on Main Street.

Luke came out of the building and asked what I needed. I
told him that I snapped the aerial off, and I wanted to know
if it could be fixed.

"Hmmmm," he said. "Your daddy's aerial."

"That's right," I said.

"Your daddy's not going to be happy if he finds out about
this," Luke said. "He really loves that car."

"Look, can you fix it or not?" I said.

"Oh, your daddy isn't going to be happy at all," Luke
said. But he said I could leave it with him. I'm afraid he's
going to screw me on the price because he knows I'll have
to pay him anything he wants to prevent Dad from finding
out.

Rode the Main Street bus downtown to work. I got a carry-
out lunch from the counter at Gray's Drugstore at Broad and
High. Then Bill Moore sent me over to UPI to pick up some
copy that we didn't get on the teleprinter machine.

Chuck and Allen called me to apologize for last night.
They said they hoped they didn't mess me up; they said they
were only doing it for a laugh. I think they were just trying
to find out what finally happened with Tina, but I didn't tell
them.

Later on George Strode from the sports desk came up to
me. He said that while I was over at UPI, Jack had called
with the message that everything was all right with the car.
Luke had welded the aerial back on, and had only charged
me five dollars. Jack paid for it and took the car back to my

house, so that when Mom and Dad and Debby and Timmy get home tonight they won't notice that anything's different.

As I was doing the fire runs I came across an item about some kids who got caught burning the shrubbery at their school. I wrote it up as a three paragraph story. Bill Keesee and Rich Lippincott showed me what I had done wrong, and then moved the story to the copy desk. I hope it gets in.

Only four more days of work before Cedar Point. I'll miss it a lot.

AUGUST 17

MY story about the kids burning the shrubbery was on page 8, inside a one-column box. It looked pretty good.

At three o'clock, Bill Keesee said he had something he wanted me to do. A man had died in a car crash; Bill wanted me to take a press car and drive to the man's house and pick up a picture of him. He said that he had already called the family to tell them that someone would be coming.

I followed the directions he gave me, but I got lost. The house was up on the north side of town. I ended up going on Lane Avenue, Northwest Boulevard, Olentangy River Road, and Riverside Drive before I finally found the house.

I sat in the car feeling very uncomfortable. How are you supposed to act when you knock on the door of a house that has just lost its husband and father? I was trying to make excuses not to do it, but finally I just got out of the car and walked up to the front door.

I rang the bell. The wife answered. Before I could even say, "I'm from the *Citizen-Journal*," she handed me the picture. I thanked her and drove back to the office.

I want to be a newspaperman—that's something I know for sure after this summer. But I don't see how you can ever get used to doing the kind of thing that I just did.

AUGUST 18

I was answering the phones at work, and a girl called to ask why the paper hadn't written anything about *A Hard Day's Night*. I figured I'd try once more with Ron Pataky.

When I went into his office, he seemed to be in a bad mood. I told him about what the girl had said, and he said, "Fuck her."

But then, an hour or so later, Pauline Taynor from the women's page said she wanted to talk to me. She said that she had been named the editor of a new monthly magazine called *Junior Prom* that is going to be sold at all the high schools in the Columbus area starting this fall. She'll keep her job at the *Citizen-Journal*, but she'll run *Junior Prom*, too. She asked me if I would review *A Hard Day's Night* for the first issue. I could feel the grin spreading all over my face. She said she needed it in a few days, but I told her I'd write it during my dinner hour tonight.

And I did. I think it's really good. I was inspired when I wrote it. I didn't write so much about the movie itself as the reaction of the crowd when they saw it.

The guys on the sports desk were getting up a pool of money to bet on the horses out at Scioto Downs at night. They asked me if I wanted to bet; I put two dollars on a horse to win in the third race. With my luck, it'll probably come in second or third.

At home after work I started on my required summer reading for school. I hadn't done any of it yet. I was reading *The Picture of Dorian Gray* and listening to WCOL when this great song, "Wendy," by the Beach Boys came on.

AUGUST 19

My horse finished out of the money at Scioto Downs.

* * *

I had left my *Hard Day's Night* review in an envelope on Pauline Taynor's desk, but today turned out to be her day off, so she hasn't seen it yet.

When I got home after work I saw this ad in *Time* magazine about children with muscular dystrophy. It really affected me; I kept looking at the picture of the little boy in the wheelchair. I got out my typewriter and wrote a story about it—kind of an editorial. In the story I was really able to capture the same emotions I felt when I was looking at the picture.

Reading my story made me start to cry. But that embarrassed me; I didn't want anyone else to see it. So I locked it up in my typewriter case.

Last day at work tomorrow. I have a feeling my passing will go unnoticed.

AUGUST 20

TALKED to Jack and Allen this morning; it's just going to be the three of us at Cedar Point, and we leave tomorrow.

The day at work was pretty uneventful. Pauline Taynor came in and picked up my *Hard Day's Night* story in the morning, but I haven't gotten any reaction yet. A few people asked about my leaving. I had dinner at Paoletti's by myself.

At eight fifty-five I went over and said goodbye to Jack Keller, the managing editor. I looked around the room—I thought I'd be bothering people if I went up to them and said goodbye.

So I started walking out the door, and as I opened it Bill Keesee called to me from the city desk. "You're not going to leave without saying anything, are you?" he said. I went over and shook his hand, and he said, "I hope I'll be printing bigger stories by you one of these days."

I started working my way around the room saying so long to people. They were all great. Ron Pataky said that I should come down and have a cup of coffee with him sometime. Tom Pastorius said that I was always welcome to come in and sit around and talk with the sports staff. Everybody had something nice to say.

It really made me feel terrific. I was so glad that Keesee hadn't let me get out of there without saying goodbye. This summer at the paper has been such a great experience. I'll miss these people.

AUGUST 21

I got up and called Judy Furman, my co-editor on the *Torch*, to make sure she could handle all the things that come up while I'm at Cedar Point. She said not to worry, and to have a good time.

At eleven Allen and Jack picked me up in Allen's blue Ford. We put our suitcases in the trunk and headed for Cedar Point.

Every teen-ager in Columbus knows the route numbers you drive on to get to Cedar Point: 71, 23, 98, and 4. The whole way up there the radio stations kept playing "Where Did Our Love Go" by the Supremes. Every time it came on the radio, we'd stick our hands out the window and bang our fists against the top of the roof when the Supremes sang "Baby, baby."

We stopped on the way for gas, and Allen bought a pack of cigarettes. None of us smoke cigarettes, but we thought it would be a cool thing to do on the trip up to Cedar Point.

Cedar Point is a combination amusement park/beach in the town of Sandusky, Ohio. We checked in at a motel called the Holmes. It's real small—just two rows of about eight units each, across a pebble courtyard-driveway from each other. There's a swimming pool out back.

Our room has one double bed and a cot. We're going to switch off nights over who has to share the bed and who gets the cot. There's two cool college guys from Dayton in the room next to ours; they were real nice when we met them, and said that they'd get us some 3.2 beer anytime we wanted it. And there's a bunch of guys about our age staying across the courtyard from us.

At night we drove over to Cleveland, where the Beach Boys

were appearing at Euclid Beach. It was weird seeing them in person—not at all like I imagine seeing the Beatles must be. They were almost corny. Mike Love kept skittering across the front of the stage like a bug. I found myself thinking that I liked them on records better.

Late at night, when we got back to Sandusky, we went to the Italian Villa for spaghetti. In our room at the Holmes we flipped, and I got the cot.

AUGUST 22

WE got up and ate at the Sandusky HoJo's. Then we attempted to catch a few rays, but it was a gloomy, overcast day.

The college guys in the next room bought two cases of beer for us. We each had a couple at night, and then we went over to Gem Beach.

Gem Beach is about twenty miles away from Cedar Point. There's a pavilion by the lake there where they have dances just about every night. When we got there the place was packed, and a band called Ivan and the Sabres was playing.

Allen and Jack and I mostly stood around. There was this one tall blonde girl about our age who I was sure kept looking at me. I pointed her out to Allen and Jack, and said she was looking at me, but they said, "Bullshitter."

Finally, as the dance was ending, I walked up to her. I think I was still feeling a little high from the beer, because I said to her, "How come you been looking at me?"

It was a perfect opportunity for her to shut me down in front of her friends and in front of Allen and Jack, but instead she said: "Oh. You noticed."

That broke the ice. It turned out that she was with a group of eight high school girls who live in a small town about halfway between Columbus and Cedar Point. They had rented a two-story cottage just down the road from Gem Beach pavilion. They asked us if we wanted to come back to the cottage.

We said sure. When we got there, the band was there, too;

apparently one of the girls had invited Ivan and the Sabres to come. We were all sitting around talking—and then this woman came down the stairs.

"It's about the noise you're making," she said. She was one of the most beautiful women I have ever seen. She was tan and had soft brown hair and was just so pretty. She went back up the stairs.

We asked the girls who she was. They said that her name was Beverly, but that everyone called her Bev. She was twenty-seven years old and married, and she had been hired by the girls' parents to be their chaperone during their trip to Gem Beach.

We kept talking, and after a while Bev came down and sat on the couch. She didn't say much, but what she did say was completely funny and smart. When she said something, everybody listened. I tried not to stare at her. But I had just never seen anyone so beautiful.

At one o'clock a deputy came around and threw all of the boys out. We drove back to Sandusky and got a carry-out pizza. As we were taking it into our room, we heard some noise from across the courtyard, where the other guys our age were staying.

We walked across to see what was up. Their room was a combination living room/bedroom. Two of them were sitting in the living room, and then the other two of them came walking out of the bedroom, with two girls.

It was pretty impressive. With us, it's always like we're trying to put something over on girls when we try to get them to do stuff with us. But these girls walked out of the bedroom with the guys, and it was like the girls were proud to be there. Like it was no big deal—like girls and guys always go into bedrooms together. I guess with us, we're not past the point where it's a big deal.

AUGUST 23

ONE of the best things about driving around the Cedar Point area is listening to Allen's car radio. At home there's just

WCOL to listen to. But up here there are three great stations we can pick up—KYW in Cleveland, CKLW in Detroit (actually we hear that it's across the river in Canada), and WBZ in Boston. WBZ comes in best at night.

The stations play the greatest songs. It seems like there's all this good new stuff coming out now, and the stations play it all the time. The whole *Hard Day's Night* soundtrack album is always playing: "A Hard Day's Night," "Tell Me Why," "I'll Cry Instead," "I'm Happy Just to Dance With You," "I Should Have Known Better," "If I Fell," "And I Love Her," "Can't Buy Me Love." Plus, there's another new Beatles song that's not from the movie—it's called "Things We Said Today," and I like it better than any of the others.

But it's not just Beatles' songs on the radio. There's "Pretty Woman" by Roy Orbison, and "Last Kiss" by J. Frank Wilson, and "Tobacco Road" by the Nashville Teens, and "Time Is On My Side" by the Rolling Stones. We just drive around with the radio blasting.

Of the radio stations, our favorite is KYW. We've already memorized the air shifts of their disc jockeys. Early in the morning there are two guys called Martin and Howard. Then, from 10 A.M. to 2 P.M. there's Jim Runyon. Jim Stagg is on from 2 P.M. to 6 P.M. After that it's Jerry G. from 6 P.M. until 10 P.M. From 10 P.M. to 2 A.M. it's Jay Lawrence—"the Jay Bird."

It already seems like those guys and their voices and the records they play are a big part of our summer. I don't think there's a minute when we're in the car and we have the radio off.

We drove over to Gem Beach again this afternoon. The girls were on the beach, along with Bev. We put our towels down and lay down next to them. Bev cracked on me about my nose, but when I looked at her she was smiling and looking at me, and it didn't even make me feel bad—it was like she was singling me out on purpose, but in a good way.

Allen already had a date lined up for tonight with Paula, the Sandusky girl he met on his trip up here earlier in the summer. At Gem Beach Jack asked out one of the girls, Linda. Paula told Allen that she'd fix me up with a Sandusky friend of hers named Betsy.

So at night we drove back to Sandusky and went to the Cedar Point amusement park. We ate a lot of food and went on all the rides. It was kind of fun, but not great. Allen and I took Paula and Betsy home early, and then we all drove back over to Gem Beach so Jack could take Linda back.

The rest of the girls were all sitting around the cottage, so we went in and talked for a few hours. Bev was down in the living room with the rest of them; every few seconds I found myself looking at her.

We left to go back to Sandusky at 1 A.M. I drove Allen's car, with KYW playing the whole time.

AUGUST 24

WHEN we woke up this morning we drove from the Holmes to Gem Beach again. The girls were at the same spot on the beach where they were yesterday. Bev was wearing this brown bikini that she was just hanging out of. Did she look cool!

Dana, the blonde girl who I noticed looking at me at the Gem Beach pavilion, is making it pretty clear that she likes me. We all went swimming in the lake, but I wasn't wearing a bathing suit—just my green plaid shorts. So when we got out of the water and went back to the girls' cottage, Dana said she would lend me a pair of her jeans.

I put them on—they were real tight on me and came up over my ankles. When Bev walked into the room she said, "Greene—it's about your pants."

We decided to go on a marathon—to stay up as long as we could without going to sleep. We all kept talking and messing around all evening. We rode in Bev's car—Bev drove and a bunch of us crammed in both the front seat and the back seat. Then, later in the evening, we walked down to Gem Beach and sat by the water in the darkness.

After midnight we went back into the cottage. Jack seems to really like Linda, the girl he went out with last night, and Allen seems to be developing a crush on one of the other girls, Julie.

It's hard for me to admit it to myself, but even though there are all of these pretty girls around, and even though we're getting close to them, and even though Dana obviously likes me, all I can think about is Bev. I know that she's twenty-seven and married, and that she's there as a chaperone. But I can't remember a time in my life when I've been so immediately knocked out by someone. The very fact that she's so out of reach makes me think about her even more.

The girls and Bev and us sat up talking all night long in the living room of the cottage. About 7 A.M. Allen and I started to conk out. He said it first: "Take me Holmes! Take me Holmes!" Then I started to say it, and we were saying it in unison: "Take me Holmes!"

Jack didn't want to go, though; he said he wasn't tired, and he seemed to want to stick around with Linda. So Allen and I drove the car back to Sandusky. We ate a big breakfast, and then went back to our room at the Holmes. I had nearly forgotten something—Jack and I had short-sheeted the double bed to trick Allen. But now we were just so exhausted, and when he got in it he said, "Goddammit." I helped him make the bed, and then we went to sleep.

AUGUST 25

BEV, Jack, Linda, and a bunch of the other girls burst into our motel room about noon. They were still on their marathon. I was so disoriented from staying up so long that I started saying a bunch of crazy things about some people I'd dreamed about.

I called Dad collect from a phone booth on the highway in front of the Holmes. He had asked me to check in sometime during the trip. He said that Nana and Mom and Debby and Timmy seemed to be having a fine time in New York at the World's Fair.

Bev and the girls went back to Gem Beach early in the afternoon. Allen and Jack and I went to HoJo's for lunch, then tried to catch some rays at Cedar Point.

* * *

At night we drove over to Gem Beach to see the girls. Bev said, "I haven't had a beer for our whole time up here." We said that we had some back at the Holmes—it was only 3.2, but that was better than nothing.

We asked Bev if she wanted to go to the Holmes and have a beer with us. She said yes. So we drove back to Sandusky, and had a great conversation. Bev told us all about what life was like in the little town where she and the girls lived, and she told us about her marriage—which didn't sound so great— and she said she was happy to be making the money as the girls' chaperone at Gem Beach. She's just such an interesting person.

When we got to our room we popped open the beer. Jack immediately got drunk, but Allen and Bev and I just got a little high. We continued the conversation we were having in the car. All four of us were lying on the double bed, drinking our beers. When Bev was lying next to me I got so turned on.

Around midnight we took Bev back to Gem Beach. The girls were all sitting around the living room of the cottage. They seemed very cold, both to us and to Bev, when we walked in, so we didn't stay very long.

On the drive back to the Holmes we kept talking about how great Bev is. We all agreed: If, when we're twenty-seven years old, we're sleeping with women who are anywhere close to as cool as Bev, that's all we'll want out of life.

AUGUST 26

HOT day. We lay out by the Holmes' pool and tried to catch some rays. We caught pretty many.

We went to the beach at Cedar Point, and the Gem Beach girls were there. So we sat out in the sun with them all afternoon, and then early in the evening we all went to the Cedar Villa for dinner.

At night there was another dance at the Gem Beach pavilion. Allen and Jack and I danced a few times with various of

the Gem Beach girls; we did the Jerk. But after every time
we'd dance, we'd walk back over to the side of the room
where Bev was. We just hung around her; the music was too
loud for any of us to do much talking.

After this had gone on for about an hour, Bev said, "If
you guys keep hanging around me, you're going to ruin any
chance I have of getting picked up." She was just kidding;
she was much older than anyone else in the pavilion. But she
could have had any male she wanted in the room.

When the dance was over we went back to the cottage. Bev
said to me, "You know, Dana really likes you. Why aren't
you spending any time with her?"

I couldn't say the truth: that the only person I wanted to
spend time with was Bev. So I just shrugged my shoulders,
and Bev said, "It's about your attitude. Dana's sitting out
behind the cottage. You should go out there and be with her."

I took it as an order. Dana was sitting under a tree, and I
asked if she minded if I sat down. She said that would be
fine. We talked a little bit, and held hands, and we kissed
once or twice. All I was thinking about was Bev, though, and
I was relieved when the deputies came around and said that
everyone had to get back inside.

We headed back to the Holmes about 1:30 A.M. Jack kept
talking about how much he liked Linda. Jay Lawrence was
on KYW, and I didn't say much, just thought about Bev.

AUGUST 27

SHOCKING.

We woke up and lay in the sun for a while, and then decided to drive over to Gem Beach. When we got there Bev
was packing.

One of the girls had called her parents and told them that
Bev had gone to a motel room with a bunch of guys—us—to
drink beer and do who knows what else. Apparently all the
girls were upset about it. That's why they had acted so chilly
to us when we had brought Bev back that night.

One of the girls' mothers had driven up to Gem Beach and

said ''Out'' to Bev. The mother and the girls were down at the beach now; the mother was going to continue as the chaperone, but Bev was through.

Bev was crying as she packed. She said that her reputation was going to be ruined in her little town. Allen and Jack and I apologized; we felt like it was our fault. But Bev said it had all been her fault; she had wanted to drink beer with us.

We felt awful; Bev said she had to hurry and finish packing because she had promised to be out of the cottage by the time the mother and the girls got back.

We sort of awkwardly said goodbye to her, and walked out the door to Allen's car. Allen and Jack said they were going to drive back to Cedar Point.

I couldn't do it. I just couldn't do it. I told them I was staying. Cedar Point was twenty miles away, and I had no idea how I would eventually get back there, but I couldn't leave yet.

So I just started walking. I walked all around the Gem Beach area—to the pavilion, down to the beach, along all the roads. About an hour had passed, and I was walking down the road that runs past the beach itself, when I heard a car honk.

I turned around. It was Bev.

''Get in, kid,'' she said.

She said she would give me a ride back to the Holmes. As we drove the radio was on, and all of the songs that had made me so happy during the past week were playing—''Pretty Woman'' came on, and then ''Things We Said Today.'' But now everything had changed. I tried to think of a way to tell Bev what I thought of her, but I just couldn't get the words out of my mouth.

She had stopped crying. ''If people are that small-minded,'' she said, ''then I probably don't belong with them anyway.''

And then she said something that I wasn't expecting.

''I'm surprised you guys didn't try to screw me that night in your motel room,'' she said.

''What?'' I said.

''Not that I would have let you,'' she said. ''But I just thought that maybe you were figuring—hey, we're alone in a motel room drinking with this older woman, maybe we'll give it a try."

"Bev, we would have never done that," I said. "We think too much of you."

"I think that's the night when I realized how much I like you guys," she said. "Because you were being so nice to me."

"Well, that's because we like you, too," I said.

When we got to the Holmes, there was a downpour. We ran out of the rain and into the room, and Jack was there. He seemed amazed to see me with Bev. He said that Allen was out on a date with Paula. We told Bev that it was raining too hard for her to drive to her town. We just sat around and talked.

When we heard Allen's car pulling in, Jack and Bev and I all hopped under the covers of the double bed and put our heads on the pillows. Allen was startled, to say the least, but he was glad to see Bev. He said that he had felt bad leaving Gem Beach knowing that she was being kicked out, but that he hadn't known what else to do.

The four of us went to the Cedar Villa for dinner. All of the men in the place were staring at us; it was like, "What is the beautiful woman doing with these kids?" It made us feel proud to be with her.

When we were finished with dinner it was still raining hard. We told Bev that it would be silly to drive home to her town with the weather still so bad; Allen and Jack said they'd share the double bed, and I said I'd sleep on the floor, so that Bev could have the cot.

She said okay. We all got in bed—I lay down on the floor between the foot of the double bed and the cot—and we turned the lights out. Bev kept saying, "Hey, Greene, stop poking the bed." Everyone laughed, and Bev seemed to be relieved that she didn't have to go home just yet.

AUGUST 28

OH, Lord.

We woke up in the morning and went to HoJo's for breakfast. Bev said that she wanted to do some shopping, so we all went into downtown Sandusky and went in and out of the stores with her.

We decided to go swimming. We all put our bathing suits on and went to the pool in back of the Holmes. It was so great—the four of us just splashing around in the water. A couple of times Bev touched me. It was just for a second, but it was something that she didn't have to do if she didn't want to.

After we went back into our room, Bev went into the bathroom and changed to a pair of white shorts and a pink cotton shirt. She sat on the cot and shaved her legs. I don't know why, but it was the sexiest thing I had ever seen.

Nobody exactly said it out loud, but all four of us started to assume that Bev would stay with us for another night. We decided to go to the nicest steakhouse in Sandusky for dinner. Again, all of the men looked at us as we were led to our table; again, we felt proud just to be with Bev. The waiter glanced at us and asked if we would like soft drinks; he asked Bev what she would like to drink, and she ordered a vodka gimlet.

Allen had a date with Paula again tonight, so Bev and Jack and I stayed in the motel room and watched a Cleveland Browns exhibition football game on TV. Jack was sitting on the floor in front of the TV, and Bev was sitting on the double bed, and I was sitting on the cot.

We kept talking as the game was being played, and at one point the talk got to kissing. I said something really stupid about being a good kisser.

"Talker," Bev said, and Jack laughed.

I didn't know how to respond, so I said, "Just you wait."

Bev turned and looked right into my eyes. "I've been waiting all week," she said.

And I knew she wasn't kidding. She looked at me and said those words, and I knew she wasn't kidding.

Jack didn't catch any of this; he was still intently watching the football game. I just sat back on the cot and wondered what to do.

About half an hour later, Allen came back from his date with Paula. He said, "Does anybody want to get a pizza?"

Jack said, "I do."

I said, "I don't."

Bev said, "I don't."

So Jack and Allen were walking out the door. I was still on the cot. Bev said, "Either move over or get off, Greene. I want to take a nap."

I was lying there like a dead man. My arms were straight down by my sides. I wasn't moving; I was hardly breathing. Bev sat down on the cot. Allen and Jack laughed at me, and then they got in Allen's car and drove away.

Bev lay down next to me. She draped one of her arms over me. A few minutes went by, and then we started hugging each other and rubbing each other. I thought I was going to go crazy.

As easy as it had been to talk to Bev all week, now I couldn't think of a thing to say. I kept trying to say something, but nothing would come out.

Finally Bev said, "What are you thinking about?"

I thought my chest was going to explode, it was thumping so hard.

Bev put her hand on my shirt and said, "It's about your heart."

We started kissing. I just couldn't believe it; I was kissing Bev. She was so willing and so passionate; I had never felt this way kissing anyone before. She kept pushing her chest against mine, and I put my hand under her shirt and she let me unfasten her bra and then she let me put my hand under her bra.

So many things were going on in my mind. I didn't know if I should attempt to go any further. Neither of us said anything about it, but somehow it seemed as if we were doing exactly what we were supposed to be doing, and that this was as far as it was supposed to go. We just kept it up—kept kissing and holding each other. It kept getting better. Time was passing, but I couldn't keep track of it. I almost felt like crying, I felt so good.

After I don't know how much longer, Allen's car pulled up outside. I got up and sat on the double bed, pretending to watch TV. Bev stayed on the cot. When Allen and Jack walked in, it looked as if nothing at all had happened.

We all talked for a while, and then it was time for bed. Like last night, Allen and Jack slept in the double bed, and Bev slept on the cot, and I lay down on the floor.

I waited a long time, until I could hear from Allen's and Jack's breathing that they were asleep. Then I got up and got under the covers of the cot with Bev.

AUGUST 29

ALL night long I kept touching her. She put her finger up to her lips, to remind me to be quiet and not wake Allen and Jack. We just kept kissing each other—not wildly like before, but we touched our lips together and looked into each other's eyes. Even though it was dark in the room, we could see each other.

She let me put my hand under her bra again, and I kept touching her breasts all night long. I kept telling myself: Don't fall asleep. Don't let yourself miss a minute of this. This is the best thing that has ever happened to you in your life; don't miss any of it.

And I had all kinds of other things going through my mind, too. The chief one was: Why me? Why had she chosen me? Allen and Jack are both better-looking than I am. But she had chosen me. Why?

And of course I thought about the moral questions, too. Bev is twenty-seven years old and she's married. I know it's wrong to be with someone who is married. The only married people I know are my parents' friends, and some of my teachers, and some of the people at the *Citizen-Journal*. And I can't imagine any of the married women in those groups of people being in bed with a seventeen-year-old boy.

But it doesn't seem wrong. It just doesn't seem wrong. What it seems like is the most wonderful thing that's ever happened to me, and all of my questions about why it was

happening sort of faded away when I thought about the fact
that *it was happening*. It was happening to me.

Just at dawn, as the sun was coming up, Bev motioned for
me to get back on the floor. She didn't want Allen and Jack
to see us in bed when they woke up. So I slept a little on the
floor, and then everyone started to wake up, and Bev said
she guessed she'd better head on back to the town where she
lived.

She packed her stuff and carried it out to her car. She got
in the driver's seat. We all leaned in her open window; Allen
and Jack said goodbye to her and told her to drive carefully.
She looked at me. She didn't say anything. She just smiled
and ran her hand through my hair, and then she drove away.

This afternoon I did probably the stupidest thing I have
ever done: I told Allen and Jack what had happened.

We went to the beach at Cedar Point and lay in the sun,
and they kept saying how great Bev had been, and I was so
bursting with the news that I told them. I told them everything. I told them exactly what had happened.

As soon as the words left my mouth I knew that I had
made a big mistake. For a few minutes they didn't believe
me, and then they both turned completely against me. They
totally condemned me. They said that what I did was an awful
thing, and that Bev was married, and that there was no excuse
for what had happened. They said that it didn't matter that
we hadn't gone all the way—I was awful for doing it. Even
as they were talking, I was furious at myself for telling them,
and I was also wondering how much of what they were saying
came from jealousy.

They wouldn't leave me alone about it. We went back to
the Holmes around dinnertime, and I got into bed at seven
o'clock. I was just so exhausted; I needed to sleep, and to
think some more about what had happened.

Tomorrow we go home to Columbus.

AUGUST 30

WE got up and packed and loaded the car; we had our last breakfast at the Sandusky HoJo's. The drive back to Columbus was easy; it felt sort of sad to hear KYW and CKLW and WBZ fading away.

The first thing we did when we got back was go to the Excelsior Club and play some basketball and swim. Chuck and Dan were there, and of course Allen and Jack told them about Bev right away. Allen and Jack seem to have changed their attitude a lot during the last twenty-four hours; now they see my experience with Bev as some sort of great adventure, or conquest, or something.

By tonight every high school kid in Bexley knew about it. We were sitting around Pongi's front yard, and everyone was coming up to me and asking me how it had happened. They all wanted to hear the story. I told them all that I didn't feel like talking about it.

That seemed to surprise them. They seemed to think that it was something I should be proud of.

But I don't like it. I don't like everyone knowing about Bev. Dumb as I am, she means a hell of a lot to me. She means a lot more than just some story to tell to a bunch of people I don't even care about. More and more, I'm mad at myself for telling Allen and Jack in the first place.

AUGUST 31

UP at nine and went to school to work on the *Torch*. It went fine; as I was leaving the football team was walking through the high school parking lot on their way back from summer practice. I saw Dave Frasch, who was sweating and breathing hard. "Miserable," he said.

Then Chuck and I took the bus up to the Ohio State Fair. I haven't skipped going to the fair since I was a little kid. It's up on the fairgrounds near Ohio State University; it's corny, but I love it. You walk past this huge cow made of butter, and then you go to the sheep-shearing contests and the cow-milking contests, and you go on the rides and play the games on the midway. Plus you look for girls.

Chuck's really learning to be cool with the girls. He's not afraid to go up to any girl at the fair and start talking. That's still hard for me to do.

The *Citizen-Journal* had a booth set up, where Al Getchell would draw sketches of people. He recognized me right away and was real nice; he drew pictures of both Chuck and me.

We got back home about five o'clock. I cut the grass, and when Dad came home he told me I was grounded for the night. He said it was because he had told me I couldn't go out last night—our first night back from Cedar Point—but that I had gone anyway. He didn't seem angry; he just seemed to be reestablishing his authority after having no control over me the whole time I was at Cedar Point.

After dinner Allen came over; we went out onto the back porch, where Dad was reading the paper. Dad said, "So, did you boys have a nice time at Cedar Point? Did you meet any girls?"

And Allen—I can't believe this—said, "Girls? Bob went out with a twenty-seven-year-old married woman."

I looked over at Dad, expecting him to be mad. But he just kind of raised his eyebrows and smiled. It was apparent that, in some way, he was proud of me.

That made me so upset that I had to walk out of the porch for a minute. Maybe this is stupid, but I just don't think of it like that. Married or not, sinful or not, I like that woman an awful lot.

Later in the evening, after Allen went home, I almost wrote her a letter. I feel so bad now that she's gone. I know I won't change. She's everything I've been looking for. I just wish to hell everyone didn't know about it.

SEPTEMBER 1

WASHED my hair when I got up. I'm rapidly becoming a Beatle again. I hope Dad doesn't make me get it cut for a while.

Dad's *Playboy* came in the mail today, and I took it in my room to read it. There were some love scenes with Elke Sommer. It reminded me so much of Bev.

We played touch football at Chuck's this afternoon. Good game. Then we all went to the Toddle House and ate.

I wrote pledge letters for Epsilons. They'll be mailed to all the freshmen, saying that we'll be having a rush party.

Dan came over, and then we went to an open house. Lindy was there, and she looked great as usual. But it was funny— after Bev, everyone else seems like a little letdown. Even Lindy. I think Bev may have ruined me for high school girls. I just don't know.

"Tobacco Road" and "Pretty Woman" were on the car radio as we drove home from the open house. Cedar Point already feels so far away.

SEPTEMBER 2

I went to the printer's with Mrs. Amos today to do paste-up on the *Torch*. It looks like the first issue will be really good. I showed Mrs. Amos the *Hard Day's Night* review I wrote for *Junior Prom*. She liked it. I still haven't heard whether Pauline Taynor is going to use it or not.

I bought a new Beatles album today. It's called *Something New*. A lot of the songs are the same ones that are on the *Hard Day's Night* soundtrack—the soundtrack was put out by United Artists records, and *Something New* is put out by Capitol, the Beatles' usual label.

I bought it because "Things We Said Today" is on it. That one song is worth the price of the whole album to me. I kept playing it and thinking about Cedar Point and Bev.

SEPTEMBER 3

JACK had to do deliveries for his dad's fruit and vegetable market today, so I rode with him.

When I got home late in the afternoon, Dad came home from the office with my Epsilons pledge letters. He had had them run off on his mimeograph machine. I signed them all, then addressed all the envelopes and stuffed the letters into the envelopes.

We had an Epsilons meeting tonight. It was hard to control things; everybody was acting like a bunch of animals.

SEPTEMBER 4

CHUCK drove me to the printer's, where I picked up the *Torch* pages and then went to Mrs. Amos' house. We went over them; they still look pretty good.

In the afternoon Dan rode over to my house on his Honda. He said that he thought he could ride it by standing up on the seat and holding his arms up in the air.

He took it down to the end of Bryden Road. He stared riding it the usual way. Then, with the cycle still moving, he put his feet up on the seat. He was standing on it, but in a crouched position and with his hands still on the handlebars.

Finally he stood up completely straight and raised his arms up above his head. The Honda immediately went off course and turned over. Dan jumped off at the last minute, but he scraped his legs and arms pretty badly. Sometimes I wonder about him.

Went to the fair again at night. Saw Donna Marsh—the high school co-hostess on Channel 4's "Dance-O-Rama." I wanted to say something to her, but people were gathered all around her.

SEPTEMBER 5

DAN and I went to the fair today. We wandered, and then we saw Pongi's little brother Eddie selling metal trays.

Because Pongi's dad owns the RC Cola distributorship in Columbus, he had the RC trays in stock, and he set Eddie up in a booth to try to sell them. Eddie wasn't doing too well—he's just a little kid, the same age as Timmy—so Dan and I said we'd help him out.

Eddie had just been standing in the booth, waiting for people to come up and buy the trays, and not many people had been coming. Dan and I got into the booth and started waving the trays in the air and shouting at the people on the midway—"Use 'em as a tray or hang 'em on your wall, do anything you want at all!"

It was great. People started coming over immediately. In an hour we sold more than fifty trays. But then we got bored, and Eddie took over the booth again.

I have to go to Hideaway Hills with the family tomorrow.

SEPTEMBER 6

MOM and Dad woke me up at nine. Instead of eating breakfast at home, we loaded the car and then stopped at the Pancake House on Main Street.

I was in a bad mood anyway—I didn't want to go to Hideaway—and then Dad jumped all over me because I ordered a cheeseburger for breakfast. He said that was not an appropriate breakfast. We got in an argument about it, and then right in front of the waitress he called me a baby.

Hideaway was no good. After unloading the car I just played albums all afternoon. I went to the lodge about five times at night, but there was no action there. I went back to the cottage and read a paperback book called *The Press*, by A. J. Liebling, which I had bought at Rogers' Drugstore.

I listened to some more records and then went to bed real early and thought of Bev.

SEPTEMBER 7

HAD a terrible lunch in the cottage, and then just wandered around Hideaway. I wanted to be home.

We drove back to Bexley late in the afternoon. At night I drove Mom's station wagon to Judy Furman's house, and Judy and I talked about the *Torch*. When I left someone had squirted mustard on the car.

SEPTEMBER 8

UP at eight o'clock to take some more *Torch* copy to the printer's. Then I went straight to Chuck's; our Epsilons pledge party is tonight. All of the incoming freshmen are invited; the party is going to be in Chuck's backyard.

We elaborated on the party all afternoon. We set up refreshment tables and put up decorations. We thought we still needed something more, though, so I drove down to the *Citizen-Journal* and talked to the head of the public service department. He lent me a sports highlights film.

At the party all of us on the executive board wore our Epsilons blazers. We talked to all of the freshmen, and then when the sun went down Chuck set up his family's movie screen on his driveway, and we showed the sports film. The freshmen seemed really impressed. I couldn't help but remember how I had gone to the pledge party when I was a freshman, and then how I hadn't gotten into Epsilons that first year.

Everybody was in a good mood after the party, and a lot of us went to Pongi's house. Later in the evening some of us tried to climb over the wall at the Excelsior Club so we could have a midnight swim, but the wall was too high.

SEPTEMBER 9

IT'S all over. This is the last day of summer. School starts tomorrow.

When I got up I called Jack, and he and I went over to Chuck's to read some plot summaries for our summer reading. I had to leave for a while to go to the printer's and pick up the finished copies of the *Torch*. The paper looks great. I took the bundles of them to school, where some other *Torch* people were waiting, and we went around to all of the homerooms and dropped them off so they'll be waiting for everyone tomorrow morning.

It was weird, being back in school. It seems like a year has passed since last spring. It's hard to believe that tomorrow I'll be sitting in classrooms.

Chuck and Dan and Jack and I went to the Toddle House for one last late-night snack before the start of school. Allen is on his way back to military school; it's going to feel different without the A in ABCDJ. We've had quite a summer.

It's a new year tomorrow. I hope we're good seniors.

September 10

BACK to the grind. My radio alarm went off at six-thirty. "Tobacco Road" was playing on WCOL, but summer's gone.

I got to school at seven-thirty. It already feels different being a senior. We all have our lockers on senior hall on the first floor of the school. I was walking upstairs and Wendy Monroe said "Hi" to me in a real friendly way. I was shocked. She's one of the girls in the class below ours who never paid much attention to us last year. But now we're seniors; we're the oldest guys in the high school.

I made sideline passes for the football games, so our *Torch* reporters and photographers can cover the games from up close. I took them down to Coach DeJong's office so he could sign them, but he refused. He said he had to think about it.

Yvette Mimieux was on "Dr. Kildare" tonight in a rerun. Mmmmmm.

I guess I knew that being a senior would be a different feeling, but I didn't think it would hit me this soon.

September 11

IN homeroom today they made an announcement on the PA system that there would be a pep rally after school.

I said to the people in homeroom, "You don't have to go." What I meant is that the people who work on the *Torch* could stay and get their stories done.

Jim Nowacki, the captain of the football team, said, "Yes you do," and gave me a hard look.

The day went fine. I knew about three answers in Physics. I wrote a glowing editorial about the football team and school spirit, and I went to Coach DeJong's office again and showed it to him. He read it and then signed our sideline passes. You'd think he'd be embarrassed to fall for something as obvious as that. Yesterday he didn't want the *Torch* on the sidelines; today he reads the editorials and he does.

SEPTEMBER 12

SATURDAY. Dan picked me up early, and we went down to his dad's fish market and I helped him work in the freezer room for a while. After that we went to Chuck's and played football in his front yard.

When I got home Judy Furman brought the first issue of *Junior Prom* over for me to see. I had never really talked to Pauline Taynor about my Beatles story after I turned it in to her at the *Citizen-Journal*. But she really played it big—she didn't cut a word, and there were pictures from *A Hard Day's Night* with it.

I hope we distribute the thing right at school, so that everyone sees it. What I'd really like is a column in *Junior Prom*, with a free hand to write about anything I want. But I don't know how to ask for it.

SEPTEMBER 13

THERE was a Cleveland Browns game on TV today. Jack came over and we watched it together. Then when it was over we went to Chuck's house and had a good time trying to kill some bees.

Chuck's older brother Bill said, "You guys are seniors now; why don't you try to get some of those good-looking girls?"

I was riding on the back of Dan's Honda about five-fifteen when I saw Lindy on the street. She said "Hi" in a stereotypical sorority manner. It's funny—we're finally going to school in the same building, but I haven't run into her at school yet.

I went to the Eastmoor to pick up dinner for Debby and Timmy. Then Jack and I went out to the TAT on Main Street and had poor boys.

God, I just thought about Bev. And what it was like being with her. Most of the summer seems so far away already—open houses, the *Citizen-Journal*, Tina Flaker. But Bev stays in my mind as clear as the sharpest photograph you could ever imagine. I just *have* to see her again.

Watched "The Rogues" on TV tonight. Really great show.

SEPTEMBER 14

BAD start today. Judy Furman didn't get the *Junior Proms* out for sale in the lobby of the high school, and then I had to go to room 109 to talk about *Torch* subscriptions, and I couldn't make myself heard.

I did get a 100 on last week's French homework, and History class with Mr. Poetker went well. And in Physics I understood perfectly what Mr. Hughes was talking about. If I can just keep it up, I won't end up in my usual academic trouble as the semester goes on.

Dan and Jack and I went to the Eskimo Queen after school. I felt crappy after having a soda there. Dan and Jack are both bugging me about getting a date for Saturday night. We talked about the cool junior girls—Sherry Smith and Susie Sloan and Carol Lowenthal and all of them. They've always gone out with older guys, and now we're the only older guys left in the high school. *We* know we're cool enough for them, but do *they*? Linda Loeffler, a senior who's a good friend of Jack's, said she'd talk to Libby Williams, another one of the junior girls, and see what's what.

SEPTEMBER 15

JUNIOR PROM went on sale in the lobby, and a lot of people seemed to be buying it. It's hard for me to think about the fact that it's being sold at every high school in Central Ohio—that's a lot of people reading my *Hard Day's Night* story.

In study hall I wrote a long letter to Allen at military school. I really feel sorry for him, having to be down there away from us.

Linda Loeffler told Jack that she had talked to Carol Lowenthal, and that the junior girls want to go out with us—but they don't think we like them. I don't quite buy that. How could anybody not like them? As it stands, though, I'm asking out Carol Lowenthal for Saturday night, and Jack's asking out Susie Sloan.

Dan and I rode his Honda after school. When we do that it still feels a little bit like summer.

SEPTEMBER 16

Aw, shit. Today was the day Jack and I planned to ask the junior girls for dates for this weekend. Jack planned to call Susie Sloan; I planned to call Carol Lowenthal.

I ate at Frisch's with Dan, then did some French homework, and then got ready to make my call. I was completely nervous; I didn't know what I'd have to talk about with Carol. So I made notes; I took a piece of paper and wrote down a lot of things that I could bring up in case the conversation lagged.

I finally got up the guts to call her at ten-fifteen. I asked her to see *Becket* on Saturday night. She said yes. But I felt like a damn queer, coming up with things to say from my notes. Even after she said yes, I was saying things like, "Well, I'll call and find out what time the movie starts and all, and then I'll let you know what time I'll pick you up. Thanks."

God, I'm an ass! I called Jack as soon as I got off the phone with Carol. He said he talked to Susie Sloan for *fifteen minutes*! But she said no. So now, in addition to being a goon on the phone, I may have no one to double with.

I wrote a column for *Junior Prom* tonight, and mailed it off to Pauline Taynor with a letter saying I'd like to write every month. We'll see what happens.

SEPTEMBER 17

THINGS might not be so bad after all. I got a B— on an English theme, and then Coach Weis asked me if I would be a hall monitor fourth period every day. So I was sitting in the hall monitor's chair, and Dianne Kushner came up. She said she had heard I asked Carol out; she laughed and said, "That's great."

Then after school I went to Jack's. He lives right across the street from Carol. Jack and I were sitting in his yard, and Lindy came walking by. It was the first time Lindy and I had really talked since the school year began. Right in the middle of our conversation, Carol crossed the street from her house and said, "Bobby? Hi." Lindy looked a little startled.

Then tonight Pongi said that Carol was telling people she was happy I'd asked her out. When I got home, our Epsilons membership cards had been delivered to my house from the printing company where we'd ordered them.

SEPTEMBER 18

BEXLEY football game tonight. I had one of the sideline passes that Coach DeJong gave us for the *Torch*. It felt cool, being down there next to the field, telling our photographer which pictures to try for.

Pat Lemmon, Lindy's older brother, came up to me at half time and said, "Who's your date with this weekend, Greene?" I don't think that he and the other junior boys like the idea of us seniors taking out their girls.

Carol Lowenthal was at the game with Chris Harbold, one of Pat Lemmon's best friends. My guess is that she doesn't care about me one way or the other.

SEPTEMBER 19

SATURDAY, the big day. Worked on the *Torch* all morning at school; Mrs. Amos told Judy Furman and me that we had to quit fighting with each other. Pissed me off no end.

Then Jack and I went to the Toddle House for lunch. I called Carol throughout the afternoon, and finally got her at five-fifteen. I told her I'd pick her up at seven-thirty.

Becket was great. It was a real long movie, with an intermission. During the first half of the movie we just watched it, and smiled at each other once in a while and said a few things. We went out for refreshments during intermission, and I decided in my head that I'd try to hold her hand during the second half.

It's funny; I think about Bev at Cedar Point, and I feel that I should never have to be nervous again about something like holding a girl's hand. But here I was, sitting next to Carol, and it took me about half of the second half of the movie to get up the nerve to try. We would look at each other and smile, and I would just about be ready to hold her hand, and then she would look back at the movie again, so I wouldn't do it. Finally I kept telling myself that I'd count up to ten and then hold her hand. I counted to 10 three times, and chickened out each time. The fourth time I did it—and she didn't seem to mind. I was afraid that she might pull her hand away, but she squeezed my hand back.

On the way out of the movie theater she held my arm. We drove to HoJo's East for something to eat; we held hands in the car. On the way back to her house, I put my arm around her shoulders.

I walked her to her door. She said, "That movie was really great. Well, I'll see you, Bobby . . . in school or something."

I think maybe I could have kissed her goodnight, but I didn't. What a nice night.

SEPTEMBER 20

WATCHED the Cleveland Browns play the St. Louis Cardinals on TV this afternoon. Good game. Then went to Mrs. Amos' to go over *Torch* pages. She says that our staff is doing a good job this year.

Jack came over at night and we watched "The Rogues" together. I told him about holding hands with Carol. We tried to figure out what it means.

September 21

I couldn't sleep last night, so I got up and watched *High School Confidential* on the late movie. In school today I wrote an English theme in study hall, and finished up a Physics graph.

Dianne Kushner and I traded senior pictures. Jack and I were at his house after school, and Carol came out of her house across the street and invited us over. Jack and I sat with her on her porch; there was a couch and two single chairs, and I purposely sat on one of the chairs so there would be no symbolism of sitting next to her on the couch.

We were talking about juniors and seniors, and Carol said, "There's no difference between juniors and seniors," and smiled at me.

Tonight I could pick up KYW in Cleveland on the radio in my room. Jerry G. said that he had an advance copy of a new Beatles album. He played two songs from it—"I'll Be Back" and "I'll Follow the Sun." Even though I had never heard the songs before, they reminded me so much of summer and Cedar Point and Bev. It was the sound of Jerry G.'s voice introducing the Beatles that did it to me. I sat on the edge of my bed and thought.

September 22

THIS morning I went down to C. W. Jones' office and made an announcement on the loudspeaker about *Torch* subscriptions being for sale. It was corny—hearing my voice going into the microphone, and at the same time hearing it come out of every loudspeaker in every homeroom in the school—but I liked it.

After school Dan and I rode on his Honda, and at night we had an Epsilons meeting. When that was over, I went to Chuck's house and read his plot summary of *Tom Jones*.

When I got home, I called Carol. We talked for ten minutes; it was all me doing the talking. She was nice enough; she said, "Your announcement on the PA system was really good this morning." When I hung up, I didn't know how I felt.

So I started thinking about it. I guess what I'm really looking for is the feeling you have when you have a girlfriend—and not Carol in particular. She's great-looking, and she's nice, and she's one of the most popular girls in the junior class. It was good for my ego that we went out together.

But I wonder if I would be doing all this stuff if Lindy and I hadn't broken up last year. The more I think about it, those feelings I had with Lindy were all that I had ever wanted. The idea of waking up in the morning and thinking about someone and knowing that she was thinking about you, too; the anticipation of the phone calls; the jolt I would get when I would be walking down the street and see her approaching from the other direction . . . when that was going on with Lindy, I was completely happy.

Now it seems that I'm in this constant search for girls, and I'm finally beginning to realize that nothing is going to replace what I had with Lindy. She's not coming back; I know that now. But I miss the feeling so much that I'm always looking for some other girl to help give it to me. And I'm finally beginning to understand that no matter how hard I look, it's probably not going to happen.

SEPTEMBER 23

DURING the summertime you lose sight of just how bad school is. This morning we had a hard French test. Then an English quiz I had studied for was postponed. Then there was a quiz in History that I know I did badly on. Then in Physics class Mr. Hughes went around the room and made each of us answer questions.

It just seems that there's never a moment when someone's not bugging you. The great thing about summer is that it's just you and your friends. Even the *Citizen-Journal* never really felt like work—it was a bunch of nice and funny people who happened to show up at the same place every day, but nobody bugged anybody else.

With school, it never ends. When the day is over I stand at my locker and automatically pick out which books I have to carry home with me to study. A lot of the times the books just sit at home all evening without me opening them, but in the morning I carry them back and put them in my locker, and at the end of the day I go through them again and lug them home. Even Dad doesn't have to bring work home from the office

I saw Carol about a dozen times in the hallways today. Each time all we did was say "Hi." Just that one word. "Hi." "Hi." Then we'd see each other again. "Hi." "Hi." And then we'd see each other again. "Hi." "Hi." She probably thinks I'm a damn goon.

SEPTEMBER 24

HOMECOMING'S coming up next month. On Homecoming night, there is a parade through Bexley—each of the five girls on the Homecoming court rides in a convertible, and the high school band marches and plays in front of them.

Each of the girls on Homecoming court gets to choose an escort. The escort rides with her in the car, and walks her out onto the field at the beginning of the game. To be an escort is one of the best things that can happen to a guy at Bexley.

There's one catch—guys who are on the football team can't be escorts. They're getting dressed for the game during the parade. So a lot of guys who would ordinarily be escorts aren't in the running, because they're football players.

Today in study hall, Dianne Kushner said to me, "If I make it to Homecoming court, I wonder who I should ask to be my escort?"

I didn't say anything. Dianne is the coolest girl in the senior class, and there's no chance that she won't make Homecoming court. We've always been friendly, although I'd never be able to get up the nerve to ask her on a date. Her boyfriend is Gary Herwald, who's on the football team, so she can't ask him to be her escort.

I wanted to say, "Why don't you ask me?" but there's no way I could have said those words. First, maybe she would have thought I was kidding, and maybe she would have laughed. And second, you don't volunteer to be an escort—it's up to the girl to ask.

Being an escort doesn't denote anything romantic—a lot of the girls on Homecoming court every year are going with guys on the football team, like Dianne and Gary. But it's such an honor—you get your picture in the yearbook with the member of the court who you escorted. I wish Dianne could read my mind.

SEPTEMBER 25

TODAY was the day of a Bexley football game, and as usual all of the lettermen from all sports in school wore their sweaters. I used to do that last year, but I haven't worn my sweater or my jacket this year because I didn't get my letter again in tennis last spring.

In Physics class I was passing notes back and forth with Dave Frasch and Tim Greiner. The three of us are getting to be great friends in Physics; Tim and I sit next to each other and Dave sits right in front of us, and Mr. Hughes doesn't seem to notice that we pass notes back and forth. Or if he does notice, he doesn't say anything.

The way the notes work is that one of us will write something, and then the other guy will write something right under it, and then the third guy will write something else, and then it will all start over again. In the middle of the note Dave wrote something asking why I wasn't wearing my sweater. Dave, as the quarterback on the football team, and Tim, as a starting end, were both wearing their sweaters.

I wrote back that I didn't think I should, because of tennis last spring. Then Dave and Tim wrote that I was being stupid— that I had earned my letter the year I won it, and that I was entitled to wear the sweater and the jacket. I wrote back that I was afraid people would knock me for it. Tim wrote, "Fuck 'em." Dave wrote that if he and Tim thought it was okay for me to wear the sweater or the jacket, who else's opinion counted?

It really made me feel good. Usually we say negative things

about people in the notes, but they were really being serious. Dave wrote, ''Wear your letter jacket to the game tonight.''

And I did. And nobody seemed to notice, much less think there was anything wrong with it.

After the game there was a party in Diane Garek's basement. There was a record album cover, and the girl on the cover had a nose that looked just like Bev's. I wonder if I'll ever hear from her again?

SEPTEMBER 26

SLEPT till eleven because it's Saturday. I went over to Jack's house, and there was a big commotion because his neighbors had gotten locked out of their house. The Bexley police were there and everything, but nobody had any idea how to get in.

Finally we saw a window that was open a crack. Jack put his hands together to give me a boost, and I pushed the window open, then crawled through it and into the house. I unlocked the doors from the inside and let the family in.

The people wanted to give me some money, but I said no. I felt like I was on ''The Rogues'' or something.

At night we drove over to the Whitehall Recreation Center, but there was no dance. When I got home I rang Lindy's number. She called me back, and said that Carol Lowenthal and Mike Luby had been seen running through the park behind the Jeffrey Mansion, holding hands. Great.

SEPTEMBER 27

WATCHED sports all afternoon. First there was a Cleveland Browns game, and then the Davis Cup was on. Dennis Ralston is the coolest guy in the world. When I see him play tennis, it makes me want to start working on my game again.

SEPTEMBER 28

JACK and I went over to his house after school today. We went up to his room and talked.

I've been going up to Jack's room since I was five or six years old. It feels almost as familiar to me as my own room at home. He's still got the bunk beds that he had when he was little; Jack's was the first house where my parents ever let me sleep over.

When his mom was alive she'd always make us tollhouse cookies and milk; we'd eat them at night when we'd stay up talking, and then in the morning she would even let us eat them for breakfast. When we were in junior high school we taped a box up above the door inside Jack's room, and we would play basketball with rolled-up socks.

I don't know how many hours I've spent in that room. I remember all the nights when I'd sleep over and his mom and dad would tell us we had to go to sleep, but we'd keep talking anyway, in a whisper. I'd sleep in the bottom bunk, and Jack would sleep in the top.

It's hard to believe that, a year from now, we'll be in college. I can't even comprehend it. It seems like yesterday, the first time Jack and I came up to his room and played. And now that's probably coming to an end.

We talked until dinnertime and then I went home.

Jack just called me. He said that Mike Luby's car is parked across the street from his house, at Carol's.

SEPTEMBER 29

I'M sick. I've got a rotten damn cold. I felt it coming on all day yesterday, and I woke up in the middle of the night with it.

When I was a kid I used to like staying home sick; I'd watch TV or play records, and it would feel like I was getting away with something. But now I go to school no matter how bad I feel; there's too much going on there, and I don't want to miss anything.

Today, for example, I went home and had a cheeseburger and a Contac for lunch. When I got back to school, Carol Lowenthal was dancing with Mike Luby in the lounge. So I guess I probably should give up on her. But I wouldn't have seen it if I had stayed home sick.

We had an Epsilons meeting tonight and elected seventeen freshman pledges. After the meeting I was supposed to call them all and invite them to join the fraternity.

It was a strange feeling. I could hear them getting excited when I called—but all I could think about was that when I was their age, I was waiting for a phone call from Epsilons and the call never came. I remember the next day in school—everybody who got in was all excited and congratulating each other, and I just tried to make myself invisible.

Now here I am, a senior and the president of Epsilons, making the calls myself. I guess things work out—I'm probably a better person for having to wait a year to get in. But even as I called the freshmen and told them that they were Epsilons pledges, part of my mind was thinking about the kids who were waiting for me to call, and were going to wait all night without the phone ringing. I don't know—with all that's happened, I still identify with them as much as I do with the guys who got in.

SEPTEMBER 30

SICK again, but I went to school anyway. There was an Ohio University conference sixth period, so a lot of us went to it to see what we thought of the school. It's down in Athens. They gave us some brochures and application forms.

After school I ran into Lindy and Janie McKenney. Janie started singing: "You can never stop me loving you . . ." That was one of Lindy and my songs last year. I looked to see how Lindy was reacting, but I couldn't tell.

At night I drove over to Mike Melton's house to read his Cliffs Notes of *El Cid*. When I got back home, the cake dialers hit, and identified themselves; they said, "This is the cake dialers," and then hung up. Five minutes later they called back and started to sing: "Oh, you've got personality . . ."

I immediately called Lindy. She answered the phone and I asked if it had been her, but she denied it.

Pauline Taynor from the *Citizen-Journal* called and said she had decided to use my column in the next issue of *Junior Prom*. She asked me to send her a picture of myself. I sent a senior picture. That would be so great, if she makes it into a really big deal.

There's a dance sponsored by the *Torch* on Friday. I had planned on asking Carol, but I hear she's got a date with Mike Luby. So I asked Candy Grossman. It will be the first time we've gone out together since last New Year's Eve; she's still a good friend of my sister's, and she knows we're just going on a friendship basis. But I couldn't not go to the dance; because I'm co-editor of the *Torch*, I have to be there.

OCTOBER 1

ALL day long I had to try to get Larry Teaburry into Epsilons. He's a neighbor of Gary Herwald's—a freshman. He didn't get in when we voted, and apparently he's been crying, and his parents talked to Gary's parents and asked if anything could be done.

Gary called me late last night and said he'd appreciate it if I could do anything to help. He said that Larry is completely crushed by not getting in. I told Gary that something like this had never been done before—once the vote's taken, it's taken.

But I thought about it—and thought again about how I had felt when I was a freshman and didn't get in. So during study halls and between periods all day, I went around to all of the members of Epsilons I could find and asked them if they wanted to change their minds about Teaburry.

Some of the guys were pissed off at me—they said that no one had a right to ask to have the vote changed. But when I said that the request had come from Gary Herwald, a lot of them said okay. Gary's probably one of the best-liked guys in the senior class.

So I spent my whole day in school trying to get votes for Teaburry, and by the end of school he had enough. Part of me felt good about doing it—I don't like to see anybody's feelings get hurt that badly. But another part of me wondered: Why didn't anybody do this for me when I was a freshman?

Mom and Dad and I had a meeting with C.W. Jones after school. They wanted to talk about college possibilities.

C.W. said that my grades were just on the borderline—I

might or might not be able to get into a really good college. He said that my grades for this semester will be a big factor in determining where I go.

It was weird to see how Mom and Dad reacted to C.W. They were both very respectful toward him—everything he said, they nodded and agreed with. It was obvious that they were trying to make a good impression on him. Mom had dressed up, and Dad was wearing his business suit from work. Usually, when I see them with other grownups—their friends—they're very loose and casual. With C.W., it was like they were waiting for a jury to make its decision or something.

I didn't say much. A couple of times C.W. would ask me something, and I would mumble an answer. I just wanted to get out of there.

On the way home Dad said to me, "Why didn't you speak up? Every time you said something, Mr. Jones turned to your mother and me and said, 'What did he say?' "

"C.W.'s not going to determine where I get into college," I said.

"Don't you be so sure," Dad said. "Just don't you be so sure. He is your principal."

"I wish you would have been a little bit more enthusiastic," Mom said.

"A Summer Song" is number one on the new WCOL survey.

Around ten o'clock tonight I started thinking about Carol, and I figured that maybe I was jumping to conclusions about her starting to go with Mike Luby. So I worked up my courage and called her house. Her little sister answered and asked who was calling; I told her, and when she came back to the phone she said that Carol was studying and couldn't talk. How humiliating. I guess there's my answer.

OCTOBER 2

WE were scheduled to have a Physics test this afternoon, and everyone in the morning classes said it was real bad. I crammed all I could in study hall fourth period for it, but in the afternoon the test was as hard as everyone had said. I may have gotten as high as a C on it, but I also may have flunked it.

Linda Loeffler, who is one of Dianne Kushner's best friends, told me that Dianne is considering asking Mark Smilack to be her escort for Homecoming. If that's true, I might as well count myself out.

There's this freshman girl named Kathy Michaels. I saw her twice today. She is absolutely beautiful—she's got long, straight hair like Marianne Faithfull's. I don't know anything about her, but everytime I see her I get turned on.

Candy and I went to the football game tonight, and then to the *Torch* dance. We had a pretty nice time. Carol was there with Mike Luby, and seemed to be enjoying herself.

When I got home, I did something that I've been wanting to do for weeks—I wrote a letter to Bev. It wasn't mushy or anything; I tried to sound grown-up in it, and I just told her what has been going on in school, and asked her what she had been doing. I'm a little scared to mail it—I don't know what her husband will think if he gets their mail first. There's nothing incriminating in there; I made no reference to what had happened between us at Cedar Point. But still, her husband might not like her getting a letter from some guy.

OCTOBER 3

I got up at eight, even though it's Saturday, because we had to go to school and work on the *Torch*. I wrote a couple of editorials, and Jack wrote a good sports column.

After we were done, Jack and I went to the Eastmoor for lunch. Then we went downtown to Marco's Records; we both wanted to get "Little Latin Lupe Lu," but they didn't have it.

We were cruising around Bexley, and as we drove down Fair Avenue there was a girl walking by herself. She yelled "Hi" at the car.

We drove around the block and passed her again. Jack said, "She's a baby." But I thought I recognized the hair.

So we made one more pass, and stopped when we got to her. Just as I had thought: Kathy Michaels. She leaned in the window and talked for a few minutes. None of us had a whole lot to say; it was the first time we had talked.

But boy, I could like her.

Tonight we went to the senior float. The floats are kind of a tradition in the weeks just before Homecoming; each class builds its float in one person's backyard and driveway. Everybody is allowed to go out at night to work on the floats; even parents who usually don't let their kids go out on school nights let them go to the floats.

Our float is being built at Judy Furman's house. Half of the people are working on constructing the actual float and covering it with chicken wire; the other people are making flowers out of tissue paper.

There's a kind of etiquette to going to the floats at night. The older you are, the more floats you can visit. For example, because we're seniors, we can drop in at the junior and sophomore and freshman floats if we want. But if you're a freshman, you can only go to your own float. If you're a sophomore, you can go to the sophomore float and the freshman float. It's probably the biggest socializing time for kids in Bexley all year.

On the way home from the float I stopped at a mailbox. I mailed my letter to Bev, plus application forms to Princeton and Stanford.

OCTOBER 4

JACK came over to watch the Browns game this afternoon. Then I finished up my college application to Northwestern and went out to mail it. After I had dropped the envelope into the mailbox, I realized that I had forgotten to write my name on the back of one of the photos of me they had requested. I wonder why a college wants your picture?

We had our first Epsilons pledge meeting tonight. We explained to them that, starting tomorrow, pledging would go into effect. One of the changes this year is that we're not allowed to make them do exercises. Before, it had been a tradition that whenever any active saw a pledge on the street, he could make him do pushups or situps or whatever. But C.W. Jones got wind of that, and even though none of it went on inside the school building, he threatened to close all high school fraternities and sororities down if it continued.

So mainly we told them that it was their responsibility to learn the names of all the actives, and to carry chewing gum with them at all times. When an active asks a pledge for a stick of gum, the pledge has got to have one, or he gets demerits.

OCTOBER 5

I was supposed to have my picture taken down at the *Columbus Dispatch* after school; they're doing a story on a high school journalism conference that is coming up, and they wanted editors of two local high school papers for the picture. It was supposed to be me and some girl from Worthington.

I didn't want to get dressed up in the morning, because we had gym class. We went outside to play football. I did okay; nothing spectacular.

I went home at noon and put on a tie and jacket. I wore them back to school with a pair of white Levi's.

I was walking down the hallway and C.W. called out my name. He said that I wasn't allowed to wear Levi's to school. I tried to tell him that there was a difference between blue Levi's—blue jeans—and white Levi's or black Levi's. I tried to convince him that it was really blue jeans he was opposed to, not other kinds of Levi's. I thought the white Levi's looked great with the sport coat.

"I don't want to hear about it," C.W. said. "Wear those to school again and I'll send you home with the rest of the babies."

In the hallways I passed Kathy Michaels twice. The first time I thought she was looking at me, so I said hi, but got no response from her. The second time she looked at me, but showed no sign of recognition. That's so strange, after she talked to Jack and me in the car on Saturday.

At the *Dispatch* they took two or three pictures of the Worthington editor—Anne Hill—and me reading a copy of the *Dispatch*. In one of the pictures they posed me in a semi-profile position. With my luck they'll run that one and people will crack on my nose.

Went to all four class floats at night. I guess I'll be doing that every night for the next couple of weeks. I looked for Kathy Michaels at the freshman float, without letting anyone know that's what I was doing. But she wasn't there.

OCTOBER 6

TOOK an early shower, because Dad's been bitching that I've been making him late because I spend too much time in the bathroom in the morning. My hair's the longest it's been in a heck of a long time.

We had lab all period during Physics, and then I used a study hall to work on the *Torch*. In the hallway, Lindy came up and said that she had to talk to me after school. I had no

idea what that was about, and I never found out, because she
wasn't around after school.

Dan and I rode on his Honda. We went to Chuck's, and
watched the very first "Superman" on a TV rerun. At night
Dan and I took his Honda to all the floats. Kathy Michaels
was at hers this time, and she talked to both Dan and me.
She knew our names.

She knew our names? What a dumb thing to feel good
about. We're seniors, and she's a freshman, and here I am
being happy that she knows our names.

OCTOBER 7

BEFORE the homeroom bell this morning I went up to the
third-floor hallway—freshman hall—to get gum from the
pledges. I walked past the lockers, and every time I saw an
Epsilons pledge, I asked him for a piece of gum.

I was talking to David Weston—Eddie Weston's little
brother, who's a freshman—and I turned around, and Kathy
Michaels was standing a few feet away. I waved to her, did
a double take, and then waved again.

Later in the day I was walking between classes, and we
passed in the hallway. We gave each other glances like we
had something going. I wish we did.

We still haven't had our *El Cid* test in English. All I know
about the book is what I read in Mike Melton's plot summary.
If I screw this one up, my whole English world could con-
ceivably cave in.

In Physics class Dave Frasch, Tim Greiner, and I made a
chart counting down the days until the end of the first semester.

Went to the floats again at night. When I got home, "Shindig" was on TV, with a film of the Beatles in London singing
a new song: "I'm a Loser." It's a great song, but I kept
thinking about how strange it is for the Beatles to sing some-

thing like that. It's easy for a high school kid to identify with—but what do the Beatles know about being losers?

OCTOBER 8

WE voted for Homecoming court today. I saw Dianne Kushner after the voting, and we talked for a while. There is not a thing that would do more for my ego than for her to pick me as her escort. But I could never tell her that, and I think it's a foregone conclusion that she'll pick somebody else.

At night Dan and Chuck and I got some 6 percent Pabst Blue Ribbon beer. We each had a couple, and we were feeling pretty good.

We were talking, and Chuck said that Craig Brandon had been going around saying that Mike Robins was looking for me. Brandon was telling people that Robins wanted to fight me. Robins is captain of the swimming team, and a member of Epsilons; I had no idea why he was after me, but I'd heard it other places, too.

We finished our beers, and we went to the senior float. We walked up Judy Furman's driveway, where everybody was working on the float, and the first person I saw was Mike Robins, walking out of the garage. He was wearing his letter jacket.

I was still feeling a little high from the beer, and I walked up to him and said, "I hear you been looking for me."

"Any time, Greene," he said.

And I slugged him in the face.

Looking back on it now, I can't believe I did it. I didn't say a word to him; I just slugged him. He put his hand up to his mouth, which was bleeding.

"You sucker-punched me," he said. "You sucker-punched me."

The real fight was just about ready to start, when I said:

"You're right. I sucker-punched you. That was a cheap shot."

And then I said, "Take your best shot at me."

"What do you mean?" he said.

"I'll stand here, and take your best punch at me," I said.

Chuck said, "Greene, are you crazy? He'll kill you."

Mike Robins is about twice as big as I am. Everyone who was watching thought I was being brave or noble or something, but actually my thinking was the opposite. I figured if we got in a real fight, he'd have me on the ground in a minute and destroy me. If I let him take one punch, then it would all be over, and I'd look good for letting him do it.

"Are you serious?" Robins said.

"Yeah," I said. "I was wrong to just punch you. Let's even it out."

"Okay," Robins said.

"Don't do it," Chuck was saying.

But I stood in the light that was coming out of the garage, and I put both of my hands behind my back and clasped them.

"Take your best shot," I said. "One punch."

So Robins stood right in front of me. Everyone was gathered around. A lot of people had their heads turned.

"I can't watch," Chuck said.

Robins wound up, put the full weight of his body behind the punch, and slammed his fist into my jaw. I was afraid it was going to break, but it didn't. That old line about "seeing stars" is really true; everything was flashing in front of my eyes. I felt myself teetering on my feet, but I was determined not to go down, and I didn't. I stood there for a couple of seconds, regaining my sense of balance, and then I put out my hand to him, and we shook hands.

Everyone was talking about what had just happened. I went home and a new Supremes song, "Baby Love," was playing on WCOL.

OCTOBER 9

DURING fourth period C.W. came onto the loudspeaker and announced the five girls who will be the Homecoming court:

Dianne Kushner, Joyce Knupke, Susan Bryant, Arloa Shultz, and Nancy Glick.

Then, during fifth period, I saw Dianne and congratulated her. She said, "Who should I pick for an escort? I have to decide." She keeps saying that to me; doesn't she know?

Saw Kathy Michaels in the lounge at noon. Her hair was different—she was wearing it pinned up. I asked her about the floats, and she said she wouldn't be at hers tonight.

After school I ran into her again, and said hi. She said hi back, but like she didn't really want to. If only I could do more than say hello to her.

That high school journalism convention began tonight at Ohio State. I went, and got home at eleven o'clock. Jack called; Susan Bryant has asked him to be her escort for Homecoming. Jack's my best friend, but somehow the news made me feel three times as bad.

Why can't Dianne just ask me? It's not like she would be giving off the signal that we were going together or anything. I feel like a damn goon—can't get a freshman, want a queen.

OCTOBER 10

THE main day of the high school journalism convention was today. I got up at seven, and picked up Jon Kaplan and Jack to give them a ride up to campus.

The big event of the day was a bunch of tours and interviews that we were supposed to write about, and then have judged for contests. My tour was of the *Lantern*, the Ohio State student newspaper; Jack took a tour of the athletic department facilities.

Then we went back to a room in the Ohio Union to write our stories. I was working on mine, and Jack came up and said he didn't know what to write. So I asked him what his tour had been like, and he told me. I wrote a two-paragraph opening for him; I said, "Just finish it from there. They won't judge anything past the lead, anyway."

Later on there was a press conference where we all interviewed an Ohio State professor, and had to write that up for the contests, too. Late in the afternoon, all the high school journalists gathered in a banquet hall, and they announced the winners.

I got a first place and a third place. But the thing that made me the happiest was that Jack got a second place, using my two paragraphs and then filling in the rest of the story. It made me want to laugh; isn't life a joke? I didn't even go on his tour, and I just had him explain to me what it was about—and based on that, he still did better than all but one other person in his category. I was prouder of the award for doing Jack's story than my own.

Anne Hill, the Worthington girl I posed with for the *Dispatch* picture, was sitting next to me during the awards ceremonies. I had heard that she was drinking last night; after I won my two awards she bet me that I'd win a third one. I didn't think I would, so she said, "What do you want to bet?" We talked about it, and she said, "If you win a third award, we'll go out drinking together."

I didn't get an award, but she said, "Let's do it sometime anyway." I said okay, and she said, "Don't forget or back down."

It didn't mean anything, and we'll probably never do it, but it made me feel really good. There's something about that kind of flirtation that can't be beat.

OCTOBER 11

FOR years there's been a rumor around Columbus—that if you drive out of Bexley at night, and take Cassady out to Fifth Avenue near the railroad tracks, and stand in a certain phone booth, a girl will come along and pick you up.

In most of the versions of the story, the girl is a whore. You're not supposed to make a phone call in the booth. You're just supposed to stand there, and wait for the girl to pull up in a car.

We've talked about it a lot, but we've never done anything about it. But tonight Jack said he wanted to try it.

So Chuck and Dan and Jack and I got in Chuck's car, and we drove out Cassady, and we parked so that we were just out of sight of the phone booth. The deal was that Jack would go wait in the booth, and we would be looking to see what happened.

Jack hopped out of the car and walked up to the booth. He got inside and stood there. At first he had the door to the phone booth closed, but then he opened it up so that the cars on the street could see more easily that there was someone in there.

We waited. And waited. And waited. Forty-five minutes went by, and no girl came. Jack stood there very patiently. Some of the time he would look at the telephone. Some of the time he would look out toward Fifth Avenue. But no car even slowed down.

Finally he got back into Chuck's car, and we went to the floats.

OCTOBER 12

THIS morning C.W. got on the loudspeakers and said that he wanted the president of every class to report to his office.

Apparently someone had painted "Class of '66" on the school parking lot, and C.W. was trying to get to the bottom of it.

C.W.'s such a strange person; for all his hard-guy attitude, he really cares about Bexley High School. I always get the feeling that he doesn't want any of us students to think of him as a person; there's a real distance that he tries to keep between him and us, and he seems more comfortable having people fear him than having them like him.

The thing this morning, for example; now how does C.W. seriously expect to find out who painted the parking lot by calling the class presidents in? In the first place, whoever painted the parking lot was obviously a junior; the juniors are the class of '66. So why does C.W. want to talk to *all* the class presidents?

And in the second place, no one is going to tell him who painted the lot. The worst thing that can happen to a person in this school is for word to get out that you've snitched to C.W. Jones about something.

But that's how he operates. He sees "Class of '66" written on the parking lot, and he takes it personally. Someone is defacing the school. His school.

I played great in football in gym today. I intercepted two passes for touchdowns. They were both called back because of penalties, but the penalties weren't my fault; I wasn't even involved in them. Coach DeJong, who's also the gym teacher, said, "Nice going, Greene." Made me feel good.

Made the usual rounds of the floats at night, but no Kathy Michaels.

OCTOBER 13

GREAT! Things are really looking up.

I went to the freshman hallway to get gum from our pledges, but I didn't see Kathy Michaels. I checked the absence list later in the morning, and her name wasn't on it.

I saw her in the lounge at noon, but we didn't talk. Seventh period I had to go to the printer's to okay the layouts for this month's *Torch*. Then at night there was an Epsilons meeting. It was lousy; there were only seven or eight people there, because everyone was at the floats.

After Epsilons Dan and I went to the freshman float. We got out of the car, and Kathy and Lindy came over to talk to us. It was a very strange feeling—all of those emotions at once. Lindy, who has meant more to me than anybody in my life, and Kathy, who I'd like to go with—mainly because I don't have Lindy anymore.

Lindy offered Kathy a piece of gum, and Kathy said, "I want a *green* piece," and smiled at me. The four of us sort of drifted apart, and I was walking around the float and Lindy stopped me.

She told me that Kathy had a crush on me. I couldn't figure out why she was telling me that; she didn't seem to be conveying the message for Kathy, and she didn't seem to be saying it just as gossip. I asked her if Kathy had a date to Homecoming this Friday (I still don't), and she said that Kathy was going out with some Tweed—a guy named Mark English who Lindy said is just a "good friend."

I took Dan home, and I was going to go home myself, but then I decided that I wanted to go back to the freshman float. Kathy was standing on the sidewalk in front of the house where the float was being built. As soon as I got out of the car, she came up to me, smiling. I asked her if she wanted to go for a ride, and she said sure.

We cruised all around Bexley. We drove for about an hour. Near the end, I drove to Chuck's house, and parked the car in the place where his driveway turns around—the same place I used to sit and talk with Lindy. Kathy and I held hands; I don't know if she really likes me or just has a crush on me, but she sure brownied. I told her that I liked her hair long better than the way she was wearing it tonight (she had it pinned up again). She told me she'd wear her hair "my way" tomorrow.

I drove her home, and she said we should meet in the freshman hallway tomorrow morning. I was really floating. I went back to Chuck's, and he and I went to McDonald's to end the evening.

OCTOBER 14

I walked up the stairs to the freshman hallway, and Kathy was waiting for me. We walked down the hall together while I got gum from the pledges. She had washed her hair and was wearing it long; she said, "Do you approve?"

Then it was time to go to homeroom. Her older brother Jerry is in my homeroom; we seldom talk, but he came over to me and said, "My sister was in a daze last night. You

really set her up. She couldn't do her homework or anything—
just talk about you.''

I kept thinking about how nice it had been—sitting together
holding hands and talking quietly.

We had a hard History test, and then at noon in the lounge
Kathy came up to me and said, ''What did my brother tell
you?'' She was kidding around, but it's obvious that she found
out that Jerry had told me stuff she didn't want him to repeat.

Then I was walking to class, and Lindy stopped me. She
said that she had heard I had taken Kathy to Chuck's driveway
last night. ''You shouldn't take other people there,'' she said.
''It's our place.'' Just like that—as if the whole last year hadn't
happened.

Dianne Kushner asked Bill Caplan, the senior class president, to be her escort for Homecoming. If it weren't for the
events of the past twenty-four hours I'd probably be depressed, but right now I don't care.

After school I was driving over to Chuck's, and I saw Lindy
on Cassingham. She waved me over and asked if she could
ride with me. She got in, and then she asked me if she could
wear my class ring while we drove, so I let her. Very strange.

''Shindig'' was great tonight. Then, at ten after ten, Lindy
called. She didn't dial for cake; she just called and asked for
me.

She said that Chet Crosby had become furious when he
heard that she had gone riding with me today. She said that
he had told her that he was going to drop her.

She also said that Mark English, the Tweed, was not just
a ''good friend'' of Kathy's—she said they have been dating
steadily for quite a while.

And then she said that she got jealous when I was with
other girls.

What exactly does she want?

OCTOBER 15

HAD a hard History test in the morning. A little more study would have helped.

At noon I saw Kathy coming down the stairs from the freshman hallway. I asked her if she was still going out with Mark English, the Tweed, tomorrow night. She said she was trying her best to get out of it.

We had a quiz in Physics, and Mr. Hughes said that all the quizzes this six weeks would combine to count as much as one test grade. Then Mr. Ridenour let Tim Greiner, Dave Frasch, and me come into his classroom and watch the World Series on television. Ridenour's really a good guy.

I saw Lindy in the hallway. She reached into her purse—and pulled out her lemon bottle to show to me. She is really reacting strangely to this thing with Kathy.

When I got home after school, there was a letter from Bev! She said she'd be coming to Columbus to shop at Lazarus on Saturday, and that she'd call me when she got to town. I can't believe it.

At night there was the bonfire at the football stadium to announce the Homecoming queen. First all of the senior football players were introduced. Then the five members of the Homecoming court were seated on a big wooden platform.

We were all in the stadium. They made the announcement: "The Bexley High School Homecoming queen for 1964 is . . . Dianne Kushner!"

The other four girls jumped on her to congratulate her, and everyone poured out of the stands. The bonfire was lit on the dirt part of the baseball diamond. Chuck and Dan and I were walking over to the bonfire, when I saw Kathy.

I went up to her, and we watched the bonfire together. It was a warm night for October; Kathy was wearing shorts and a sweater. After we had stood by the bonfire for a few minutes, I said, "Let's go."

I had parked Mom's station wagon on Stanwood; we got in the front seat and I started to cruise around Bexley. At first she sat sort of close to the door, but I put my arm up on the seat, and she moved right next to me.

We had been driving and talking for about fifteen minutes, and then I said, "Wanna stop for a minute?"

She said, "I don't care."

I parked on a street next to Commonwealth Park. We started making out, and kept it up for fifteen or twenty minutes. She is just so pretty. My friends have been teasing me that she has no body—meaning she's flat-chested—but she is really a beautiful girl.

After a while she said that she'd better get over to the freshman float, where she was supposed to be. I dropped her there, and then went to the senior float. I hung around with Jack, Chuck, and Dan until about twelve-thirty, then went home. I feel on top of the world.

OCTOBER 16

THINGS just couldn't be going any better. When I got to school this morning, Kathy was waiting by my locker. She said that she had broken her date with Mark English, and that if I still wanted to go to Homecoming with her tonight, she could go. Of course I said yes.

The *Torch* came out, and everyone was reading it. I passed Lindy in the hallway, and she was very polite and formal. I figure she must have heard about last night.

At noon in the lounge, Kathy had us stand back-to-back so we could measure up next to each other. She said she had to decide whether to wear heels or not tonight. Then I bought tickets to the Homecoming dance for us, and a ticket to the football game for her. I already had mine.

I got a 100 on a Physics quiz—with the help of Mr. Hughes, who answered a question for me in the middle of taking the quiz. Then after school Dan and I went out on his Honda and saw all four of the finished floats.

Dan and I watched the parade early in the evening. Dianne looked terrific as she rode in the queen's convertible. When you grow up in Bexley, your image of the Homecoming queen is always formed from the pictures you see in the *Bexleo*. Even when you're a little kid, you get hold of the yearbook and turn to the pages where the queen and her court are featured. They always seem so old and so gorgeous. It's hard to believe that now it's our turn—we're the seniors, and we have our own queen, and she is every bit as glamorous as all the queens in the old *Bexleos*. I felt good for Dianne.

Dan and I doubled, and we picked the girls up—he had a date with Melanie Frank. The four of us sat together in the stands. Kathy and I held hands the whole game. It got to the point where I didn't know whether I should stop or not—a whole football game is a long time to hold somebody's hand. But if I stopped, I figured she might think I didn't like her or something. I sensed she was thinking the same thing. So we just kept holding hands until the game was over. Bexley won.

We took the girls home so that they could change into their good clothes for the dance. While we waited for them, Dan and I went to his house; he had a beer and I had three-fourths of a beer. Then we went back to pick the girls up again.

At the dance Kathy really looked the greatest. We did the Jerk when the music was fast, and danced every slow dance. For a while we went out of the gym and into the lounge and sat and held hands some more. I felt proud to be with her.

When the dance was over the four of us went to HoJo's East for food. When we finished I drove to Kathy's house, and walked her to the door. She said, "Thanks for a really wonderful time," and we kissed at the door for a long time.

OCTOBER 17

I slept late after last night, and at eleven o'clock this morning Mom knocked on my door to wake me up. She said there was a phone call for me.

"It sounds like a woman," she said, and she had a quizzical expression on her face.

I got out of bed and went to the phone. It was Bev.

"I'm in town," she said.

I pulled the phone into my room and closed the door. It

was unbelievable—hearing her voice. She said she was calling from a pay phone at Lazarus, and that she wanted to know if she could see me.

I tried to completely wake up, and I tried to figure out what to do. Mom and Dad would be going to the Ohio State football game at about noon. Debby was already out with her friends, and I knew that Timmy would be gone by early afternoon, too.

"Do you want to come over?" I said.

"Is that possible?" Bev said.

"Yeah," I said. "Nobody's going to be home." I gave her directions to our house.

I took a shower and got dressed and waited. I was pretty nervous. I didn't know what to expect. I sat in the den and watched "Dance-O-Rama" and then "The Lloyd Thaxton Show." Every few minutes I would look at the clock, and then go to the front windows and look out toward the street.

At two-thirty I saw her car coming down Bryden Road slowly, as she looked for the right address. She was driving her husband's green Austin-Healey; she had told us all about the car when we were at Cedar Point. Finally she found our house, put the car in neutral, gunned it for a moment, and then turned off the ignition.

I watched her get out of the car. It was Bev, all right. She was wearing a short silk dress with dark patterned hose and high heels. As she walked up to our front door, I found myself breathing irregularly. Was this really happening?

She rang. I answered.

And there we were—standing there. Finally I moved out of the way and let her in.

But we were still just standing there—right inside the front door, at the foot of the stairs.

"Hi," she said.

"Hi," I said.

It was apparent that she wasn't going to make the first move—after all, it wasn't her house—so I walked back to the den, and she followed me. We sat on the two chairs—the ones that Mom and Dad sit on when they watch the news at night.

It was very difficult. The television was still on, and we alternated between talking and looking at it. At one point I said, "Would you like something to eat?" and she said, "No, thanks, I ate downtown."

We talked about anything we could think of—my life in school, her life in her town. During the summer, up at Cedar Point and Gem Beach, I only saw her in shorts or swimming suits or jeans. Now that she was sitting here in her fancy dress, it was all the more obvious how much older than me she was.

I think we were both getting uncomfortable. It struck me that maybe I should reach out to hold her hand, or ask her if she wanted to go upstairs. But I really didn't feel like doing that. This was so different than that last night at Cedar Point. For one thing, the sun was streaming through the windows, and sitting there in the light didn't seem all that conducive to romance. And I *couldn't* just ask her to go upstairs. I kept thinking: What if Mom and Dad were to see me right now?

Finally I said, "Do you want to go see Jack?"

Bev smiled, as if relieved. "That would be great," she said.

So we went through the kitchen, and I got the keys to Mom's car off the key rack by the back door, and we got into the car and drove over to Jack's. I honked the horn and he came out. He couldn't believe it, either. I mean, think about it—I show up at Jack's house in Mom's station wagon, just like I do almost every day of our lives, and who's sitting with me in the front seat but Bev. I think Jack actually slapped his hand against his forehead.

He got in the back seat, and for the next hour or so we cruised around Bexley. It was much easier than before; we all had plenty to say, and there wasn't that tension that was there when we were alone at my house. I think that both Bev and I realized that we had probably gotten ourselves into a situation there was no easy way out of, and now things were okay again.

It's funny how your life changes so quickly; it wasn't so long ago that the thought of having Bev alone at my house would have been my idea of heaven. But when she was there, all I could think about was what a remarkable distance there was between summer and now. Once in a while, as I drove around Bexley, I would glance over at Bev. She was smiling a sort of private smile.

I dropped Jack off back at his house, and took Bev back to my house. She said she'd better be heading home. I walked her out to the Austin-Healey; I wondered if any of the neighbors were looking. We didn't kiss goodbye or anything. I just said that it had been good to see her, and she said it had been good to see me, and she got in the car and drove off.

Around five o'clock I called Kathy. She seemed glad to hear from me. She said that she had to baby-sit tonight, but if I wanted to come over I could.

So I had dinner with Mom and Dad and Debby and Timmy, and then I went to Kathy's. There was a fire going in her living room; her little sister was already upstairs in bed. We sat on the couch, and I put my arm around her, and with the lights out we listened to WCOL and kept an ear out to make sure her sister didn't come down to explore. We talked and we kissed. WCOL was playing three new records—"Dance, Dance, Dance" by the Beach Boys, and two sides of a new Beatles single: "She's a Woman" and "I Feel Fine." Once in a while I thought about Bev driving back to her hometown, but mostly I thought about Kathy.

OCTOBER 18

WHEN I woke up it was as if yesterday hadn't happened. Mom and Dad were eating in the breakfast room, and Debby was on the phone, and Timmy was running around the living room. Had Bev really been here? It didn't seem possible. Mom asked me what I was thinking about, and I said nothing.

I drove down to the *Citizen-Journal* and gave a recommendation form for Northwestern to Bill Moore, and asked him to fill it out. Standing there in the city room gave me the same kind of funny feeling that waking up in our house had this morning. Did I really used to work here every day? Time goes by so fast.

* * *

Watched the Browns play the Dallas Cowboys on TV, and then I played some records and talked to Chuck and Dan on the phone. It seems that Pongi got into some kind of tussle with a man over on Dale Avenue. I guess Pongi was driving too fast and squealed up to a stop sign, and the man yelled at him from his front yard, and Pongi jumped out of his car and tried to back the man down. All in a day's Bexley entertainment.

Mom cooked steak and spaghetti for us for dinner. The Animals were on "Ed Sullivan," but they only got to sing one song before they were cut off by a speech by President Johnson.

OCTOBER 19

EASY French and History tests this morning, and then I played pretty good in football in gym. At noon I sat with Kathy in the lounge; we said we'd give each other notes after sixth period.

So during Physics I wrote her a note—one side of a page. When we traded in the hallway after class, hers to me was three pages. At the end of it she said that she'd write me a longer one tomorrow.

I went home and called her at five o'clock. We talked for about fifteen minutes, but then Dad got home from work and told me that I had to get off the phone, because he had to talk to me.

He asked me if I had gotten Mom a birthday present yet— her birthday is tomorrow—and I said no. He bawled me out, so after dinner Dan and I went over to Rogers' Drugstore and I got her something.

The Blackboard Jungle is on TV tonight. I'll watch that and write a note to give Kathy in the morning.

OCTOBER 20

KATHY gave me an *eight-page* note before school!

I really like this—our trading notes in the hallways. It's a sure way of knowing that we're thinking of each other during the day. Usually you have to guess—does a girl like you? What does she say to her friends behind your back? Are you bugging her too much?

But with the notes, you know where you stand. It doesn't matter exactly what's in the notes—the fact is, she took the time to write them to you, so you must mean something to her. I love it when she hands me the note, all folded up, and then I stick it in my back pocket and take it to the next class where I can read it in private.

After school Jack showed me this place he found—the Hideout. It's way north on Cassady, past the Bexley limits, past the railroad tracks, on the way to Winding Hollow Country Club.

That's mostly wooded area and farmland out there. We got in his car, and as we were driving he slowed down. There was something sticking out of the woods that looked like a driveway. It was just dirt, but it led to somewhere.

Jack took a right and we turned into it. The driveway went for about twenty yards back into the woods. Then there was the remains of a chimney—like a house had been there once, but had burned down or something. The driveway made a circle around the chimney—you could slowly steer your car all the way around it, and then head back toward Cassady. Once you were in there, there was no way anyone could see you from the road.

Jack said it's the perfect place to park with a girl. He's already done it. You're completely alone—no cop is going to come by and shine his flashlight in your car. And since you have to really look to see the dirt driveway, nobody else is going to know about it. I've been driving on Cassady for years, and I never noticed it.

We got out of the car and explored the area for a few minutes. I don't know who must have lived back here. But it's totally overgrown now—except for the old chimney and the dirt path that winds around it.

At night I went to the library to study, and Kathy was there. We went right up to each other, and I asked her how much she had to study. She said not very much.

I told her about the Hideout, and asked her if she'd like to see it. She said yes.

So we went to Mom's station wagon, and I drove through Bexley, and then out Cassady. I had to drive real slow—it's dark on that road, and I didn't want to miss the driveway.

I turned into it, and edged the car forward. The bushes and overgrowth on both sides were scraping against the car. Then the headlights focused on the chimney. I drove all the way around the chimney, so that the car was pointed out toward Cassady.

We were there for about an hour. We talked and kissed; at one point I put my hand under the back of her sweater, and it ended up beneath her bra strap. She thought that I was trying to reach around toward her front, and she took my hand away. She didn't seem mad about it, though. Finally we both had to get home. So I slowly worked the car out to Cassady again, and we were gone.

I wouldn't mind spending every night like this.

OCTOBER 21

KATHY was waiting by my locker this morning, and handed me a note, which started the day out right. Got a B— and a C+ in English, but then I really shone in History. In French language lab, I wrote Kathy a note back.

I was carrying it in my pocket at noon, when I saw her sitting in the lounge with Steve Gutter, a junior who's in Epsilons. They seemed to be having a deep discussion.

She saw me across the room, and walked up to me.

She said, "Promise you won't be mad if I ask you this?"

I was sure she was going to say that Gutter had asked her out, and that she wanted to know if I'd mind if she went.

But then she said, "I've heard that you're using me. Is it true?"

I told her that it wasn't. I wonder who's telling her that; was Gutter saying that?

Next period I wrote her a long note telling her not to believe it when people said stuff like that. I said that the only thing that should matter was how we felt when we were together. Other people were just trying to start trouble.

I also wondered whether Lindy was behind any of this.

In study hall they were passing around a "Purity Test." You were supposed to fill out how far you've gone with members of the opposite sex. The last question on it was about "going all the way." Chuck's still the only one of us who can honestly say yes to that one.

After sixth period Kathy gave me a great note, so I guess things are okay there. Went home after school, and at dinner Mom and Dad asked me if I'd go out with some girl on Saturday night—the daughter of a relative. I said that I had a date with Kathy.

After dinner Jack and I went to the TAT for poor boys. I just got home again; I'll write Kathy a note and then go to bed.

OCTOBER 22

KATHY and I exchanged notes before school again today. That's really something that makes me want to get there in the morning. Usually I hate getting out of bed and getting up. But now I go to school with the expectation of our note exchange.

We usually pass each other in the hallway before fourth period. I didn't see her today, but one of her friends, Terri Colton, passed me and said, "Kathy said to say hi."

I really like this—going with her and having other people know that I go with her.

We exchanged notes at noon, and then again sixth period. She really wrote good today.

After school Pauline Taynor called and said that the new *Junior Prom*s had just been printed. She said that she had used my column, and that she would drop off an issue at my house tonight.

She did, and it really looked great. The column is called "Speaking Out." There is a big picture of me—my senior picture—and my by-line. You definitely can't miss it. I just hope Judy Furman doesn't screw up the circulation when the issues get to school.

Tonight I read some Physics and wrote a report about it. Then I wrote Kathy a note for tomorrow morning. I'm really tired, but now I have to do some History.

OCTOBER 23

I felt crappy all day because I took a Contac in the morning and it made me drowsy. At noon in the lounge I sat with Kathy, and she was in a bitchy mood. We were mean to each other.

After school I went to Chuck's house to watch "Superman," then went over to Dan's. His parents weren't home; he had something called Colt .45, which comes in a can like beer, and looks like beer, and sort of tastes like beer, but which he says is much more powerful than beer. It's malt liquor; we split a can.

I went home, showered, and changed clothes, and picked Kathy up to take her to the Bexley football game. It was freezing; we held hands and I hinted about leaving the game and going to the Hideout, but she said no.

The dance afterwards was poor. When it was over I asked her if she was hungry, and she said, "I don't feel well." I drove out to the Hideout and we were there for about an hour. It was great—but in the back of my mind I had the feeling that she wasn't all there. I don't know what that means.

OCTOBER 24

THE day started like a typical Saturday. I got up at eleven, went over to the barber shop and got a bad haircut, then went home and ate lunch and watched "Lloyd Thaxton." Chuck and I cruised for a while, and then I called Kathy. She had said yesterday that her parents were going out tonight, and that I could come over; now she said she wasn't sure if they were going out, and that I should call later.

Mom and Dad had some guests for dinner, which made it longer than usual. Some of them were relatives of Dad's; he asked me to take them to another house in Bexley where they wanted to see some people, so I did. I went to Dan's; he and Chuck were having Colt .45s, and I had one with them.

Then I called Kathy. She said her parents had gone out after all, and that I could come over. I got there, and we sat on the couch and put records on and kissed a little. But then her two brothers barged in. They had gotten some six-packs of beer. Her two brothers and I had some—even Kathy had one, and she's only a freshman. She told me she'd had beer before.

Her brother who's my age, Jerry, said he was going over to his girlfriend's house. He asked us if we wanted to come along. Since her other brother was going to stay home, ruining our privacy, we said yes.

Jerry's girlfriend's parents weren't home. The four of us went into their den and turned the lights out and sat on couches. Jerry started making out with his girlfriend, and I started making out with Kathy.

It was great, as usual, but I thought something was really weird. Here I was making out with Kathy—and on the other couch, ten feet away, her brother Jerry was making out, too. It made me a little uncomfortable—I don't understand how they can do that in front of each other. It didn't seem to bother Kathy or Jerry. But if I was in a room with a girl, and my younger sister Debby was on the other couch making out with a guy, I would feel really creepy. I mean, I assume she does that, but I don't want to know about it. And I certainly don't want to see it.

Kathy was much friendlier tonight than she was last night. Right now I like her an awful lot. I am one very happy guy.

OCTOBER 25

DAN came over and woke me up at ten forty-five. The two of us went to the Pancake House for breakfast, then went out to the Hideout on his Honda to check it out in daylight.

We cleaned it up—there were beer bottles and beer cans and liquor bottles all over the place. It took us about twenty minutes to clear all the junk off the dirt driveway. It's obvious that we're not alone out there—all that stuff wasn't ours.

Went to Chuck's to watch the Browns game. Then I cruised for the rest of the afternoon. I kept listening for "Dance, Dance, Dance"—everyone's going crazy over that song. WCOL finally played it at four-thirty.

The Rolling Stones were on "Ed Sullivan." They're pretty disgusting. I started writing a column for *Junior Prom* about them. Speaking of *Junior Prom*, the new edition with my first column should be on sale at school tomorrow. I hope a lot of people see it.

Called Kathy at night. She was okay, but a little distant and a little flippant. I may have to cool it with her for a while.

I don't want to, though. I really like her. I don't tell anyone what I do with her—that's between her and me.

OCTOBER 26

I talked to Kathy on the third floor when I went up there to get gum from the pledges. She was friendly, but not as good as usual. That worries me.

* * *

At noon *Junior Prom* went on sale in the lounge, and they sold about a hundred of them. A lot of people were carrying them around.

I got a 100 on a Physics quiz sixth period. On the way out of the class I sneaked a look into Mr. Hughes' gradebook, which was lying open on his desk. I got a B for the six weeks! That makes me feel great.

Looked for Kathy after school, but she wasn't around. Dan and I went over to Chuck's. His dad was at work and his mom wasn't home, so we each had a bourbon and Coke. It was delicious, and we were all feeling pretty high. Dan and I rode out to the Hideout again on his Honda, and we fell off as we turned into the entrance. We were sprawled out on the ground, and we couldn't stop laughing.

Mom asked me to go over to Rogers' Drugstore after dinner to get an assignment book for Timmy for school. When I got back I called Kathy. She was really wising off a lot on the phone—I didn't like it. But when we had hung up I wrote a nice two-page note to give to her tomorrow morning.

OCTOBER 27

BEFORE school I exchanged notes with Kathy. I told her that she was in a bitchy mood; she said that I was.

In her note she said that Lindy had given her all the memory stuff that she had saved from me. Kathy said that Lindy thought that Kathy should have all of that now.

During seventh-period study hall I wrote a new column for the November issue of *Junior Prom* about the first anniversary of President Kennedy's death. It's really an emotional column. It starts out, "It has been a year now, and being young, we tend to forget." I really think I did a good job on it.

* * *

After school I saw Lindy. I asked her what she thought she was doing, giving our stuff to Kathy. She said she thought I'd want it that way. I told her to get the stuff back.

Late in the afternoon I was cruising down Cassingham and I saw Kathy walking home with Joe Thiebert, a junior. They were laughing and talking. She put her hand on him, and then he grabbed her, and then she pushed him away, but they were kidding around while they did it, and obviously having a good time. I hoped they didn't notice my car.

I went to Chuck's house. His older brother Bill was there, and he asked me to go to the drugstore and get cigarettes for him. I did, and when I came back I told him what was going on with Kathy, and I asked him what he thought I should do.

"The biggest mistake you can ever make is to let a girl know you have emotions toward her," Bill said. "Once she knows that, she's got you."

I said that Kathy already knew I cared a lot about her.

"Then she's in control," Bill said. "The only way for you to regain control is to let her think you have no emotions toward her. Then she'll want you back."

At home tonight I typed up my *Junior Prom* story about President Kennedy. I showed it to Mom and Dad, and they said they loved it. But then Jack came over, and I let him read it, and he said it was no good. I think he's just jealous.

I'm not calling Kathy tonight, per Bill Shenk's advice. And I'm not writing a note to give to her tomorrow morning. She's going to have to shape up. I'm not being a fool this time.

OCTOBER 28

TROUBLE.

When I got to school, Kathy came up to me in the first-floor hallway and asked me if I was mad at her. I told her no; I had to go back with her.

We got our six-weeks report cards. I got B's in French and English, but that damn Mr. Duffey gave me a C in History.

I walked to English class with Kathy, and gave her a note at noon. She didn't give me one.

There was an assembly in the auditorium about safe driving. Tim Greiner and Dave Frasch and I sat together and made jokes during the whole thing.

Sixth period I gave Kathy another note, in which I asked her out for Friday night, and again I didn't get one back from her.

I saw her after school, and asked her to go to the library tonight. I said I'd meet her there.

When I got home from school there was a letter from Allen at military school. I wrote him one back.

Debby and I got in a big fight after dinner. She spit on me. Mom and Dad blamed it all on me.

I went to the library. No Kathy. I waited around. Finally, I went home and called her at nine-thirty.

She said that I was bitching and sounded just like Mark English, that Tweed she went with before I came along. And she said that she might have to go out with her friends on Friday night.

I don't know what to do. Maybe she's just a weekend girl. Don't let me blow this one.

OCTOBER 29

WELL, I've done it again.

I looked for Kathy in the morning, but I didn't see her until noon. She didn't have a note for me, and I said, "Don't ever give me a note again." She walked away.

I complained about my six-weeks History grade to Mr. Duffey. He said that I was lucky to get a C.

Then, sixth period, I waited for Kathy in the hallway.

"I'm sorry for what I said at noon," I said. "Let's meet after school."

She just smiled.

So school ended, and I waited in the first-floor hallway for her to come downstairs. When she came, it was with Lindy and a bunch of other girls.

"Kathy, come here," I said.

"Wait," she said.

Jan Gebhart, one of the girls who was with her, said, "Kathy, you're mean."

Finally she came over and I said I wanted to talk with her.

"I can't right now," she said. "I have to go with Lindy." And the two of them left the school building together.

I felt like a complete fool. I went to the Toddle House with Dan, and told him the whole story. He was sympathetic, but what could he say?

At night I sat around my room, and finally I called Jack and asked him what to do. He said to just call her up and find out what was going on. I knew by calling her I'd be making myself seem even more persistent, but I had to do it.

I called. She answered.

I said, "You've been acting different."

She said, "So have you."

I took a deep breath and said, "Maybe we should call it off." I was hoping that by saying that she would tell me that she didn't want to break up.

But she said, "It probably wouldn't last anyhow. We're different. Lindy and I were told different things by you."

I had no idea what she meant by that. But obviously Lindy has gotten involved in ways I didn't know about.

"Well," I said, "I guess we'll call it off."

"Can we still be good friends?" she said.

I thought of what Bill Shenk had told me.

"I have no emotions," I said.

"You don't even want to be my friend?" Kathy said.

"I have no emotions," I said, and hung up.

I felt so low I could have cried. I know that technically I dropped her, because I brought it up first, but that didn't help the way I was hurting inside. I called Jack again, to tell him what had happened. He said that if things had gotten that bad, then it was probably better to end it sooner rather than later. Then I called Dave Frasch and told him. He said that I should just forget about it; in Physics class he and Tim Greiner have always been telling me that I was going too crazy over Kathy, anyway.

Mom and Dad were asleep in their bedroom. So I went downstairs and poured myself some orange juice from the refrigerator, and then filled the rest of the glass up with vodka from the bar in the living room. I drank it all.

I went back up to my room, pulled the phone inside, and called Lindy.

When she answered, I said, "Listen, just stay out of my life, will you?"

"Bobby?" she said. "Is something wrong?"

"Yeah," I said, and then I said goodbye.

So now I'm sitting here looking out the window. The born loser strikes again. My heart feels like it's breaking in two.

OCTOBER 30

I didn't see Kathy in the morning; I did see her at noon in the lounge, but we didn't talk.

In the hallway before fifth period, Robin Lindsey said that Kathy told her that we broke up because of Lindy. She talked as if Kathy still liked me, which gave me some hope.

After school I saw her hanging around with Bruce Byrnes, another junior who's in Epsilons, for a long time. Then I was riding on the back of Dan's Honda, and I saw her and a bunch of other girls walking home with Byrnes.

At night Jack and Chuck and Dan and I cruised in Chuck's car. We went to the Hideout and drank some beer. After that we went to Robyne Finke's house, where a bunch of people were hanging around. Pongi was there, and he wised off to Mr. Finke, and Mr. Finke threw him out.

Mike Robins came up to me and said that Kathy was going around saying that she dropped me, and that she had said that I was scum.

I didn't know whether to believe him; he might still be holding a grudge against me because of the punches we exchanged at the float that night.

But then Ned Peters said he had asked her about me, and that she had pointed thumbs down.

I don't know what to believe. I know one thing; I don't

want to make her into another Lindy goddess. But I still like her a hell of a lot, and I wish I could go back with her.

OCTOBER 31

SATURDAY. I got up at ten, played the radio for a while, and then watched "Dance-O-Rama." Dave Frasch called and said he and Tim Greiner and Kenny Stone and Eddie Weston were going to go downtown, and then up to campus. He wanted to know if I wanted to come along.

I said sure. We all bought some stuff—I got a copy of "Dance, Dance, Dance"—and then we went back to Greiner's house. Everybody was talking and kidding around, but I just sat there feeling bad.

When I got home the phone rang, and it was two girls who said they went to Westerville High School. They asked me if I was the same Bob Greene who wrote a column in *Junior Prom*.

I said I was.

"I can't believe it," one of the girls said. They were on separate phones. "We've tried half the Greenes in the Columbus phone book."

They said they really liked the column, and wanted to talk to me about it. That's such a strange feeling. I'm really not very good at breaking the ice with people, and if these girls saw me standing around a dance they probably wouldn't even look twice. But because of what I wrote, they got in touch with me. Writing is the most private thing I do—it's just me putting my words down on paper. And yet here these girls were, responding to those words. It's very hard for me to think about the beginning of the column I wrote—me sitting there in my room with the door closed, writing my thoughts down—and then to think about the end of it—these girls from halfway across the city taking the trouble of finding my phone number just so they could talk.

We stayed on the phone for a few minutes. The call reminded me that I hadn't sent the President Kennedy column to Pauline Taynor, so I went out and mailed it.

At dinnertime I went to Chuck's house, and we went to Rubino's and got a couple of carry-out-pizzas. We took them back to his house.

Bill Shenk was there with some fraternity brothers of his from Ohio State.

I told Bill that I had taken his advice about Kathy; I hadn't let her know that I had any emotions toward her. I said to him, "I dropped her even though I still liked her." I'm still saying that; still hanging onto the idea that technically I told her we should break up before she told me.

Bill looked at me sort of oddly. I got the impression that he had forgotten the whole conversation we had had.

Tonight I sat home. All I could think of was Saturday night, when Kathy and I were together. I thought of the things we did—and I thought that tonight Bruce Byrnes or Mark English or somebody would be doing the same things in the same place to the same songs. I read the notes she had given me in school, and thought about the things we'd said, and recalled the little things—like rubbing her back underneath her bra strap, and her putting her head on my shoulder in the car at the Hideout.

If only she'd come back. But she'll probably be smiling with Byrnes in the lounge at school Monday noon, and I'll be the fool. It has been quite an October, hasn't it?

NOVEMBER 1

THERE was an Epsilons football game this morning. Steve Gutter said that he and some other guys had been at Kathy's house last night. She had said that she was thinking about going back with Mark English. Gutter said that Kathy had said, "I wonder if he'll take me back."

After the game Jack and I rode around in his car. These other guys passed us in their car, and yelled "Pussy" out the window at us. I don't think they were from Bexley; we didn't recognize them.

Had steak for dinner with Mom and Dad and Debby and Timmy, then watched the Dave Clark Five on "Ed Sullivan." I kept watching TV; "The Rogues" was the best episode yet, about a rocket plant. That would be so cool, to be as suave and self-confident and debonair as David Niven and Gig Young. I bet they wouldn't sit around feeling sorry for themselves over some girl.

NOVEMBER 2

BEFORE school I went to the third-floor hallway to get gum from our pledges, just like I had done when I was meeting Kathy up there every day. She was there. I said "Hi Kath," and she waved and smiled. Nothing there—just a friendly wave, like before we went together.

I played great in football in gym. It was like I needed some outlet for the way I've been feeling—I was all over the field, both on offense and on defense. I was panting and tired out by the end of gym period, but I felt like I had let off a lot of steam.

At noon Kathy was on the pay phone in the lobby, with a lot of girls around her. Ron Shkolnik said he had seen her talking to a bunch of guys last Friday night, and that when someone brought my name up she said she "could do better." Now how am I supposed to react when someone tells me a story like that?

Dan and I cruised on his Honda after school. At dinner, Mom and Dad asked me about Kathy; they said I hadn't mentioned her in a while. I hadn't told them that we broke up. I didn't want them to get into it. So I just mumbled something.

Nighttime is the hardest. Without her to call, or to meet at the library, the hours drag by. I called Dave Frasch, Jack, Chuck, and Dan tonight, and finally I realized that I was making all those calls just to get me through to bedtime.

NOVEMBER 3

I'M completely lost in Physics, and we have a test coming up on Thursday.

After school I walked by Kathy. She said "Hi." It could have been a repulsed hi, or it could have been like before we went together. I won't interpret.

President Johnson won the election tonight.

NOVEMBER 4

ALLEN'S mother called me; she said that he was coming home from military school for the weekend, and she invited me to have lunch with her and Allen and Allen's dad on Saturday, and then to go to the Ohio State football game.

Epsilons has been talking about having a meeting devoted to civil rights, so I called a Columbus Negro civil-rights leader, Reverend Zebbs, and asked him to come talk to our meeting next Tuesday night. He said he'd be happy to do it.

Saw Kathy a few times in school today. We both said hi. After school I went to Chuck's to shoot baskets. We're planning a big party at Allen's parents' apartment on Saturday night. Chuck said I should just take a chance and ask Kathy. He said she might surprise me and say yes.

So tomorrow I'm going to ask her. If she says no, I'm not going to tell anyone but Chuck.

Gene Pitney was on "Shindig" tonight. Great.

NOVEMBER 5

TOMORROW should write the book for fall. I went up to the third floor to get gum, and Kathy wasn't there. So I went back down to senior hall, then went up there again five minutes later. She was standing by her locker.

I took a deep breath and walked up to her.

"Hi," she said.

"Hi," I said.

There were a couple of seconds' silence, and then I said, "Remember when I told you about my friend Allen, who goes to military school? And the great parties we always have at his apartment?"

"Yes," Kathy said.

"Well, he's coming into town this weekend," I said. "And we're having a party there, and I thought maybe you'd like to go."

"I don't know," she said. "It sounds like fun, but I might have to baby-sit."

"Do you know when you'll know for sure?" I said.

"I'll tell you in school tomorrow," she said.

I know she doesn't want to go. But I won't ask anybody else until tomorrow anyway, just in case.

After school Dennis MacNeil let me ride his Vespa. I had been riding for about half an hour when I passed the corner of Fair and Roosevelt—and there was Allen in his mom's car! It was so great to see him. I had him follow me so that I could give Dennis his cycle back, and then I got into Allen's car and we cruised for the rest of the afternoon.

Everything feels different when he's in town. ABCDJ is really together. For the first time since school started, today I felt like it was summer again.

Allen said that his party was going to be the best ever Saturday night—his parents are going to be out, and we're going to go crazy. I hope so much that Kathy says yes. But chances are she'll say, "I have to baby-sit," and I'll be down in the depths once again.

NOVEMBER 6

WELL, hell.

I went up to the third-floor hallway twice before school, but Kathy wasn't there either time. I told Mr. Munselle, the French teacher, that I had to go to the boys' room, but what I really did when I left class was to check the absence lists that are stuck outside the classroom doors every first period. Kathy's name wasn't on the list.

The morning was a drag, and at noon I saw Kathy in the lounge talking to Steve Gutter. I motioned her over.

"Did you decide about tomorrow night?" I said.

"I'm sorry, but I have to baby-sit," she said.

I told myself to show no emotion.

"That's okay," I said. "I have another date anyway."

I was pissed off and depressed the rest of the day. Allen showed up at school seventh period, and we all went to Pongi's after school. I knew I had to get a date, and I thought of

Tina Flaker. I hadn't talked to her since last summer, and I knew that she was back at Bishop Hartley, probably going with some guy there. But I called her number anyway.

Her mother answered. I asked for Tina, and her mother asked who was calling.

"Bob Greene," I said.

That was my first mistake. Tina's parents made it clear they didn't like me last summer, and there's no reason they should have changed their minds.

"Tina's on probation," her mother said. "She's not allowed to go out, and she's not allowed to get phone calls from boys." And she hung up.

That's a new one—being shot down by a girl's mother.

At the Bexley football game tonight Kathy was with Steve Gutter; they were doubling with Bruce Byrnes and his date. I couldn't even look.

My sister Debby was there with all of her friends. I went up to them and called Candy Grossman aside; I asked her if she would go to Allen's party with me tomorrow night. She said yes. Candy's awfully nice. She must know what I've gone through with Kathy—everyone in the school does—and it would be easy for her to say no to me just to be cool. But she didn't. I really appreciate that.

I went home after the game and played the radio as I lay in bed. "I'm a Loser" came on. The lyrics say so much: ". . . and I'm not what I appear to be . . ."

NOVEMBER 7

I got up at ten. Allen came over and we went to get pretzels and other supplies for the party. Then we drove downtown to the Athletic Club, where his mom and dad were waiting for us in the dining room.

My dad and Allen's dad were best friends when they were growing up in Akron; they both moved down to Columbus after they got old enough to work. Allen's dad owns a big towel supply company in town. It means a lot to our dads that Allen and I are friends, but the funny thing is, I think we'd be friends anyway, even if our dads never knew each other. We just have always gotten along that well.

We ate our lunch and then went to a boring Ohio State game. I remember when I was a kid, the first time I ever walked into Ohio Stadium. Before you get to the seats, you're in this dingy, dark, gray concrete area underneath the stadium. Then you walk up some concrete stairs—and you're in the middle of bright sunlight and seventy-eight thousand screaming people, wearing all the colors in the world, and down on the huge green field are the two teams. The first time I made that trip from the grayness below into the stadium itself I think it was the most thrilling thing I had ever seen. My heart started beating faster.

But I guess you get used to everything. Today we just went to our seats without thinking about it, and Allen and I bitched about how cold it was. We weren't even looking around the stadium; we were thinking about the party tonight.

I went to the Eastmoor with Jack and Al for dinner. Then I stopped off at the drugstore to get Mom and Dad an anniversary card; their anniversary's today, and they went out to dinner, so I'm going to leave it on the table in the front hallway for when they get home.

Dan has a new theory. He says that if you eat a lot of ice cream before you drink, you can handle the alcohol better. So we went to Baskin-Robbins on Main Street and each had a cone.

Allen dropped me off at my house after that. I showered and put on my white Levi's. Then I went downstairs and had about one-fourth of a bottle of vodka with orange juice, and a shot glass of Scotch and water. I was really feeling great by the time Allen picked me up again, but I was worried that Mom and Dad will notice the missing vodka.

I was so high in the car. We picked up Candy, and "Dance, Dance, Dance" came on the radio. For the first time in days I felt okay.

We got to Allen's, and eveyone showed up with their dates. I had some more vodka with orange juice, and Candy had some, too. In Allen's parents' den there is a big brass eagle over the doorway; we stuck a cigarette in the eagle's mouth.

We were all dancing and feeling terrific. Everyone was doing the jerk with their arms up in the air, dancing real close together. Then ABCDJ told the girls to sit down on the couches and chairs. We put "Dance, Dance, Dance" on the record player, and then we made a circle and put our arms over each other's shoulders. As the Beach Boys sang the song, we sang the words to a song we had made made up to the same tune: "Drink, Drink, Drink."

There was Allen; there was me; there was Chuck; there was Dan; there was Jack. We held onto each other and sang: "After five days of school, we've had enough of the class/ We get a six-pack of Colt, and get drunk on our ass . . ." And: "At a weekend dance, we never show up first/ We gotta wait a while, so we can quench our thirst . . ."

I had never felt closer to those guys. We played the record over three times, and then we started dancing with the girls again. I started feeling really drunk and spilled a whole glass of orange juice and vodka. At first it seemed great, but then all of a sudden I felt a little dizzy. I sat down. I opened the window in the den, but that didn't help.

I walked into Allen's bedroom and threw up all over the place. I just couldn't stop. I would try to get some breath, and I would throw up some more. I lay in the stuff for about two hours. People kept coming in to see if I was okay, but I felt too bad to get up.

Finally Allen said I had to do something before his parents got home. So I struggled up, and got some paper towels from the kitchen to clean up my mess. I took my clothes off and took a shower in Allen's bathroom.

When I got dressed again, it was time to go. I really felt like I had been an ass to Candy; for two hours I had left her all by herself. But she couldn't have been nicer to me; the whole way home in the car she kept asking if I was okay, and when we got to her house and I walked her to her door I tried to apologize, and she said there was nothing to apologize for. I really respect her a lot for that.

NOVEMBER 8

WHEN I got home last night I tried to be quiet going up the stairs so that Mom and Dad wouldn't see me drunk. I slept fitfully all night; I still felt horrible. At six in the morning I went to the bathroom and threw up again.

Around eight o'clock Timmy knocked on my door. He said he had gone into the bathroom and found my shoes where I had left them there last night. He said they had been covered with dried-up vomit. He told me that he had taken some Kleenex and cleaned them up so that Mom and Dad wouldn't see them before I got out of bed. He's really a pretty good little brother.

I stayed in my room most of the morning, just thinking. What's come over me? A year ago I didn't know anything about girls other than the fact that I was in love with Lindy; and a year ago I'd never even tasted a beer. Now look at me. So messed up over a girl I went with for less than a month that I get drunk on hard liquor and pass out in my own vomit. If, a year ago, I could have somehow seen forward to last night, I wouldn't have believed it.

At least I learned one thing last night: Getting that drunk may take your troubles away for a couple of hours, but the next day the troubles are still there and you feel even worse. I don't imagine it will take long for the word to spread around school about my escapade.

There's one thing I'm sure of. I will never again be able to take a sip of orange juice and vodka.

This afternoon there was a big touch football game at the school. I played and it helped get some of the poison out of my system. Already people were making jokes. Candy and some of the other sophomore girls came by. I was embarrassed seeing Candy, but all she said was, "You missed quite a party last night." She was smiling, though; she said it in a nice way.

NOVEMBER 9

AT the end of morning classes today, Allen was waiting outside the school. He drove me home for lunch, and he came
in and ate with me.

I've been going home for lunch ever since I started school.
I never liked eating in the cafeteria—although in seventh
grade, because all the other boys were doing it and thought
it was cool, I washed dishes in the junior high school lunch-
room once in a while in exchange for a free lunch. But I like
going back to my house at noon.

Mom is always there; she has sandwiches and soup ready
in the breakfast room by the time that Debby and Timmy and
I get home. Debby and Timmy have never gone in for the
cafeteria, either. Our house is only about a ten-minute walk
from the school building, so we can make it home, eat, and
make it back in plenty of time.

There's something about eating in the cafeteria—and not
leaving the high school from morning until afternoon—that
feels a little like being in jail. By the end of the morning,
I've got to get out of the building. And Mom never seems to
mind fixing lunch for us; she never suggests that we eat in
the cafeteria.

It's really the only time we have to be alone with her. In
the morning Dad's there, and by the time I get home after
messing around after school he's usually home from work.
So the times that Mom and I talk together are usually at lunch.

I sort of feel sorry for the kids who eat in the cafeteria
every day. It would drive me nuts. I don't know if their moms
just don't like to cook for them in the middle of the day, or
if they actually like the cafeteria and the cafeteria food.

Today Mom made egg salad sandwiches and tomato soup.
We gulped it down and hurried back so we could hang around
the lounge for a few minutes before afternoon classes started.

After school Allen and I went to the Toddle House for
cheeseburgers. He's going back to military school tomorrow.

Dad told me last night that I had to get another haircut. So

I got one. I thought it was pretty good, for once, but when Dad got home he said it was too long.

NOVEMBER 10

KATHY was absent for the second day in a row.

Steve Gutter, trying to get a rise out of me, said, "She must have the syph." I said, "I didn't give it to her."

Tonight was the Epsilons meeting to talk about civil rights. We had a real good turnout to hear Reverend Zebbs. But Reverend Zebbs didn't show up.

After Epsilons, Chuck and Jack and I decided to go to the Hideout. We had a six-pack of beer, and we thought it would be fun to sit around the Hideout without girls, just shooting the shit.

I had Mom's car. We drove out to Cassady, and I took the right turn into the Hideout, and inched the car up the dirt driveway—and there was another car in there! It was really spooky, being back there in the woods and finding someone else using the place. I slammed the car into reverse and got out of there fast. I think I scratched the car on the tree branches as I did it. I dropped Chuck and Jack off and went home and read the Cliffs Notes for *Macbeth*.

NOVEMBER 11

IN Physics class Dave Frasch and Tim Greiner made a rating list—names of different people in the high school who we were supposed to rate on a scale of 1 to 5, 1 being the lowest and 5 being the highest. Kathy's name was on the list and I gave her a 5. Greiner wrote in the margin, "You're hopeless, Greene."

After school I called Reverend Zebbs. He said he had completely forgotten about the Epsilons meeting last night. I said that we had another meeting next Tuesday night, and he said he would be there for sure.

Tonight Frasch, Gary Herwald, Kenny Stone, and I went up to Mershon Auditorium on the Ohio State campus to see the Kingston Trio in concert. Kenny had gotten us tickets.

Our seats weren't good—they were in the very back row—and whatever excitement I had expected to feel wasn't there. I've been listening to the Kingston Trio for years, and I thought it would be a huge kick to see them on stage. But they weren't five minutes into their show when I realized that the whole thing felt very old-fashioned.

I think the Beatles and the other English groups have ruined me for folk music. I remember back to the beginning of the year, when I used to listen to ''Hootenanny'' on WBNS radio every night—I never do that anymore. Dave is just about the only guy who still does; and he still buys chord books of folk songs to learn on his guitar.

As I was sitting there watching the Kingston Trio, I hated to admit it, but I was bored. They sang ''Tom Dooley'' and ''M.T.A'' and ''Scotch and Soda'' and all of their other hits—and all I could think about was how cool it would be to see the Beatles live, and how this wasn't even any fun. Just three guys in striped shirts with wooden guitars that weren't even electric. We got in an argument about it on the way home. Kenny agreed with me, but Dave and Gary said the concert had been great. Oh, well. At least now I can say that I've seen the Kingston Trio in person.

NOVEMBER 12

WE pissed in Donny Elias' Canoe.

Donny Elias is an obnoxious guy who has real rich parents, and even though he goes to Bexley he hangs around with Tweeds all the time. He's always acting like he's too good for the people at Bexley. We talk to him, but five minutes with him is usually enough.

For the past couple of months he's been coming to school drenched in Canoe every day. When he walks down the hallways he reeks of the stuff. And he's always talking about it; it's like he thinks he's the only guy in the world who wears Canoe. He'll say stuff like, "Canoe is made in France, you know," as if that's big news or something.

Anyway, today after classes Jack and Dan and I were hanging around outside the school, and Donny Elias came up and started talking about some tests that we're going to have next week. None of us had a car at school, so we got in Donny's car and he cruised for a while, then went to his house. We went inside with him, and sat around his bedroom.

Donny said that he had forgotten some books at school. He said he'd be right back.

So we were sitting there in the bedroom, talking about how weird it was to be at his house, and Jack looked over at Donny's dresser and said, "There's the famous bottle of Canoe." It was just sitting there.

"Yeah, it looks like piss," Dan said.

And it was like one of those cartoons, where a light bulb goes on above the character's head. In that one second we stopped talking and looked at each other and broke into big grins.

I went over to the dresser and picked up the bottle of Canoe. It sure did look like piss; the liquid was bright yellow.

We didn't have to make any plans out loud. Jack went into the hallway to make sure that Donny or his parents didn't come home. I took a piece of notebook paper and rolled it into a funnel.

Then Dan and I went into the bathroom. We held the bottle of Canoe over the toilet. First I held the funnel in place and Dan pissed into it. Then he held the funnel in place and I pissed into it. We didn't piss very much; just a few drops each. Just symbolic pisses.

We quickly screwed the white plastic cap back on the top of the bottle, and put it back on Donny's dresser. We couldn't stop laughing. In a few minutes Donny got back from school. It was really hard to keep straight faces. Donny kept making normal conversation, and we were all biting the insides of our mouths to keep from breaking up.

Finally we left his house and started walking. People who

were driving by must have thought we were nuts. We were howling the whole way, doubling over as we tried to keep from falling down.

We stopped at the school to watch basketball practice. Coach Millard nodded at us and said, "Hello, men," which made me feel good.

At night I stayed home and studied. My mind was never too far from Kathy. I thought about that first night with her, and how the next morning her brother said I had "really set her up." Boy, a lot can happen in a month.

Maybe I shouldn't fool around with crushes. Maybe I blow it instinctively. Maybe I just like the "love feeling."

But probably I like her a hell of a lot.

NOVEMBER 13

MRS. Barr got mad at us in English today and said she'd had enough. She's a very nice old lady who has been at Bexley forever. Every day she'll talk about the novel that we're supposed to be reading, and will ask questions and call on people in the class.

Most of the time no one knows the answers. Marcia Ziskind and a few other people have actually read the books, but I'd say that most of the class is not up on the reading assignments. So Mrs. Barr will ask her question, and call on someone. At the beginning of the year we were all scared that we'd get in trouble for not knowing the answers. But gradually we found out that Mrs. Barr was just too nice a person to blow up. So now, when she calls on someone who doesn't know the answer, the person will usually just say, "I'm sorry, Mrs. Barr, I'm behind in the book. I don't know the answer." And Mrs. Barr will accept it.

That seemed to work, until today. For the first time all semester Mrs. Barr got really angry. She said, "I hate to say this, but I think you people are taking advantage of me." And she gave us a pop quiz right on the spot.

I can't blame her. She's right.

* * *

In the lounge at noon today, Donny Elias came in smelling of Canoe as usual. He passed by Jack and Dan and me and said hello. We managed to keep straight faces.

This is great. Every time from now on when Donny comes to school in the morning wearing his Canoe, we'll know that we've pissed on his face.

Tim Greiner came over to my house tonight. We've started to be good friends. He said he knew about a Tweed party over on Parkview—boys from the Academy and girls from the Columbus School for Girls.

We drove over to it in his Volkswagen. We thought they might throw us out, but when we got down to the party in the basement everybody was drunk, and they welcomed us. We saw Janie Dinkelaker, a senior at Bexley, and we teased her about having a date with a Tweed.

It made me think, though. We all assume that all of the crazy things that are happening to us at Bexley are unique, and that they're not happening to anybody else in the world. But here the Tweeds were—and they were drinking behind their parents' backs just like we drink behind our parents' backs, and trying to score with girls just like we try to score with girls, and being close with their buddies just like we're close with our buddies. Their world is self-contained just like our world is. All this stuff that's been going on with us— some version of it has probably been going on with them, too, and it's probably been going on with kids our age all over Columbus, and all over the country. Maybe all over the world.

A Tweed offered me a beer and I accepted it. I sat down in the corner, just watching and thinking.

NOVEMBER 14

NORMAL lazy Saturday. Pauline Taynor came over in the afternoon to drop off the first copies of the new issue of *Junior Prom*. My Kennedy column is in there. It looks pretty good.

After dinner I drove over to Jack's house. I had some dessert with him and his dad, and after we were finished his dad asked Jack to drive Carrie, their maid, home.

Carrie has been with Jack's family for years—I've known her ever since Jack and I were kids. She always cooked and cleaned for them, but it seems like she's even more important now that Jack's mom is dead. I don't see how Jack and his dad would get along without her.

For all the time that I've been coming over to Jack's house, I don't think I've ever had more than a few sentences of conversation with Carrie. Most of my memories are of her standing by the sink in the kitchen, peeling potatoes or cleaning carrots or getting something ready to put in the oven.

There are women like Carrie all over Bexley—maids who ride the bus to work in the morning, ride it home at night, week after week, year after year. Sometimes I wonder what they must think—spending their days in nice suburban houses, and going back to their own places at night. In Carrie's case, I don't have a hint. She just doesn't seem to be much of a talker.

Anyway, it was raining tonight, and Jack's dad said that he should take Carrie home. So we went out to the garage, and Jack got behind the wheel of his dad's big blue Pontiac, and we drove Carrie down to the Negro section of Columbus. She was quiet the whole way down there. When we got to her place she thanked Jack for driving her, and said that she would see him on Monday.

NOVEMBER 15

WE played football at Chuck's all afternoon. When I got home Dad asked me to go over to Rubino's to get us pizzas for dinner.

I did, and we were all sitting around having a pleasant dinner when Dad told me that I'm not allowed to take showers in the morning anymore.

"What?" I said.

"You have abused the privilege," he said. "You take

twenty-minute showers, and you make me late, and when I finally do get into the bathroom it's like a steam bath."

"But I can't go to school without taking a shower," I said.

"Take one the night before," he said.

"That's no good," I said. "If I don't take a shower in the morning I feel grubby all day."

"Then take a bath," he said. Mom's and Dad's bathroom has a shower, but the children's bathroom just has a bathtub.

"I hate baths," I said. "They don't make you feel as good as showers."

"This situation is your own fault," he said. "If I've told you once I've told you a million times—you're free to use our bathroom if you take a five-minute shower. I don't know what you do in there, but it's going to stop."

I looked over at Mom. "Mom . . ." I said.

She just grimaced and shrugged.

"This decision has nothing to do with your mother," Dad said. "It's my decision, and it didn't have to be necessary. You made it necessary with your long showers. I'm tired of getting in the shower and having no hot water."

"I can't believe this," I said.

"Well, start believing it," he said.

Real nice.

NOVEMBER 16

I took a shower before bed last night, and this morning I just got dressed and went to school. It made me feel terrible all day. I have to work out a solution to this.

C.W. Jones cracks me up.

Today Mr. Duffey was sick, so C.W. came in to teach our history class. No one could remember this ever happening—substitute teachers, yes, but not the principal teaching the class.

We were sitting in the room for about three minutes after the bell rang, wondering where Mr. Duffey was. That's when C.W. came barging into the room. He stared around like he was looking for a fight—that's what C.W. does every time he walks into a room of students—and then said, "All right, what have you been studying in here?"

Someone said, "World War I."

C.W. said, "I know a little bit about World War I." And then he started talking about the tinderbox theory of how World War I began.

He asked the class a question, and George Beltzhoover, in the front row, raised his hand.

Jones pointed at him and said, "Beltzcraft?"

George said, "The name is Beltzhoover, sir."

Now, you'd think that most principals would be a little embarrassed if they got a student's name wrong.

But C.W. just waved his hand in the air and said, "Beltzhoover, Beltzcraft—I never know." And went on to the next question.

The guy's amazing.

Had a long *Torch* session after school, working on the page proofs for the next issue. Kathy walked by the *Torch* office, talking to Bruce Byrnes. More and more, I'm beginning to accept the fact that it's all over.

NOVEMBER 17

LAST night I had a talk with Dad. I told him that I just couldn't take going to school without a shower in the morning.

"What possible difference could it make whether you take a shower at night or in the morning?" he said.

"Night molecules," I said.

"What?" he said.

"It doesn't matter if you take a shower the night before," I said. "When you're asleep, you get night molecules on you, and you feel grungy all day if you don't take a shower in the morning."

He shook his head. But we made a deal. If I set my alarm for a half hour earlier than I usually do, then I can take a shower. That way, he said, by the time he got out of bed the bathroom wouldn't be steamed up, and the hot water heater would have built up some more hot water. I agreed to do that.

So this morning I took a shower. I felt 100 percent better than I did yesterday.

Junior Prom, with my story about President Kennedy, went on sale at school today. Everybody was walking around with copies of it.

It's something, the effect of having a column in there. Lindy came up to me and flipped open the magazine and flashed my picture at me. And then Sherry Smith, one of the prettiest junior girls—she'll probably be Homecoming queen next year—passed me in the hallway and said, " 'Speaking Out,' by Bob Greene." Sherry never talks to me.

And Mr. Ridenour made a special point of congratulating me for the column and saying he thought it was really good. I've been going to Bexley High School for four years, but now, whenever *Junior Prom* comes out, people treat me as if they've discovered something new about me. I don't get it.

We had an Epsilons meeting tonight; it was the rescheduled one for the civil-rights discussion. But Reverend Zebbs didn't show up again, so we just read the minutes from the last meeting and then everyone went home.

Timmy knocked on my door tonight. He said he had been over at the Bexley Public Library, and Kathy had been there. She had said to him, "Is Bobby here, too?" When he said no, she said, "Tell him I said hi."

Then, Timmy said, a librarian asked him his name, and Kathy was standing behind him and said "Greene'" and smiled.

I don't want to get my hopes up.

NOVEMBER 18

MOM let me drive her car to school this morning, so I took Debby and Timmy with me. I dropped Timmy at the elementary school, then parked on Fair Avenue, and Debby and I walked the half block to the high school.

I feel kind of responsible for them, in a weird kind of way. In Bexley, you're always known by who your big brother or big sister was. Most kids, when they get to high school, already have a reputation to deal with—and the reputation is that of the big brother or big sister who has gone before them.

Chuck, for example, will always be Bill Shenk's younger brother. Jack will always be Benson Roth's younger brother. Dan will always be Dicky Dick's younger brother.

But I don't have that. I'm the first one in my family to go to the high school, and there's no history I have to live up to. But Debby and Timmy—they're always going to have to live up to my history. Debby is always going to be Bob Greene's little sister, and Timmy is always going to be Bob Greene's little brother.

It's kind of a tough role for me to have. Last spring, for example, when I didn't letter, as bad as I felt for myself, I felt just as bad for Debby and Timmy. They had a big brother who had lettered once, and then who didn't letter the next year. That's the kind of thing that doesn't go away. It's almost as if everything I do will have repercussions for them.

Sometimes I envy Chuck and Jack and Dan. I remember freshmen year, when we all had our first classes at the high school. All their teachers recognized their names and asked them if their big brothers were so-and-so. Me, I was just some kid whose name no one had ever heard of.

I just hope when Timmy gets to high school, and the teachers say "Was Bob Greene your big brother?" he'll be proud to say yes.

· C.W. kicked Chuck out of school today. Chuck was wearing Beatle boots, and C.W. made him go home and change back to regular shoes.

* * *

We had to fold "Dial-a-Dates" after school. The "Dial-a-Date" is a mimeographed publication that the *Torch* puts out: It has everyone in the school's name, address, and phone number. It's an extra way for the *Torch* to make money, because I don't think there's anyone in the school who doesn't buy a "Dial-a-Date."

So today's the day that the *Torch* staff had to fold the pages, put them in their covers, and staple them together. We finally got done at about five-thirty, and when I walked out of the *Torch* room Lindy was in the hall. She must have had a detention or something. She hooked her arm through mine and we walked all the way down the hallway together. I don't understand anything anymore.

NOVEMBER 19

IT rained most of the day. School dragged by. Tonight I was getting restless at home, so I asked Mom if I could take her car. She said it was late to be going out, but I promised I'd be home before too long.

Sometimes you see a lot of guys cruising around Bexley, but tonight I seemed to be the only car on the street. I cruised down Fair and then up Remington and then along Main Street and then back down Gould to Broad Street. The streets were still slick from the rain, and the streetlights gave everything a kind of spooky glow.

I thought about stopping off at Chuck's or Jack's, but I didn't. I just played the radio and thought about all the things that have been going on with my life. It was cold out, and I had the windows rolled up. WCOL played "She's Not There" by the Zombies, and I listened to it and drove until I knew Mom and Dad would be getting mad. I went back home and left the car in the driveway and went in the back door. I really didn't feel like being home. For some reason, tonight I could have cruised all night.

NOVEMBER 20

PAULINE Taynor called today. She said that she was thinking about printing my *Junior Prom* column about Kennedy in tomorrow's *Citizen-Journal*. The anniversary of his death isn't until Sunday, but the *C-J* doesn't print a Sunday edition so she wants to try to get it into the Saturday paper. She said she thought it was so good that more people deserve to read it.

I hope she puts it in.

Tonight was a Bexley basketball game. I went with Tim Greiner, Kenny Stone, and Tom Williamson. Chuck and Dan came in by themselves, and they sat in a different part of the stands. I think they thought I was screwing them by going to the game with those other guys. It's funny; we've all been best friends for so long that when any of us spends time with other guys, it's almost like we're cheating on a girlfriend.

At half time I made a point of walking up to them and asking them to sit with us the second half. Then after the game we all went to HoJo's East together, and then back to Kenny's to listen to records. I could tell that Chuck and Dan were uncomfortable. I'm becoming pretty good friends with Greiner and the guys he runs around with, but Chuck and Dan aren't. So everybody was trying to joke around and have a good time, but after about a half hour at Kenny's, Chuck and Dan said they had to leave. I know I'll hear about this tomorrow.

I could tell Chuck was mad at me, because when someone brought up Kathy Michaels' name, Chuck said, "I'm only going with her," just to get to me. I wish I only was.

NOVEMBER 21

MOM woke me up at seven-twenty with a copy of the *Citizen-Journal* in her hand. My Kennedy story was in the paper; it ran six columns wide. There was a headline running across the top of it in small type that said, "A Teenager Remembers JFK." Then, underneath the small headline, was a bigger headline that said, "November Returns With Sad Memories."

Mom and Dad were all excited, and then the phone started to ring. It seemed that every person in Columbus who our family knows was waking up, picking up the paper from the front doorstep, and seeing my story. The phone literally didn't stop ringing for three hours.

Mom and Dad kept saying "Thank you very much" to the people who called, and then putting me on the phone to say something. The call that made me feel the best was from Allen's father; he said he wanted me to know how proud he was of me.

One thing sort of bothered me. A couple of people told Mom that they thought she had written the story. They thought that it was too good for a high school kid to have written. Mom seemed really furious when they said that; I wasn't so much furious as kind of flattered. After all, I know that I wrote it, and if they think it's so good that I couldn't have written it, that means it must be pretty good.

I kept thinking as the phone continued to ring: Isn't this something? A couple of weeks ago this idea popped into my head about President Kennedy. If I would have just kept it in my head, no one would have known that I was thinking about it. But because I wrote it down, everyone's going crazy. It's like the things that I walk around thinking about don't matter until I write them down. That's okay with me. But you'd that all of these people who called today might have taken an interest in me before they read my story. They've all been friends with my parents for years. And now, for the first time, they're paying attention to me.

I wonder if Kathy saw the paper?

Jack came over for lunch, and then we went over to Rogers' Drugstore, where I bought ten extra copies of the paper for seven cents apiece. I put them up on my top closet shelf, just to have them.

We shot some baskets in the afternoon. Tonight Chuck and Dan went to the Hideout to drink beer; they've been here twice so far, honking in the driveway and calling me a buddy-fucker for hanging around with Greiner and his friends last night. But they're not serious about it; they're laughing when they say it. We'll be okay.

NOVEMBER 22

GOT up at eleven, showered, made myself peanut-butter-and-jelly sandwiches for lunch, and watched the Browns game.

After the game, some friends of Mom and Dad called to say that they had collected a lot of bottle caps for Timmy. There's this soda pop promotion going on where you look under the bottle caps, and there's certain letters, and if you can get the letters to spell out the right word then you win a Cleveland Browns pennant, or even an autographed football from the Browns.

So I got the bottle caps for Timmy, then went to my room and tried to think of a column to write for the next *Junior Prom*. It's funny; as good as I feel about the reaction to the Kennedy column, the deadline for the next issue is already here, and I can't sit around and think about how nice it is that people liked the last one. I have to write a new one, and fast.

Nothing was coming to my mind. I looked around my room. It's gone through so many changes during the years that I've lived in it.

When I was a kid, there was a big framed portrait of Superman on the wall. It was drawn by the guy who actually draws it for the comic books; Mom and Dad got it for me at an auction or something. When my friends would come over, they would think that was the coolest thing in the world.

Then I got too old for that, and the Superman portrait went into storage in the basement. For a while, every inch of my walls was covered with color photographs from *Sports Illustrated* and *Sport*. I would go through each new issue of the magazines and carefully cut the pictures out, and then Scotch-tape them to the walls. It was really something; all four walls were totally covered, from the floor to the ceiling.

A few years ago I took all the pictures down. That was when I was really getting interested in tennis, and I had only one thing on the wall: an article called "Don't Be a Good Loser," from *World Tennis* magazine. The point of the article was that a good loser was still a loser, and that there was no satisfaction to be derived from telling yourself you were a good loser. The important thing was to become so good that you would win your matches, and then you wouldn't have to worry about being a good loser or a bad loser. You'd be a winner.

Now there's nothing on my walls. Just the wallpaper with the marks from all that tape that used to hold the sports photographs up. I sat at my typewriter and tried to think of a column, but nothing came.

NOVEMBER 23

ON my gum trip to the third-floor hallway this morning, I got up my courage and asked Kathy to the Bexley basketball game Wednesday night. She said she already had a date with that Tweed she used to go with, Mark English.

After school I got Mom's car and followed Dan over to Dick Klamfoth Honda on Main Street, where he had to leave his cycle to get repaired. After he had dropped it off I gave him a ride back home. Everything's fine with us again.

Pauline Taynor called tonight and said she really needed the column if it was going to make it into the December issue of *Junior Prom*. I still didn't have any idea what to write about, but there wasn't any time to agonize over it. I just sat down and wrote one about Timmy's bottle cap contest. It seemed sort of silly, after the one on President Kennedy, but I finished it by nine o'clock and then took it over to the mailbox on Main Street so that it will be picked up first thing in the morning.

OUR French test was postponed, but the History test is still on for tomorrow.

In Physics Tim Greiner and Dave Frasch and I were having our usual round-robin note exchange. Tim and I started writing stuff teasing Dave about always being with his girlfriend, Sue Rosel. I think Tim wrote the first thing, and then I added to it. At first Dave was his usual sardonic self when he wrote his part of the note.

But Tim and I kept it up. Tim was harder on Dave than I was; he kept writing that Dave was deserting all his old friends to spend every possible minute with Sue. I just wrote some stuff that I meant to be funny.

All of a sudden Dave blew up. Not out loud; but in the note. He wrote, "If I'm not mistaken, Tim, you—the great expert on romance—don't even have a date for Friday night. And Bob—isn't it a little hypocritical for you to criticize me when it is well known all over the school that you are totally whipped over a certain freshman girl who has already bid you goodbye?"

I could tell that Dave was serious, but Tim kept pouring it on. The note got more and more heated. The odd thing about it was that all this was going on in the middle of Mr. Hughes' lecture. The note kept going around the triangle from Tim to me to Dave and back to Tim, getting angrier each time. But we didn't speak; we just exchanged momentary looks and kept the note going. Finally, with about ten minutes left in the period, Dave wrote, in big capital letters, "TRUCE," and underlined the word three times.

If Mr. Hughes noticed what we were doing, he never said a thing.

Dave was obviously right about me being whipped. After dinner tonight I wanted to call Kathy's house to see if she was home, but I didn't want to do it at my house where someone might pick up the phone while I was on. So I went to Rogers' Drugstore, and went to the phone booth in the back of the store by the pharmacy counter. I called her house and disguised my voice as I asked for her, so whoever answered wouldn't know it was me. Her mom answered; she said Kathy was out and asked who was calling. I hung up.

NOVEMBER 25

HISTORY test was fairly easy. It was raining this morning, so we had gym inside. We played Bombardment—I played great. At one point the ball got stuck up in the rafters and Coach DeJong accused me of throwing it up there on purpose. He was just kidding, so I wised off back to him. It was pretty funny.

I said hi to Kathy in the lounge at noon, and then I got an inspiration. I thought if I wrote her a note telling her that someone had called my house asking for her, then she'd have to write me back, and maybe that would start up communications again.

So fifth period I wrote the note. It felt funny doing it—we used to write each other notes two or three times a day, without even thinking about it, but this time I took my time and tried to make it perfect. I started it "Kath—" and signed it "Love."

I gave it to her in the hallway after fifth period, and she smiled. After sixth period I saw her in the hallway again, and she just mumbled something about it not being her—meaning that it wasn't her that called my house. My guess is that she knows that no one really called my house and asked for her.

Oh, well. It was worth a try, I guess. After school Dan and I rode his Honda in the rain. We were soaked by the time we went home.

NOVEMBER 26

THANKSGIVING. I woke up at about eleven, and I walked out into the hallway in my pajamas—and there were Candy

Grossman and Marcia Smilack, who were visiting Debby. We all laughed, but I was really embarrassed.

This afternoon was the Turkey Bowl, the annual fraternity-league football game. Epsilons won. Then we rode cycles and shot baskets for another couple of hours.

When I got home, Dad said he wanted to see me in his and Mom's bedroom. I thought that I was in trouble or something, but he said that he was cleaning out his closet and that he wanted to give me one of his old cashmere sweaters and some ties. That was nice of him, although he kept holding the sweater up to my chest and then the ties up to the sweater and telling me which ties went with the sweater and which ones didn't, as if I couldn't figure it out myself.

We had Thanksgiving dinner at Nana's. All of my aunts and uncles and cousins were there, and Dad kept making us line up so he could take pictures with Nana's Polaroid. There was one big dinner table set up, and then two card tables for the overflow kids.

As the turkey was being served I thought to myself: This is where I came in. I remember last Thanksgiving so vividly. Lindy and I had just broken up, and I was so upset that I couldn't even talk to anyone or even look them in the eyes. No one knew what was wrong with me—maybe Debby did, but I hadn't told Mom and Dad about what had happened with Lindy and me—but they could tell that something was definitely on my mind. Everyone kept asking me what was wrong, and I kept saying, "Nothing." It was a pretty dismal day for me.

Now tonight here I was again, after breaking up with another girl. But I must have seemed okay; no one said anything to me about acting morose or anything. And I took part in conversations well enough, and I even laughed a lot. As bad as I've been feeling about Kathy, I have to admit that it's nothing compared to the way I felt after Lindy. I had a great time with Kathy, and I wish we were still going together—but with Lindy I felt that a bomb had been dropped on me, and that I'd never be able to get up from it. This isn't like that.

I guess you could even consider this progress. Even though I'm still feeling down about Kathy, it could be worse—this

could be the second straight Thanksgiving that I sat at the
table in a daze over Lindy. At least I'm not doing that.

We had pumpkin pie with whipped cream for dessert. When
we were done, Debby and Timmy and I went into the kitchen
to see Jean, the cook who's been with Nana for years. We
said the same thing we say every Thanksgiving—the thing
Mom taught us to say when we were little kids: "Thank you
very much for a lovely dinner." Then we all went home.

NOVEMBER 27

I feel so ashamed of myself.

We had the day off from school because it's the day after
Thanksgiving. At noon I took Mom to the beauty parlor, and
then Jack and I went downtown to Marco's Records to buy
"Gone, Gone, Gone." It's a new song by the Everly Brothers
that they sang on "Shindig" the other week, and it's great.

Tonight Chuck and Dan and I were together. We got to
talking about "The Rogues," and how cool those guys are.
We said that it would be the best thing in the world if we
could pull off escapades the way they do on TV.

The more we talked about it, the better we liked the idea
of trying something daring like the Rogues do. We didn't
want to do it at some point in the future—we wanted to do it
tonight.

We thought and thought. Finally we came up with an idea.

On Friday nights in Bexley, there are usually adult parties
all around town. You can tell where they are by looking for
houses where a lot of cars are parked in the driveways and in
the streets out front. If you don't recognize the cars as be-
longing to high school guys, you can assume it's a grown-up
party.

The men and women get pretty bombed by the end of the
parties. And that's where our idea came in.

Dan and I were wearing our letter jackets. If there's anything that Bexley grown-up men like to talk about, it's Bexley
sports.

So we figured it this way: Late in the evening, Chuck and

Dan and I would go to one of the houses that had a lot of cars in front of it. We'd ring the doorbell, and when the people answered we'd ask for someone with a made-up name. The people would either say that the person didn't live there, or would think that the person was a guest at the party.

Either way, we figured, the people would be drunk enough that they would talk to us. They'd probably ask us what sports we'd lettered in. And we'd use that as an excuse to get in the front door and start a conversation with the people.

Two of us would stay with the people at the party, talking about Bexley High School and Bexley High School sports. We would be the diversion. Then the third of us would wander off to find the people's liquor cabinet. That third person would open the cabinet, take a bottle of liquor, and quickly slip out the front door and back to our car. Then the other two would say goodbye and leave.

It seemed like a perfect scheme. Something that the Rogues could carry off with no trouble at all. But the main thing was, did we have the guts to make it work?

As the evening got later, we wavered back and forth about whether to do it. One minute we were saying yes; the next minute we were worrying about what would happen if we got caught.

Finally Dan said, "Look. Do we have balls or don't we?"

So we started driving around, looking for parties. The first one we found was over on Dawson.

We walked to the front door. We were all so nervous we could hardly talk. Finally we rang the bell—and it worked just like we thought it would. The people invited us in, and they were drunk, and they started asking us who our parents were and what life at the high school was like.

Chuck and I talked to them, and Dan slipped off. Chuck and I talked to the grownups for about ten minutes. We figured that Dan had had his chance by then. So we said goodbye and went out to the car.

Dan was in the front seat, laughing and holding a half-full pint bottle of vodka. "It isn't much," he said. "But they hardly had anything in the liquor cabinet."

We drove off, and we really felt like we had gotten away with something. I wanted to stop now that we'd carried it out, but Dan said that he'd proved he could do it—now it was our turn.

We stopped off at another party and went to the front door. This time the people weren't drunk; they just said we had the wrong place and closed the door in our faces.

Now I was really ready to call it off. But Dan said, "Come on, Greene. Don't pussy out now."

So we went to another house, on Merkle. This time I was completely nervous—the people who lived there knew my parents. We walked up to the door, and this time it worked again. They welcomed us in and had us come into the living room and started talking to us.

This time I was the person who was supposed to slip off. After a few minutes of conversation, I did. I looked around the first floor, and found the liquor cabinet in the dining room.

I had to do it quickly. I bent down, and at first I was afraid that the cabinet was locked. But I opened it—and there was a whole array of booze.

I could feel my heart pounding. I reached in and took the first bottle that I touched. I didn't even look to see what it was. I slipped it under my letter jacket, closed the liquor cabinet door, and walked quietly to the front door and out to the car. I was so scared that someone from the party would see me and ask what the bulge under my jacket was. But no one did.

I waited in the car for about ten minutes, and then Chuck and Dan came out.

"Did you get anything?" they said.

I pulled the bottle out from under my jacket. It was seven-eighths full—a fifth of 151-proof rum.

Chuck and Dan saw it and whooped.

We agreed that we had pressed our luck enough for the night. We headed for home; Dan said that he would sneak the vodka into his house, and I said that I would sneak the rum into mine.

I put it under my letter jacket again, and managed to get it upstairs. I've just locked it in my typewriter case.

But I'm sitting in my room, and I feel terrible. I know I had to do it—I had to prove I had balls. I feel so guilty, though.

The only other thing I ever stole in my life was when I was, about ten years old. I was at Rogers' Drugstore, and there was no one at the counter, and I took a pack of gum and put it in my pocket. I got home with it, and I felt so bad that after about a half hour I told my mom.

She told me to go right back to the drugstore, to ask for the manager, and to tell him what I had done. She said to tell him how sorry I was, and then to hand over the gum to him. I did it. As I remember it now, he tried to hold back a smile, and told me that it was wrong to steal, but that he was glad I was being honest, and that he hoped I would never do anything like that again.

Well—this time there's no chance I can tell Mom about what happened. What could I say? That we wanted to be like the Rogues so we decided to steal liquor that we could drink later? I'm going to have to live with this one. If we go back to the houses where we stole the vodka and the rum and tell the people what we did, we'll probably just set ourselves up for real trouble.

Like it or not, we did it, and the liquor is here. I really feel like a low person. I guess I don't deserve anything now in the way of grades, love, or honors. The next time I watch "The Rogues," I'm going to wonder if they ever feel this way.

NOVEMBER 28

WHEN I woke up this morning I had the vague feeling that something was wrong. It took me a second to realize what it was. Last night. I rolled over and went back to sleep.

Chuck and Dan came over around noon and we went to the Burger Boy Food-O-Rama for lunch. Then we went to Pongi's and played records for most of the afternoon. Chuck and Dan said that they're feeling the same way I am about stealing the liquor last night. We all wish that we hadn't done it. But the main thing now is not getting caught.

* * *

Mom and Dad went to a dinner party tonight. At six o'clock I made myself two turkey TV dinners, and I was eating them when Chuck and Dan showed up again.

They have dates tonight, and I don't. We were sitting around, and they asked me where I had hidden the rum. I told them about the typewriter case.

We decided we'd might as well try it to see how it tasted. So I went up to my room, unlocked the case, and brought the bottle down to the kitchen. I set it on the counter.

We all looked at it. None of us had had rum before. The "151," as in "151 proof," was in big letters on the label.

"That sounds pretty strong," Dan said.

I agreed. I don't know too much about the different strengths of alcohol, but I had never heard of anything higher than 100 proof.

We all talked about how we should drink it. We had heard of rum and Coke; we were going to pour each of ourselves a glass of Coke with some of the rum in it, but we were a little worried about the 151-proof thing.

"Maybe you're not supposed to drink this stuff like regular liquor," I said. "If it's 151 proof, maybe too much of a dose could kill you."

We didn't know what to do. And then Chuck got a good idea.

There is a restaurant on Main Street, just outside the Bexley line, called the Top. All of our parents go there sometimes for steak. We decided to call the Top, ask for the bar, and then ask the bartender his advice.

So we went to the phone in the back hallway. I looked up the number of the Top and dialed it. When someone answered, I lowered my voice as deep as I could and said, "I would like to talk to the bartender, please."

In a second another man picked up the phone.

"Bar," he said.

"Is this the bartender?" I said, still in my deep voice.

"Yes," he said. "Can I help you?"

"Yes," I said. "I have just purchased a bottle of rum. I happened to notice that it is 151 proof. Could you tell me how to mix a rum and Coke with it?"

The bartender laughed. "You're asking me how to make a rum and Coke?" he said.

"Well," I said, "I have made many rum and Cokes with

regular rum. But I need to know if you make it differently with a hundred fifty-one proof rum.''

"Put some ice in a glass," the bartender said. "Pour a shot of the rum into the glass. Then fill the rest of the glass with Coke.''

"And I don't have to be careful about how much rum I use?" I said. "I mean, because it's a hundred fifty-one proof?''

The bartender laughed again. "I think you'll be all right," he said.

So we each had a rum and Coke. It tasted good—real sweet. Then Chuck and Dan went off to get ready for their dates, and I cleaned up the kitchen, locked the rum in my typewriter case again, and, feeling a little high, settled down for a night of TV.

NOVEMBER 29

WHILE I was watching the Browns game today, Jack came over in his new pair of Wellingtons.

Wellingtons are black boots that we think C.W. can't kick us out of school for. The bottoms of them are plain—they aren't pointy like Beatle boots, and they don't have raised heels like Beatle boots. But they're definitely boots—the tops go up past your ankles for about a foot.

Jack said that C.W. would have no case if he tried to kick people out for Wellingtons, because once the boot tops are tucked under the bottom of your pants, it's not that obvious that they're boots. There would be a problem if you tried to wear the boots outside your pants. But once they're tucked inside, C.W. shouldn't be able to say anything.

They really look cool. I'm going to get a pair next week.

I studied for a while tonight, and then went out to the driveway. I took a tennis ball with me. I turned on the driveway lights. I threw the ball up onto the roof of the garage, and then caught it as it came down.

Our garage roof is sloped, so that if you throw a ball onto

it, the ball will bounce down to you. The higher you get it on the roof, the better the bounce is. But if you throw it too far, and it goes over the top of the roof, you've got a problem. It will bounce down the other side of the roof, and end up in the Fenburrs' yard next door.

I've been throwing balls up onto our roof since I was a little kid. When I first learned how to play baseball, I would take a hardball out onto the driveway, put on my mitt, and practice catching as the ball rolled off the roof toward me. It seems that no matter what else was going on in my life, part of my time was always spent out there, throwing balls onto the roof.

I was thinking about that tonight. Part of me doesn't feel like a kid any longer. But another part of me—the part that was out there on the driveway, positioning myself so that I would be in the right place when the ball came bouncing down—is the same as when I was eight years old. I don't expect anybody else to understand that, because I really don't completely understand it myself.

NOVEMBER 30

WE had a French test this morning, which I didn't think was hard—but then I didn't think the last one was hard, either, and it turned out that I got a C on that one. Also, Mr. Duffey gave back our History tests, and I got an A on mine—which gives me hopes of bringing my grades up this semester.

In gym we played basketball. Coach DeJong called me over and told me that I had to wear socks with my gym shoes.

After school I walked to Main Street and went to Rogers' Drugstore to look at the magazines.

The magazine rack is right beside the machine where you test your batteries. I come to Rogers' at least once a week to see what new magazines are in. The one that I always make a point of looking at is *Time*.

We get *Time* at home, but it looks different on the rack at Rogers'. Every time I see an issue, I think of what it must feel like to be the person on the cover. Think of that—your picture staring off the rack in every drugstore in America. I wonder what you do during the week when you're on the cover of *Time*? If it was me, I'd be tempted to just walk around letting people recognize me all week.

DECEMBER 1

FOURTH period I was a hall monitor, and Chuck got out of study hall to come up and talk with me. We have to decide what the Epsilons seniors should put in their senior sketches in the *Bexleo*.

In the senior section of the *Bexleo*, each person has his or her senior picture, and then a short sketch that he or she writes. The sketches are just short items—significant phrases, names of brothers and sisters, things like that. It's the best-read part of the yearbook.

The problem is getting a reference to Epsilons in there. C.W. Jones absolutely hates the idea of high school fraternities and sororities, and in past years he has gone over the senior sketches and taken out any references to the fraternities and sororities. There's no way, for example, that we could just write "Epsilons" in our senior sketches. C.W. would delete that right away.

So the trick is getting something in there that tells the *Bexleo*'s readers who the senior members of Epsilons are—but that we can sneak past C.W. It's a tough one—it can't be too bizarre a phrase, because if C.W. sees it pop up in so many different senior sketches, he'll catch on that it's a code word for a fraternity.

All fourth period Chuck and I thought of ideas. We had to come up with an answer today, so we can tell the seniors at the next Epsilons meeting what to put in their sketches. The *Bexleo* deadline is coming up.

Finally, we decided on something: "51 Men." There are fifty-one members of Epsilons, counting all four classes, and maybe that phrase sounds innocent enough that C.W. will overlook it. Maybe he'll think it's a reference to the Bexley football team or something. We'll see. In any case, we couldn't think up anything better, so that's what it's going to be.

DECEMBER 2

AFTER school today I went straight home, and Timmy had come home from school, too. He had one of those little rubber peewee footballs, and we started throwing it around the living room.

I stood near the front window, and told him to go out for a pass. I threw the ball and he missed it, and the ball hit one of the framed portraits above the couch. We were afraid for a second that we had broken the glass.

There are three of the portraits—one of me, one of Debby, and one of Timmy. They were drawn in 1957 by a lady artist who Mom and Dad hired to do them. She worked with colored chalk. The reason I know that they were drawn in 1957 is that the lady included the date next to her signature on each portrait.

It's funny how vividly you remember some things. The lady came to our house and had us pose for the portraits. Each of us had to sit still for a couple of afternoons while she drew. I remember one afternoon in my room, she was drawing, and she asked me if I would be more comfortable if I played some records. I said sure, and put on the turntable a new record that I had just asked Mom to buy for me. It was an Elvis Presley record—"All Shook Up" was on one side, and "That's When Your Heartaches Begin" was on the other side.

The lady was drawing the picture, and she said to me, "You look sharp as hell today." That was the first time that a grownup had used a cuss word in a conversation with me; I had heard grownups use cuss words talking to each other, but no one had ever said one to me. I think the lady was trying to make me feel older, but I remember being very uncomfortable about her using that word to me.

I overheard Mom and Dad talking about the portraits one night during the time they were being drawn. They said that the lady was charging $75 apiece for them, and that $225 seemed like a big chunk of money to pay all at one time. But they said it was worth it; the portraits would be part of the family forever.

Timmy and I went over to the portraits this afternoon to make sure we hadn't cracked the glass. Everything was okay. The portraits are so pure-looking. In them I'm ten years old, and Debby is eight, and Timmy is four. I'm wearing a yellow V-neck sweater in mine. We look like the most ideal little kids in the world. I guess that's the purpose the portraits will always serve—to capture us looking perfect and sweet, no matter what really happens to us in life.

DECEMBER 3

Two things happened today that made me start thinking hard about Lindy for the first time in months.

The first came when we were cruising in Chuck's car, and "Bobby's Girl" came on the radio. That did it to me. Chuck noticed it right away; he said, "What, are you back in the daze again?"

And then, later, I was walking around the neighborhood and I saw Kent Nitz walking, too. Mr. Nitz is the man who owns the house at the corner of Bexley Park and Gould, where Lindy and I used to go and sit all day during that summer. I remember lots of times when Mr. Nitz would come out of his house, and there Lindy and I would be, sitting in his front yard by his bushes, listening to a transistor radio. A lot of people in Bexley would have told us to get out of their yards, but Mr. Nitz always pretended not to see us—although I would notice him smiling as he walked down to the sidewalk.

When we passed each other today, he didn't give any sign that he recognized me. He probably didn't; it's been a long time since those mornings and afternoons in his front yard, and he's undoubtedly forgotten. But I never will.

DECEMBER 4

DAVE Frasch wrote a great absence list in English this morning. People in school have been doing that for the last few weeks—getting hold of the absence lists that the principal's office sends out, and then writing cutting things after the sick people's names. It makes you scared to stay out of school for a day—you don't know what people are going to write by your name when you're on the absence list.

There was a pep rally in the gym after school. Frasch got the biggest hand when they introduced the basketball team. Dave and I have been friends for so long that it's hard to imagine the fact that he is now the official Bexley High School hero. There's always one guy in each senior class who fills that role, and you go through elementary school and junior high school knowing their names. When you're a kid, they seem as important and unreachable as professional athletes. I still remember the names from when I was younger: Bob Babbitt, Mike Benis, Jerry Hockman, Karl Kumler—and now it's Dave. All the kids in the elementary school must idolize him. That's hard to think about as he and I and Tim Greiner sit in Physics class every day and pass our notes around. I wonder if Dave ever tries to put it all in perspective? For all the kidding around we do, he never talks about it directly.

After the pep rally we had *Torch* paste-up, and then I went downtown to get Wellingtons. First I tried on a pair of size 9½ D, and they were too big, so I tried on a pair of size 8½ D and they fit perfectly. I didn't wear them to the basketball game tonight, but I'll wear them around the house over the weekend and then wear them to school on Monday morning.

DECEMBER 5

CHUCK and Dan came over in the morning, and we cruised. We could pick up KYW on the car radio; they're playing songs from a new Beatles album about once every half hour. George Harrison sings lead on one called "Everybody's Trying to Be My Baby" that's really good.

In the afternoon Mom and Dad asked me to take Debby to Marcia Smilack's and then to pick her up again. I said I'd do it if Dad let me drive the Thunderbird. He said okay. Boy, I love that car.

Trouble with the Wellingtons. They look fine when I'm standing up—but every time I sit down, my pants ride up and the tops of the Wellingtons pop out, and then when I stand up again the pants bunch up against the top of the boots. I don't look cool at all; I look like a farmer.

I've got to figure out a solution before Monday.

DECEMBER 6

I watched the Browns game today, then listened to KYW and WBZ—for some reason I could pick up the Cleveland and Boston stations real clearly. And then I solved the Wellingtons problem.

I took all my pants to Mom, and told her that they were bunching up on top of the boots. So she took a scissors and some thread, and did something so that the pants didn't have cuffs anymore—she folded the cuffs down so that they made the pants longer. Then she ironed them so that you couldn't even tell where the cuffs had been.

Now my pants go all the way down to the tops of my feet, and even when I sit down the boots don't pop out. I polished the Wellingtons around dinnertime; I'll wear them to school tomorrow.

Tonight Bill Emig, a man who is a Princeton alumnus, came over to talk to me. That's how they work it—if you apply to Princeton, an alumnus in your town visits your house and writes an evaluation that he sends to the school.

Mom and Dad were nervous about it. They kept telling me to speak up, and to make intelligent conversation with Mr. Emig. He was due at our house at seven-thirty, and he rang the doorbell right on the dot.

He was wearing a business suit, even though it was a Sunday night. Mom and Dad shook his hand and tried to make some jokes with him, while at the same time making sure that he realized how seriously we were taking this occasion. I could tell that they didn't know whether it would be appropriate to offer him a drink or not. Finally Dad asked him if he'd like one, and Mr. Emig said no.

Mom and Dad went into the den and closed the door so that Mr. Emig and I could be alone in the living room. One of the first things he said to me was, "Didn't I used to hear your name on Jimmy Crum's broadcasts of the Ohio State basketball games?" I said yes, that had been me.

We mostly talked about Princeton, and what a good school he thought it was. I said that I'd never been there, but I heard it was great, etc., etc. I managed to keep up my part of the conversation, being as pleasant and interested as I could. It exhausted me. He left around eight o'clock.

He hadn't been out the front door more than thirty seconds when Mom and Dad burst out of the den.

"What did he say?" Dad said.

"I don't know," I said.

"Well, did he seem to like you?" Mom said.

"I guess," I said.

"Come on, Bob," Dad said. "Don't make us pull teeth. Tell us what it was like."

"We just talked," I said. "I don't know."

This went on for a few more minutes. Mom and Dad seemed disappointed that I wasn't telling them more, but what could I say? Some guy shows up because he's been told to do it, and I talk to him because I've been told to do it, and then we say goodbye. I suppose we liked each other well enough. But I still don't think I have the grades to get into Princeton.

DECEMBER 7

I wore my Wellingtons to school with a pair of black pants. The boots really looked cool. A lot of people saw them and said nice things. Even Kathy came up and said she liked them—it's the first time that we've talked in school for a long time.

We had a History quiz, in which I got six out of ten right, and then I knew some answers in class in Physics, and Mr. Hughes said "very good."

I got out of seventh-period study hall and went down to the *Bexleo* office. I joked around with Susan Koebel, a senior girl who's on the yearbook staff. She's cool.

Right as school was ending, Jack and I were talking in the hallway. He was wearing his Wellingtons, too. All of a sudden we heard a voice: "Come here, you two."

It was C.W. Jones.

He put his hands on his hips and stared down at our feet. "Well, well," he said. "What have we here."

"They're Wellingtons," Jack said.

"They look like boots to me," C.W. said.

"Look," I said, pulling one of my pants legs up. "They're not like Beatle boots at all. Look at the heels. The same as the heels on a regular pair of shoes. Look at the toes. The toes aren't pointed."

C.W. kept looking down and shaking his head. Finally he said, "I don't know why I'm doing this, but I suppose you can wear them." He made it clear that the conversation was over.

We started walking away when we heard his voice again.

"Greene?" he called out.

I turned around.

"Get a haircut."

DECEMBER 8

WHEN I got to school today, Tom Hill was wearing Wellingtons, too. It looks like we've started a fad.

People kept saying things about them. I walked past Steve Stout in the hallway and he looked down at my feet and smiled. "Hey, Greene," he said, "you can't be a hood and a writer." And then Kathy Liefield looked at my feet and laughed in a friendly way and said, "I like your boots."

I'm afraid that if this thing spreads too far, C.W. will change his mind and outlaw Wellingtons. There's no way he's going to allow a whole school full of people to wear them.

Tomorrow could be the night.

Ever since I came back from Cedar Point and everyone started talking about what had happened between Bev and me, different people have treated me in different ways. Most of the guys seem to love it. The girls who hear about it say that it was disgusting and immoral—to be in bed with a married woman. They don't get seriously down on me and bawl me out; in a way they're kind of funny about it. But they make it clear that they don't approve.

Some girls, though, seem . . . interested. That's the first thing I started to notice. Some girls talk to me who had never talked to me before. It's almost as if I've moved up a notch or two in their estimation because of Bev.

I'm not sure how much they really know. I've made a policy of not talking about it, so I think some of them assume that Bev and I actually did it. But there have definitely been girls who have been very flirtatious with me in a way they hadn't been before Bev.

One of the girls is Monica Curry, a senior. In study halls and stuff all fall, she's been saying that we ought to get together sometime. She's always said it in a teasing way, so I didn't want to make a fool of myself and ask her out and find out that she was only kidding.

When Monica was a sophomore she went with a senior, and it's pretty much common knowledge around Bexley that they did it. Her old boyfriend's gone now, and she doesn't have a steady new boyfriend.

Today in the hallway she stepped in front of me and said, "Nice boots." I said thanks, and then she said, "My parents are out of town on vacation. Would you be interested in coming over tomorrow night?"

"Coming over?" I said. I expected her to give me some logical reason.

"Yes," she said. "Coming over."

I got the point. I told her that I'd be there, and she said, "Good."

DECEMBER 9

BOY.

All day long in school, all I could think about was what might happen at Monica's tonight. Why else would she be asking me over unless she wanted to go to bed with me? It made perfect sense—she was used to it with her old boyfriend, and she heard about Bev and me at Cedar Point, and she decided that I would be a good substitute for the guy she used to go with. It's pretty clear that she doesn't want to be my girlfriend or anything—she just wants me to come over to her house while her parents are away.

I couldn't concentrate in classes. After school I went to Dan's and told him about what was up for the night. He gave me a can of Colt .45 to drink before I went over to Monica's. I took it home and left it out in the garage, behind the garbage cans, where it would stay cold but no one would see it.

We had dinner, and I told Mom that I needed her car to go to the library. She said that was fine.

I took the keys off the key rack, got the can of Colt, drank it, and then drove over to Monica's. I was really revved up. Finally it might come true for me.

I parked my car on the street a few houses down from her house, so that people cruising by wouldn't think I was at Monica's. Then I walked up to her door and rang the bell.

It was unbelievable. She answered the door in this pink

satin negligee thing, and said, "I was afraid you wouldn't come."

She lives in a one-story house; she led me right to her parents' bedroom and closed the door behind us. The TV was on, facing her parents' huge king-sized bed.

She sat down on the bed. I couldn't get over this. She didn't even seem to want me to talk.

"So," she said, patting the bed next to her.

I sat down, and she draped one of her arms over me. I put my arms around her, and we started making out and then we both lay down.

It was great. She knew exactly what she was doing—it was clear that she had a hell of a lot more experience at this than I did. I reached down and took my Wellingtons off; she was already barefoot. We stretched out on the bed and started rubbing against each other. I thought I was going to go crazy.

"There's no need to hurry things up," she said. "We have all the time we want."

So we kept it up, and we both kept getting more excited, and I thought I was going to burst. Her negligee and her skin felt wonderful; I didn't want this to stop, but I didn't want the big chance to get away from me, either.

Finally she said, "Why don't you take your shirt off?"

I sat up and started to unbutton my shirt. Out of nowhere, there was a knock on the bedroom door.

"Monica?" a woman's voice said.

"Shit," Monica whispered.

I felt as if my heart and brain had frozen.

"Monica, are you in there?" the voice said.

"I thought you said your parents were out of town," I whispered, buttoning my shirt and putting my Wellingtons back on as fast as I could.

"They are," Monica whispered. "That's my grandmother. She lives with us."

"Then why didn't you tell me about her?" I whispered frantically.

"She never comes out of her room at the back of the house," Monica whispered. "I don't know what she's doing."

"Monica, are you in there alone?" the voice said. Her

grandmother tried the doorknob, but fortunately Monica had locked it.

"I'm all by myself, Grandma," Monica said.

"I thought I heard a boy's voice," her grandmother said.

"It's just the TV," Monica said.

"Monica, I want to come in there," her grandmother said.

I was dressed and had my jacket on. Monica motioned to her parents' bathroom, which was attached to the bedroom.

I walked into the bathroom. There was a window that cranked open, and angled out toward the house next door.

"Monica, let me in this minute," her grandmother's voice said.

I waved goodbye. I cranked the window as far open as it would go, stood on her parents' toilet seat, and jumped out onto the grass. I put my head down and ran as fast as I could to the car. I drove away without looking back.

This had to be fate. I have a feeling it's never going to happen to me.

DECEMBER 10

I wore a yellow shirt, black pants, and my Wellingtons to school this morning. C.W. looked down at my feet and said, "You can go home and change if you want to." I said, "No, thanks."

In the first-floor hallway I ran into Monica Curry. At first we just exchanged glances, but then we both started to laugh.

I said, "Did you get in trouble?"

She said, "No. Right after you went out the window, I opened the bedroom door. My grandmother walked in and I said, 'See, Grandma? I'm just watching TV.'"

"Pretty close call," I said.

"Yeah," Monica said. "It's a good thing that Grandma didn't go into the bathroom and find the window wide open."

Tonight I was sitting around my room and Mike Melton called. He wanted to know something about an English assignment we both had.

It's a funny thing about Mike. When we were doubles partners we were so close, we might have been the same person. When we were on the court together, it was almost as if we could read each other's minds. Sophomore year, when we lettered, we were magic. We would see each other move toward the net or across the court, and the other guy would automatically know where to go. However good each of us was singly, we were more than twice that good as a doubles team. We would easily beat guys in doubles who could have beaten both of us at singles.

Now, because of what happened with me and tennis last spring, Mike and I don't see each other too much. We're still friends—but there's nothing that can replace that feeling that you absolutely depend on each other. I think sometimes Mike is a little embarrassed when we talk—he knows that if he would have stuck with me as a doubles partner, I would have lettered again last spring. I don't blame him, though. He's a better player than I am, and he deserved a chance to play singles.

When we got off the phone, I looked across the room, and my Jack Kramer racquet was propped against my desk. I wonder if I'll try out again for the team in the spring. I don't know. I just don't know.

DECEMBER 11

I was a hall monitor fourth period. I got a book out of the library to read while I sat there. It's a play called *The Front Page*, about old-time journalism in Chicago. It's great; it really inspires me.

We had a Physics quiz this afternoon. I did well on it, but after class I went up to Mr. Hughes and asked if I could talk to him.

"You know that quiz we just took?" I said.

"Yes?" he said.

"Well, I knew one of the questions to it before you handed

the quizzes out," I said. "I found out from one of the people in your morning class."

"So you knew the answer to it already?" he said.

"Yeah," I said. "I don't know what to do, but I didn't want to get a good grade by cheating."

He was really nice about it. He said that he appreciated my honesty, and that I could make the quiz up some day next week after school. He said I wouldn't be penalized.

I think I know why I told him. I think I'm still trying to get over that guilt for stealing the bottle of rum.

DECEMBER 12

Mom had me do some Saturday errands in the morning, and when I got home from doing them Dan called.

He wanted to make a deal with me. He has a date tonight with a girl he thinks he can do pretty well with. He wants me to ask Mom for her station wagon, and then he'll ask for his family's T-Bird. Then we'll meet somewhere and switch. That way he can go to the Hideout and use the big back seat of the station wagon, and I can drive his Thunderbird around all night.

I said it was fine with me. But right around dinnertime he called back and said the switch was off. Something about his dad finding out that he was going to lend the Thunderbird to someone else, and telling Dan absolutely not.

We all went over to Chuck's after dinner and had poor boys. Chuck told me that he knew for a fact that Kathy Michaels was making out with David Herwald—Gary Herwald's younger brother—last night. That totally depressed me.

But later on we ran into Gary Herwald, and I told him what Chuck had said. Gary laughed. "David wasn't even out with Kathy Michaels last night," he said. "I was with him the whole evening."

I think Chuck just likes to screw me up sometimes.

DECEMBER 13

I decided not to shave this morning.

Dan and Jack came over, and we were messing around downstairs, and then Dad came into the room.

"What are you doing, trying to grow a beard?" he said.

"I don't know," I said. "I think I'll let it grow for a few days."

"A real lumberjack, huh?" Dad said.

"I probably can't get away with it," I said. "C.W. will say something about it in school tomorrow."

"Well, if he does, why don't you just dab a little milk on your face and let the cat lick your whiskers off," Dad said.

Dan and Jack cracked up laughing. I started to get mad, but I had to admit it was pretty funny.

DECEMBER 14

THE Dave Clark Five are going to be in Columbus next Saturday night, to give a concert at the State Fairgrounds Coliseum. In the afternoon they're supposed to hold a teen press conference down at the Deshler-Hilton Hotel.

The promoters sent one pass to the press conference to every high school newspaper in the city. Judy Furman opened the envelope that came to the *Torch*, and took the pass. I told her that I wanted to go, but she said that as co-editor she had as much right to the pass as I did.

I argued with her, but she said she was keeping the pass. So I called Pauline Taynor at the *Citizen-Journal*, and asked her if she could get any passes because of *Junior Prom*. She said she'd check on it and call me later in the week.

DECEMBER 15

NONEVENTFUL day in school. After the last bell, Jack and Dan and I went to the Pancake House. Then we went back to my house, where Debby taught us how to play "The Name Game."

"The Name Game" is a new song—I think it's by Shirley Ellis—that they're starting to play a lot on WCOL. You take a name and do funny things with it. We've heard it over and over, but we haven't been able to figure out how to do the names.

So we sat in the living room and Debby went through it with us. It's actually pretty easy, once you know how. "Debby, Debby, Bo Bebby, Banana-Fana Fo Febby, Fe-Fi Mo-Mebby, Debby." Or "Jack, Jack, Bo Back, Banana-Fana Fo Fack, Fe-Fi Mo-Mack, Jack."

We went out cruising after that, and every time "The Name Game" came on the radio we sang along with it. We started using other people's names, and when we did Chuck's name it went, "Chuck, Chuck, Bo Buck, Banana-Fana Fo Fuck . . ." That broke us up.

Every time we'd see someone on the street, we'd stop the car and yell out their name in "The Name Game." Every person we did it to asked us to teach them how to do it—although a few of them had already figured it out from listening to the song.

When I got home for dinner, Debby and Timmy and I kept doing it at the dinner table, until Dad told us to stop. He said it was giving him a headache.

But then, during dessert, he asked us to teach him how to do it.

DECEMBER 16

EVERYBODY was in a bad mood in school today. Kids, teachers—everybody.

Seventh period I worked on *Torch* page proofs. They were really sloppy—a lot of typos. I may have to go down to the printer's an extra time this issue to make sure everything gets in right.

I was watching "Shindig" in the den tonight, and Mom came in and bawled me out for not studying. She asked me how I could expect to get into Princeton or Northwestern or any good school if I didn't even do my homework.

I know she's right, so I started doing some English home-work. But then *Salome*, that old movie with Rita Hayworth, came on, and I had to watch. When she does that Dance of the Seven Veils, it's so sexy.

DECEMBER 17

HAD a test on *Henry IV* in English this morning. I think I did crummy. I can blame it on Rita Hayworth.

I'm starting to worry about getting a New Year's date. New Year's Eve is two weeks from today. We'll have a party at Allen's parents' apartment, but I have no one in mind to ask. And for girls, New Year's Eve is the most important date night of the year—most of them have already been snapped up.

One piece of good news—Pauline Taynor called tonight to say that she'd gotten me a pass to the Dave Clark Five teen press conference. She said I could represent *Junior Prom*. So at least I'll be going to that on Saturday.

DECEMBER 18

ALLEN's home from military school for Christmas vacation. ABCDJ got together tonight, and for some reason we started talking about which of us would get married first.

Dan said, "It has to be Greene. He's always in a damn daze over some girl or other."

But Chuck said, "I'll bet it's Jack. I just have a feeling."

We argued over it for a while, and then we came up with an idea.

We're each going to get twenty dollars, and put it in a savings account in the Bexley branch of the Ohio National Bank, over on Main Street. So there'll be one hundred dollars in the account, and then we'll let it gather interest. As each guy gets married, he'll become ineligible for the money. The last of us who's not married will get to take it all.

All of us being married . . . it seems like that will be a long time from now.

DECEMBER 19

THE Dave Clark Five teen press conference was today.

I rode the bus downtown so that I would be there at two o'clock. The intersection of Broad and High, in front of the Deshler-Hilton, was absolutely mobbed with kids. Traffic couldn't move.

The only people they were letting into the hotel were guests with keys, and kids with passes to the press conference. I fought my way through the crowd, and showed a security guard my pass. He said I should go up to a ballroom on the second floor.

When I got there it was already filling up with other kids from all the schools around Columbus. I made sure I got a seat, but soon enough it became pretty obvious that we were going to have a long wait. Three o'clock came, and then four, and still no Dave Clark Five. All the kids stayed in a pretty good mood; we introduced ourselves to each other and messed around. Nobody wanted to leave before the Dave Clark Five showed up.

Finally, at four-thirty, they came into the room. Were they cool! They were all wearing suits and boots, and they stood at the front of the room to answer questions.

It was amazing, seeing a group in person who had actually appeared on ''Ed Sullivan.'' I was pretty impressed last summer when I met a member of the Marauders, a local Columbus band, but this was different. This was the big time. The promoter called for everyone to quiet down, and then introduced the members of the group one by one—Dave Clark, Mike Smith, Lenny Davidson, Rick Huxley, and Denny Payton.

It was sort of like a White House press conference. The kids all raised their hands, and the promoter would pick someone out, and the person would ask his or her question. Mostly it was stuff like what was their favorite color, and what did they think of American girls.

I didn't want to let the opportunity pass without getting to ask a question. So I rehearsed my line over and over in my head, and then I raised my hand and the promoter was pointing at me.

I stood up, cleared my throat, and then said it:

''Where to from here?''

Dave Clark said ''We're going to Cleveland tomorrow, and then I think we go to Detroit.''

As he answered me, the whole group looked at me. It was really great.

After about fifteen minutes the promoter said that the group had to go upstairs to their rooms. Off to the side of the ballroom were five girls in short red costumes with white fur trimming. The promoter had brought them with him. They wore sashes across their fronts that said they were ''Miss Christmas and Her Snow Princesses.'' They looked pretty trampy; they all had beehive hairdos and seemed bored as they chewed gum and waited for the teen press conference to end.

When the Dave Clark Five got onto an elevator, Miss Christmas and Her Snow Princesses went with them.

DECEMBER 20

IN the morning Jack and Chuck and Allen came over. We had pizzas at Rubino's for lunch, and then went over to the high school, where the choir was having its annual Christmas concert.

We didn't have tickets, so we went up to the balcony to watch from the aisles. All the choir members were standing on risers in their blue robes.

C.W. Jones was talking with a bunch of parents when he saw us. We were all wearing Levi's and Wellingtons. Usually you get kicked out of school for Levi's, but since this was a Sunday he couldn't do it.

So, with all the parents watching him, C.W. looked us up and down and said in a loud, disgusted voice, "Well, there's some real nice people." He made his point.

Nana came over for dinner tonight, and when we were done I went up to my room.

I was thinking about the Dave Clark Five press conference yesterday. It had seemed exciting at the time—but now I remember back to the beginning of the year, when Steve Pariser said that his uncle was going to arrange for us to interview the Beatles when they came to Columbus.

The Beatles never came to Columbus; I guess we're too small a town for them. So we had to settle for the Dave Clark Five. I suppose the Beatles are for the New Yorks and Chicagos and Los Angeleses; the Dave Clark Five are for the Columbuses.

Every time I watch TV and they mention something that's going to be on the air at a certain hour "Eastern Standard Time," I think about what that means. Columbus is in Eastern Standard Time, just like New York, but sometimes I think that Eastern Standard Time is the one and only thing we have in common.

I wouldn't even know how to handle New York. It would intimidate me too much. Last summer, when I went to Cedar Point with Allen and Jack instead of going to the New York World's Fair with Nana and Mom and Debby and Timmy, I told everyone it was just because I really wanted to go to Cedar Point. But the truth of it is, I was a little scared to go to New York. I was looking for any excuse not to have to make the trip. I didn't know what to expect, or how I would deal with it. I was relieved when I didn't have to go.

I'm sure someday, when I'm older, I'll go visit New York. But something about me makes me feel safer in Columbus. Even if the Beatles never come here.

DECEMBER 21

ENGLISH and French were both futile this morning. In study hall I read as much History as I could. Then we had lab in Physics, which I faked my way through as best I could.

At night Allen and Dan and I went to Rubino's again for pizzas. When I got home the cake dialers hit; I called Lindy back and she said it had been her.

She told me that she was going with Chet Crosby to New Year's—I had assumed that much all along—but then she said, "You know, Bobby, you're still the only boy I can really talk to."

We stayed on the phone for a half hour. Now I feel I can fall asleep.

DECEMBER 22

LAST day of school before Christmas vacation. We had a party in French class. It was pretty corny—Mr. Munselle had a big bowl of punch and everything—but it was better than a test.

The rest of the day went pretty fast. It's nice to be out of school until the new year.

Tonight Chuck and I drove up to the Ohio State campus and cruised around the streets where the fraternities and sororities and bars are.

Chuck has just about decided to go to Ohio State next year. The way I figure it, ABCDJ will end up going to five different colleges. That will be so strange.

A lot of people from Bexley go to Ohio State, and as soon as they enroll there, it seems that they change. Their world shifts from the halls of the high school to the Oval at OSU; when you're still in high school you hear about them, but it's like you never knew them. It's like Bexley instantly becomes a part of their distant past.

I tried to explain that to Chuck tonight as we drove around, but he didn't seem to understand. He's sick of high school and can't wait until June when we graduate, and then September when he goes to OSU. I told him that what he was talking about probably meant the end forever of ABCDJ, but he said that we'd still have summers.

I guess maybe that's true. But as we cruised the streets of the campus, I had sort of a sad feeling. I was glad when we drove away and got back to Bexley.

DECEMBER 23

GOT up around eleven, and then Allen picked me up and we went downtown to Lazarus to buy Christmas gifts. The store was so full of people that you could hardly move.

When we got back to Bexley we picked Jack up and went to the TAT for poor boys. Then we drove by Candy Grossman's, and there were a lot of cars in front, so we went in.

Candy and all of her friends were there, but there was another girl I had never seen before. She was blonde and really cute.

It turned out that she was Alexis Mayer—and that her father was Lex Mayer. Lex Mayer is a household name in Columbus; he's a Chevrolet dealer, and for years he was the host of "Lex's Live Wrestling," which was broadcast on Saturday afternoons on Channel 4. At first they put up a ring in the parking lot of his Chevy dealership and telecast the wrestling matches from there, but pretty soon it got too big for that, and they moved it to Old Memorial Hall downtown. Lex and a Channel 4 guy named Clark Smith did the ringside announcing, and then between falls Lex would stand next to used Chevys and do commercials.

I don't think there's one person in Columbus who never saw "Lex's Live Wrestling"—and all of a sudden here was Lex's daughter. She lives in another city, and has just come in for Christmas vacation. She seemed sort of shy and very nice. It must be tough to be the kid of someone as famous as Lex Mayer—especially when your name is Alexis, so everyone can figure it out right away.

I got the idea that this could be the perfect solution to my New Year's dilemma. I called Candy aside and asked her if she could fix me up with Alexis for New Year's Eve. She said she'd try. I know Candy will do her best, because she has her own date for New Year's, so she can do me the favor knowing that she's already taken care of.

What a cool thing—New Year's Eve with Lex Mayer's daughter. Candy promised to call me tomorrow and tell me what's up.

DECEMBER 24

DAMN! Dan's going out on New Year's with Alexis Mayer. He showed up at Candy's yesterday after we were already there, and by the time he left he asked her and she said yes.

Son of a bitch. Now why couldn't I have just gotten the nerve up to ask her when I first saw her, instead of trying to get Candy to do it for me? Here I am—a week from New Year's, and no date.

Tonight Bob Kaynes, our neighbor who lives two doors down, came over and asked me to help carry a Ping-Pong table over to his house. He had bought the table for his two sons, Bobby and Tommy, and had hidden it in our garage. Now it was Christmas Eve, and his kids were asleep, and he wanted to set it up so it would be a surprise in the morning.

I put my letter jacket on and went out to our garage, and we each picked up one end of it and lugged it to his house. It made me feel sort of grown-up; now, instead of waiting on

Christmas Eve for someone to bring me a surprise, I was bringing some other little kids a surprise. I don't know exactly why, but I liked it.

DECEMBER 25

TIMMY woke all of us up at seven-thirty, and we went downstairs for the present-opening. It wasn't all that exciting; I guess I'm getting too old for that.

Allen came over around noon, and he and I went to the Toddle House for lunch. The Toddle House on Christmas Day is pretty lonely; the woman behind the counter asked us what we wanted, and we said what we always say—cheeseburgers, Cokes, and banana cream pie—and she didn't say anything, just got it for us.

When we got back to my house Debby said someone had called for me who didn't leave her name, but who sounded like Lindy. So I pulled the phone into my room, locked the door, and called her.

She said that it was she who had called. She said that she just wanted to wish me a Merry Christmas, and I wished her a Merry Christmas back.

"Do you want to come over?" she said.

"Who's there?" I said.

"My whole family," she said.

"I don't think I'd better," I said.

"Well, I just want you to know that you're always welcome," she said.

"How long does that extend?" I said.

"All of Christmas vacation," she said.

I said I just might take her up on it. Her call was the nicest Christmas present I got.

We all had dinner at Nana's. The food was great, as usual. Dad had us pose for some more Polaroid pictures.

As we were driving home I asked Dad to drop me off at Chuck's. He did. Allen and Dan were already there.

Chuck had gotten hold of some plastic Beatles masks, and we decided to put them on and go for a Date With Nature.

The idea of Dates With Nature started a few weeks ago. We had been cruising around, and we couldn't find Dan, and finally he showed up back at his house around midnight.

"Where have you been?" we said. "Did you have a date tonight?"

"Yeah," he said, laughing. "A Date With Nature." He explained that he had had nothing to do, and had just been walking around Bexley by himself, and the phrase was born.

So we decided to go on a Christmas Night Date With Nature. We each put on a Beatles mask—I was George Harrison, Chuck was Paul McCartney, Allen was John Lennon, and Dan was Ringo Starr.

It was freezing out, and there was snow on the ground. We had thought it would be funny—all the cars on the streets seeing the Beatles walking around Bexley. But there was hardly anyone out. So we just walked the streets, passing all the houses with their Christmas lights on. We talked, but it sounded funny—because of the masks, our words were sort of trapped, so the person who was talking could hear himself clearly, but it was hard to hear the other guys.

We walked for about an hour, and then the Date With Nature ended and we all went home.

DECEMBER 26

ALLEN has a friend at military school, a guy named Phil Clark, who lives over in Newark, Ohio. Phil's home for Christmas vacation, too, so today we drove over to Newark to see him.

He's a good guy. It's strange seeing him and Allen together—it makes you realize that Allen has a whole different life down at military school. The way he and Phil joke around, it's obvious that they have their own friends down there, and their own world. I always think of Allen as the member of ABCDJ who's sort of in exile, so it was kind of a surprise to see how close he is to Phil, and how many stories they share about military school. He must have other friends down there like that, too.

We mostly bombed around Newark all day in Phil's Oldsmobile 442. It was nice to be on streets other than Columbus streets, and to see sights other than Columbus sights.

DECEMBER 27

I got up and showered and was ready to leave the house at nine o'clock this morning. Uncle Fred, down in Cincinnati, was having his annual holiday party for the whole family, and we all had to go.

Dad drove. The party was at a country club; it was mostly for old people. I snuck away during the middle of it and found a little room where the Browns game was on TV. I stayed there and watched the whole game. The Browns were great.

The drive back was really boring. I had to piss and I had a headache, and Dad wouldn't play the radio. He gets real serious when he drives, and he never lets us hear the radio, and when Debby and Timmy and I start messing around and talking loud in the back seat, he tells us to settle down because of the "treacherous driving conditions."

We got back to Bexley. Mom and Dad had another party to go to, and Debby and Timmy went out with their friends. Allen and Chuck and Dan were supposed to come over later in the evening.

I thought about it for a while, and then I dialed for cake at Lindy's and she called back. She invited me to come over, and I said I'd come in, but that then we should leave.

I got there and her parents were real nice to me; her brother Pat and his girlfriend Linda McClure were there, too. Lindy and I said goodbye and left.

We drove all around Bexley, looking at the Christmas lights. It was a real dark, quiet night. We didn't say much; it really wasn't necessary. Here we were together in the car, and the lights on the houses were so beautiful, and I felt so good.

I asked Lindy if she wanted to come to my house, and she said that would be okay. I pulled Mom's car into the driveway, and I unlocked the back door of the house and then there we were.

We went into the den and turned the TV on. We lay down on the floor next to each other and watched the show. I don't even remember what it was. All I could think about was the fact that Lindy and I were alone in my den, and it was night-time, and that this is what I had dreamed about for the whole last year.

We talked about a lot of stuff, but really about nothing. We said things about school, but what was really on our minds was how amazing this was—after all this time we were here.

We went into the living room. I sat on the couch—the one with the portraits of Debby and Timmy and me above it—and Lindy sat next to me, and after a couple of minutes had passed she stood up like she was going to leave, but instead she took the two steps toward me and sat on my lap.

We just sat there like that for I don't know how long. I thought: This is perfect. All the wishing and all the hoping and all the screwing around with other girls, and this is per-fect. I thought: I don't want this moment to end. Just let Lindy be here sitting on my lap, and nothing else needs to happen—just freeze this in time and let it last forever.

I knew that my friends were coming over, and I knew that when they did the mood would be broken, and that Lindy would say that she had to go back home. So we kept sitting there, talking and then being silent for a few minutes, talking some more and then being silent again. My thoughts re-mained the same: Just don't let this end. When it finally hap-pened—when the front doorbell rang—Lindy quickly hopped off my lap and sat back on the couch, and I walked to the door and opened it, and Allen and Chuck and Dan came in.

They were shocked to see Lindy there, and I could tell that she was a little embarrassed. We all sat around talking awk-wardly for a few minutes, and then, just as I had guessed, Lindy said that she probably ought to be getting home.

I told the boys I'd meet them later, and Lindy and I got back into the station wagon and I drove her home. She didn't say anything when she got out, and I didn't either. We didn't have to. Funny, funny year.

DECEMBER 28

ABCDJ drove over to Newark again today. Chuck and I are the only ones without New Year's dates, so Phil Clark said he'd try to fix us up with Newark girls. But I'm not very confident about it.

Jerry Lee Lewis has a new album out. I hear he sings "Hound Dog" on it. I want to get it just to see if he does it as good as Elvis did. I've always liked Jerry Lee Lewis, but my friends say I'm crazy.

Allen, Chuck, Dan, and Jack went to the Hideout to drink beer tonight, but I didn't feel like going. I walked over to Main Street and went to Rogers' Drugstore to look for something to read. I got the new issue of *Esquire* magazine with something called the Dubious Achievement Awards on the cover. I'm reading it now. It's really funny. It must be great to be that witty.

DECEMBER 29

ALLEN and Chuck and I were cruising around tonight; we went to the TAT for poor boys, and then just drove aimlessly.

WCOL was on the radio, as usual; Bob Harrington was hosting his nighttime show. We all got the idea at the same time—we'd drive downtown and try to meet him.

I don't know why we hadn't thought of that before. We listen to him every night of our lives. The front of the WCOL building is on Broad Street, but there's another street—really just an alley—called Young Street that runs along the side of the building. Allen pulled his car onto Young Street and we got out.

We could see a light in the window upstairs. We took pennies from our pockets and started heaving them at the window. Some of them missed, but most of them clanked against the glass and fell back down to us. We kept it up, and after about five minutes someone appeared at the window.

We couldn't see him very clearly. He was a pudgy, dark-haired guy. He opened the window and said, "Who's throwing that stuff?"

Chuck yelled, "Are you Bob Harrington?"

He answered, "Who wants to know?"

We counted to three, and then did what we had rehearsed in the car: "Bob, Bob, Bo-Bob, Banana-Fana Fo Fob, Fe-Fi Mo-Mob, Bob!"

Up in the window he laughed. "Do that again," he said.

This time we did it real loud:

"BOB, BOB, BO-BOB, BANANA-FANA FO FOB, FE-FI MO-MOB, BOB!"

Now he was really laughing. "Who are you guys?" he said.

"Chuck," Chuck shouted.

"Al," Allen shouted.

"Bob," I shouted.

Bob Harrington stuck his head out the window.

"Chucklebob?" he said.

"Yeah," we yelled back. "Chucklebob!"

"What school do you go to?" he said.

"Bexley," I yelled.

"Well, thanks for coming down," he said. "I have to go play another record." And he closed the window.

We drove back toward Bexley, talking about what a cool thing that had been to do, and all of a sudden, right after the next song, Bob Harrington's voice came on the radio again.

"A good friend of mine just came down to the station," he said. "His name's Chucklebob, and he goes to Bexley High School. Chucklebob's a real swinger."

We whooped and yelled in the car. We couldn't believe it. Not only did he like us—but all over Columbus, in the car of every kid who was cruising tonight, people were hearing about us. Unbelievably cool.

DECEMBER 30

CHUCK and I don't have dates for New Year's. Phil Clark called Allen this morning to say that he had struck out trying to get us Newark girls. So tomorrow night ought to be uneventful.

Allen and Chuck and I went to Wentz's Pharmacy for chocolate sodas right after dinner. Since Chuck and I won't be coming to the party at Allen's parents' apartment, Allen said he's inviting a bunch of people who aren't in ABCDJ—Pongi, Dennis MacNeil, Phil Clark, and a lot of others. I feel kind of bad that I'll be missing it, but it wouldn't make any sense to go to the party without having a date.

After Wentz's we came back to my house and watched "Shindig." Jerry Lee Lewis was on—he really looked old. After that we went to the Pancake House. Pongi's dad and mom were eating in the restaurant part, and Chuck and Allen and I were eating at the counter, and when Pongi's dad was leaving the restaurant he came over and paid our checks for us. That was nice of him.

When I got home, Debby and some of her friends and their dates were in our living room and den, so I just went up to my room. I thought a lot about the past year. So much has happened. When I really think about it, I realize that the calendar is sort of an artificial way to measure your life. But I can't help getting this feeling that a very special time is just about to end. I got in bed and rolled that around in my mind. Downstairs I could hear Debby and her friends and their dates laughing and watching TV.

DECEMBER 31

GOT up early this morning and went to the eye doctor's. I don't have to get glasses.

In the afternoon, Jack and Chuck and I shot baskets at Jack's. It was really cold, but it felt good working up a sweat outdoors. After that we went down to Allen's, where he was making preparations for the party.

He was really being a good guy about the whole thing. His parents had left some bottles of champagne in a closet, and Allen took one of the bottles and gave it to Chuck and me and told us to enjoy it tonight.

Chuck and I didn't know where to store it, and then we thought of the refrigerator in Pongi's garage. We drove over there and made sure that no one was around, and then we stuck it in the refrigerator and made plans to retrieve it at night.

I had dinner with Mom and Dad and Debby and Timmy, and then around eight o'clock Chuck came by and picked me up. We drove back over to Pongi's, made sure the coast was clear again, and picked up the champagne.

We just drove. We made jokes about not having dates, but both of us knew that we wished we did. We cruised for about two hours, and then we went to the Toddle House for cheeseburgers.

We were sitting at the counter eating them, and Chuck asked me what Kathy Michaels was doing for New Year's.

"I heard she had a date with Bruce Byrnes," I said.

"Yeah," Chuck said. "But I talked to Byrnes yesterday, and he told me that Kathy had broken the date because she had to baby-sit."

"I don't know anything about that," I said.

"Why don't you call her?" Chuck said.

"Right," I said.

"No, I'm serious," he said. "See what she's doing."

So I went to the Toddle House pay phone and dialed her number. I was prepared to hang up if Kathy's parents answered, but Kathy herself picked up the phone.

She seemed surprised to hear from me. I told her that Chuck and I were cruising around with a bottle of champagne, and that we wondered if she felt like having company.

She said sure; she said to come on over.

So we got back into Chuck's car and drove to Kathy's house. We rang the bell and she let us in.

It was weird. If you would have asked me to make a bet, the surest bet I could have made was that I wouldn't be with Kathy Michaels on New Year's Eve. But here we were in her house; Chuck asked her if she wanted to drink the champagne with us, and she said she'd try some, so we popped open the bottle.

If I was having any illusions that her letting us come over was a sign that she wanted to start going out with me again, those illusions went away pretty quickly. It was quite obvious that she was letting us be there just because she was bored, and she didn't like baby-sitting on New Year's Eve, and she wanted to kill some time. She showed more interest in Chuck than she did in me.

The whole time we were there we listened to WCOL. Bob Harrington was counting down the top forty records of the year, and every song he played reminded me of something that had happened during the past twelve months. When "House of the Rising Sun" came on—that was a song that was playing the first time Kathy and I parked at the Hideout— I looked over at her to see if she would react, but it was clear that the song meant nothing to her.

During the hour between eleven o'clock and midnight I paced around the first floor of her house. Chuck had a pack of cigarettes, and we both smoked some. And then, right at midnight, to mark the beginning of the new year, Bob Harrington said he was going to play the number one song of 1964. He shouted "Happy New Year!" and then "I Want to Hold Your Hand" came on.

Kathy made no move like she wanted to kiss either Chuck or me, so I went over to the far side of her living room and smashed my fist into the wall above her fireplace. It didn't even make a dent.

"What was that for?" Kathy said.

"Nothing," I said. "Just welcoming in the new year."

Chuck and I sat around for a few more minutes, and then we thanked Kathy for letting us come over and we left.

We decided to drive down to Allen's. The major part of the party was over by now—they had already danced and done whatever drinking they were going to do and kissed at midnight—so we figured we wouldn't really be intruders. We parked Chuck's car on Broad Street and rode the elevator up to Allen's parents' apartment.

Everyone was in a great mood. They were still dancing, and a couple of guys lent us their dates, so Chuck and I danced a few fast ones, and some of the girls gave us New Year's kisses.

All of this was going on in the den. After a while I walked out to the living room, which was empty, and looked out at downtown Columbus. This is just where I was last year at this time—seventeen stories up in Allen's apartment, looking down at the city. I just stood there, with Columbus in front of me and the music coming from the other room. I guess you can't predict anything for sure about your life, but here comes 1965.

ABOUT THE AUTHOR

BOB GREENE is a syndicated columnist for the *Chicago Tribune*; his column appears in more than two hundred newspapers in the United States. He is a contributing editor of *Esquire* magazine, where his "American Beat" column appears each month, as well as a contributing correspondent for *ABC News Nightline.* He has written seven previous books, including the national bestseller GOOD MORNING, MERRY SUNSHINE.